RtI in Math

Other Eye On Education Books
Available from Routledge
www.routledge.com/eyeoneducation

RtI in Math

Evidence-Based Interventions for Struggling Students

Linda L. Forbringer and Wendy W. Fuchs

Routledge
Taylor & Francis Group

NEW YORK AND LONDON

First published 2014
by Routledge
711 Third Avenue, New York, NY 10017

and by Routledge
2 Park Square, Milton Park, Abingdon, Oxon OX14 4RN

Routledge is an imprint of the Taylor & Francis Group, an informa business

Library of Congress Cataloging-in-Publication Data
Forbringer, Linda L.
  Rti in math : evidence-based interventions for struggling students / Linda L. Forbringer and Wendy W. Fuchs.
      pages   cm
    1. Mathematics—Study and teaching (Elementary)—United States. 2. Response to intervention (Learning disabled children) 3. School failure—Prevention. 4. Remedial teaching. 5. Effective teaching. I. Fuchs, Wendy W. II. Title. III. Title: Response to intervention.
    QA13.F67 2013
    372.70973--dc23   2013014937

ISBN: 978-0-415-73530-8 (hbk)
ISBN: 978-1-59667-254-3 (pbk)
ISBN: 978-1-315-85227-0 (ebk)

Typeset in Palatino, Formata, and Rockwell
by click! Publishing Services

■ Contents

Meet the Authors

Dr. Linda Forbringer is an Associate Professor and Special Education Program Director for the Department of Special Education and Communication Disorders at Southern Illinois University Edwardsville (SIUE), where she teaches undergraduate and graduate courses in methods of teaching mathematics, classroom management, and instructional methods for students with disabilities. Before joining SIUE she taught for the Cleveland Public Schools and for the Positive Education Program, an agency which provides integrated educational and mental health services throughout Northern Ohio for school-age children and youth who have been diagnosed with an emotional disturbance. Dr. Forbringer served as a classroom teacher, a liaison teacher-counselor, and then administrator of a day treatment center serving kindergarten through twelfth grade students. She has presented on Response to Intervention in mathematics, differentiating instruction, and motivation at a variety of national and international conferences, including the Learning Disabilities Association, Council for Exceptional Children, International Council for Learning Disabilities, National Council of Teachers of Mathematics and National Council of Supervisors of Mathematics. Her research interests include methods of teaching mathematics, effective teaching practices, and strategies to support students in inclusive settings.

Dr. Wendy Fuchs is an Assistant Professor in the Department of Special Education and Communication Disorders at Southern Illinois University Edwardsville. She teaches the beginning and advanced reading methods courses for pre-service special educators. Dr. Fuchs also serves as the Principal Investigator and Project Coordinator of the Illinois Institutes of Higher Education Partnership, a federally-funded Statewide Professional Development Grant that assists teacher preparation programs integrate MTSS into course content and field experiences. In addition to her work with the IHE Partnership, Dr. Fuchs provides professional development and educational consulting to school districts in Southern Illinois in the areas of Response to Intervention/Multi-Tier System of Supports (MTSS), school improvement, and maximizing student engagement. Dr. Fuchs is a member of the PBIS Statewide Leadership Team, and serves as an executive board member for the Illinois Teacher Education Division of Council for Exceptional Children. Her research interests include effective teaching practices, teacher perceptions of students with disabilities, data-based instructional decision making.

The authors wish to thank Melissa Landwehr, a special education teacher in Fort Zumwalt, Missouri, for her wonderful contributions!

■ Introduction

Students in the United States are struggling in mathematics. According to the National Assessment of Education Progress (NAEP), in 2011 only 34 percent of U.S. eighth-grade students, and 40 percent of fourth-grade students, scored at or above the proficient level in mathematics (U.S. Department of Education, 2011). Although the No Child Left Behind Act states that no child would be left behind, clearly many children have been left behind in mathematics.

One model for providing early intervention and support for struggling learners is Response to Intervention (RtI). RtI is a multilevel prevention system that integrates data-based decision making, high-quality instruction, and intervention matched to student needs in order to maximize student achievement. The initial focus of RtI has primarily been on improving reading achievement, but schools are now expanding RtI to mathematics. While a multitude of books and articles have been written about RtI, most of them describe beginning the RtI process, recommendations for universal screening and progress monitoring, and instruction and interventions for reading. As schools begin to look beyond support in reading, there is a need for resources that address interventions for mathematics.

This book is for classroom teachers, special educators, math specialists, math coaches, teacher aides, administrators, related service providers, and other professionals who directly or indirectly support elementary and middle-school students struggling to master mathematics. We begin with an overview of the RtI process and discuss how to use assessment to make instructional decisions in mathematics. Chapter 3 provides an overview of the evidence-based practices for teaching mathematics in the general classroom and the interventions that support students who are struggling with core concepts. Because a large body of research suggests that careful attention to both lesson design and motivational strategies can significantly improve struggling learners' mathematical achievement, we address these foundational topics in Chapters 4 and 5. In the remaining chapters we provide a detailed description of interventions to help struggling learners master concepts and operations involving whole numbers and rational numbers. Some of the intervention strategies we describe differ from the way material would be presented in the core curriculum. Other strategies represent best practice for all students, but their systematic implementation becomes essential for individuals who are not meeting benchmark expectations. The evidence-based interventions discussed in this book address recommendations from the Institute of Education Sciences Practice Guide, *Assisting Students Struggling with Mathematics: Response to Intervention (RtI) for Elementary and Middle Schools*. Using these strategies can help prevent difficulties, support struggling learners, and allow *all* students to be successful in mathematics.

Chapter 1

Overview of Response to Intervention in Mathematics

What Is Response to Intervention?

Response to Intervention (RtI) is an innovative framework for school improvement that is designed to help *all* learners achieve academic and behavioral proficiency. Its goal is to prevent learning difficulties through the use of effective, high-quality instruction, early identification of problems, and tiered intervention services. All students' progress is monitored two or three times each year in order to identify individuals who may need additional support *before* they fail. Students who are experiencing difficulty receive targeted, research-based interventions through a tiered support system. Their progress is monitored frequently, and data from these assessments inform instruction decisions. In addition, districts monitor instructional delivery, assessment, and intervention services to ensure that they are implemented as intended.

The landmark legislation of No Child Left Behind (NCLB, 2001) focused on increased accountability of schools, the use of research-based curriculum, highly qualified teachers, and communication with parents regarding their child's academic proficiency. The reauthorized Individuals with Disabilities Education Improvement Act (IDEA, 2004) also required states to include frequent monitoring of students' progress in the general curriculum as part of, or prior to, the special-education referral process. Both laws emphasize the key principles of RtI: progress monitoring, high quality, research-based instruction, application of a research-based process of problem solving, and increased accountability. While RtI includes a process used to determine students' educational needs, it is not synonymous with the special-education referral process.

In the past ten years, practitioners across the country have worked to refine the general principles and guidelines for implementing RtI. While the details of implementing a multi-tiered model may vary based on local context, the critical components are constant: (1) providing evidence-based instruction to all students, (2) using data to guide instructional decision making and evaluate instructional effectiveness, and (3) using multiple levels of support to provide increasingly intense and targeted interventions for students at risk of academic failure.

Evidence-Based Instruction

A core principle of RtI is that all students should receive high-quality instruction using methods that have been validated through rigorous research. In the past, pedagogy was often based on educational theory rather than scientific research. However, researchers have increasingly focused on identifying effective instructional practices. As a result, educators have access to a growing list of instructional procedures that have been shown to significantly increase student learning during rigorous scientific experiments.

Unfortunately, evidence-based pedagogy is sometimes slow to make its way into our classrooms. Studies document that many evidence-based strategies are not routinely included in textbooks and teacher guides commonly used in our schools (Bryant et al., 2008; Hodges, Carly, & Collins, 2008; NMAP, 2008). While most publishers provide research and testimonials claiming that their products will achieve miraculous results, many of the studies quoted do not meet the methodological criteria required of high-quality research. To qualify as "scientifically based" research, a study must meet rigorous standards, including the use of systematic observation or experiment, measurements or observation methods that have been shown to provide valid and reliable data, and rigorous data analysis. The participants, setting, and methodology must be described in sufficient detail to allow other researchers to replicate the study and compare results. The study must have been accepted by a peer-reviewed journal or approved by a panel of independent experts who apply rigorous, objective review criteria. In addition, for a scientifically based practice to be labeled as "evidence-based," the practice should be supported not just by a single study, but by multiple studies that meet the standards of methodological rigor (Gersten et al., 2005).

While high-quality research evaluating complete math programs is currently sparse, a significant body of research describes instructional procedures that have been found to be effective for teaching mathematics. These methods have produced significant positive effects in multiple high-quality research studies. In Chapter 3 we provide an overview of key evidence-based instructional methods for mathematics. Each strategy is described in greater detail in subsequent chapters.

Data-Based Decision Making

Data-based decision making is a cornerstone of RtI. Assessment data are collected and used to evaluate instructional materials and programs, and to guide instructional decisions for individual students and groups of students. Within an RtI framework, three types of assessment occur: (1) universal screening, (2) progress monitoring, and (3) diagnostic assessment.

  ♦ **Universal Screening:** Universal screening is the first step in the data-collection process. The information obtained allows a district to evaluate the effectiveness of its core instructional program and identify students who are struggling or at risk for mathematical difficulty. Universal screening is usually administered two to four times per year. School personnel may review students' performance on recent state or district tests or may administer a math screening test. The results are used to identify students who are not making adequate progress in mathematics and who need additional support in order to attain mathematical proficiency. The National Center of Student Progress Monitoring (www.studentprogress.org) provides guidelines for selecting assessments and includes reviews of numerous assessment instruments. The National Organization on Response to Intervention (www.rti4success.org) also provides guidance for selecting assessment instruments.

♦ **Progress Monitoring:** Students who are not making adequate progress, as indicated by the universal screening results, receive more frequent progress monitoring. Typically this involves administering short assessments that can detect small changes in student learning. Student responses to intervention are used to evaluate the effectiveness of the current interventions and guide the decision to either increase or decrease the level of support provided or to maintain or change intervention strategies.

♦ **Diagnostic Assessment:** Diagnostic assessments provide more detailed information about students' strengths and weaknesses in specific skill areas. This formative assessment helps teachers identify the specific mathematical content to be addressed and select appropriate instructional strategies and activities.

Each of these types of assessment will be discussed in greater detail in Chapter 2.

Tiered Support

In an RtI model, tiers are used to provide increasingly intensive support for struggling learners. The term "intervention" is used to describe the instructional procedures used to support individuals who have not made adequate progress in the core curriculum. Intervention is "extra help or extra instruction that is targeted specifically to skills that a student has not acquired" (Pierangelo & Giuliani, 2008, p. 80). Generally RtI is described as a three-tier model of support, but variations using more than three tiers also exist. Regardless of the number of tiers used, the basic format of tiered support remains the same, with each tier representing increasingly intense levels of intervention. Figure 1.1 provides an overview of the increasing support provided at each tier.

Tier 1: General Classroom

Tier 1 represents the general classroom, where a high-quality, evidence-based core curriculum is delivered according to state standards. Research has not clearly identified an optimal amount of time for Tier I math delivery,

Figure 1.1 Tiered Support

Tier	Students	Grouping	Time	Curriculum	Service Provider	Assessment
1	All students in the general education classroom	Flexible grouping: whole class and small group	60 minutes per day	Core curriculum evidence-based program with differentiated instruction	General education classroom teacher	Universal screening 3 times per year
2	Students performing below grade level who have not responded to differentiated instruction in Tier 1	Small group: 3-5 students with similar needs	120 minutes per week in addition to Tier 1 instruction (for example, 30 minutes per day 4 days a week)	Targeted to skill deficits	Personnel determined by school: math specialist, Title 1 teacher, intervention specialist, etc.	Progress monitoring weekly or every two weeks
3	Students below grade level who have not responded to Tier 2 intervention	Individual or small group: 1-3 students	120+ minutes per week in addition to Tier 1 instruction	Targeted to skill deficits; matched to student need	Personnel determined by school: math specialist, Title 1 teacher, intervention specialist, special education teacher, etc.	Weekly progress monitoring

but generally fifty to sixty minutes are allocated daily. Teachers are expected to differentiate instruction to meet the needs of students who function at varying levels within the general education classroom. The core curriculum should allow at least 80 percent of students to achieve proficiency in mathematics. Since the goal of RtI is to reduce the number of students needing more intensive interventions, at Tier 1 teachers must be proficient in providing high-quality instruction and the evidence-based intervention strategies described in subsequent chapters.

Universal screening is administered at least twice a year, and the results are used to evaluate the effectiveness of the core program and to provide early detection of individuals who may need additional support. Schools typically decide on cut-off scores to determine the level of academic proficiency. Some schools use national norms, but many schools determine their own local norms. Students performing at or above the "proficient" level continue to receive instruction in the general classroom, including differentiated instruction. Students falling below the "proficient" level—that is, those who have not made sufficient progress in the general classroom setting—may require additional instructional support (Tier 2 or Tier 3) depending on the severity of need.

Tier 2: Supplemental Support

Students who have not made sufficient progress receive supplemental support in addition to the math instruction provided in the general classroom. Homogeneous groups of two to five students meet for approximately thirty minutes per day to receive Tier 2 targeted instruction that supplements what they receive in the core curriculum. The content of this supplemental instruction addresses gaps in the students' knowledge or focuses on extended instruction in key concepts. It is not a tutoring session to help students complete the general classroom assignments, but rather an opportunity for students to develop or solidify missing concepts and skills that they will need in order to obtain mathematical proficiency. In the RtI model, a multidisciplinary team of professionals uses assessment data to identify students' specific deficiencies and then targets interventions to remediate those deficiencies. While some publishers are promoting a "Tier 2 Program" packaged for all students at a particular grade level who are in need of additional support, such a one-size-fits-all approach is incompatible with RtI's emphasis on data-based decision making. Seldom will all students who experience difficulty at a given grade level have identical skill deficits. Since the time students spend receiving Tier 2 support is time they are out of the classroom and therefore not participating in other instructional activities, it is important to spend this time providing focused support in skills the student needs to learn.

Tier 2 instruction is provided by trained personnel, such as a mathematics coach, general education teacher, or other professional who has received special training. The progress of students receiving Tier 2 services is monitored frequently, and the data are used to determine whether students still require intervention. Once the child makes sufficient progress, Tier 2 support can be gradually faded. About 95 percent of students should make adequate progress through the combination of Tier 1 instruction and Tier 2 support. For students who are still making insufficient progress after receiving Tier 2 services, problem-solving teams design a Tier 3 intervention plan.

Tier 3: Intensive Interventions

Students who have received high-quality instruction but have not made sufficient progress in Tier 2 need more intensive interventions targeting their individual skill deficits. It is generally expected that, if Tier 1 and Tier 2 are implemented successfully, no more than 5 percent of students will require these intensive interventions. Students receiving Tier 3 services generally meet for a minimum of fifty to sixty minutes per day in addition to the core curriculum. Tier 3 may include one-on-one tutoring, or instruction may be provided for small groups of two or three students who demonstrate similar needs. The instructional strategies used are generally similar to Tier 2, but by decreasing group size and increasing instructional time, interventionists can target instruction to more precisely meet individual student needs. Progress is still monitored weekly.

Occasionally students who receive special services may follow a different curriculum in place of the core mathematics program. The decision to remove a child from the core program can only be made by an individualized education plan (IEP) team. Except for students who have an IEP specifying that the child will not participate in core math instruction, all students receive Tier 3 support in addition to the core curriculum.

The method of delivering intensive support varies. Some districts equate Tier 3 with special-education placement; others view Tier 3 as the beginning of the special-education referral process, while others use Tier 3 to provide intensive support prior to considering a special-education referral. For example, Texas uses a three-tiered model of RtI, while in Georgia four tiers are used. Regardless of the number of tiers, the data collected at each tier reveal the student's responsiveness to intervention, and these data are used when making decisions about eligibility for special education. However, parents have the right to request a formal evaluation for special education at any point in the process, and the RtI process cannot be used to delay or deny this evaluation.

Models of Implementation

Two approaches to RtI are described in the literature: a problem-solving model and the standard treatment protocol. Both approaches provide evidence-based instruction to all students, use data to guide instructional decision making and evaluate instructional effectiveness, and use tiered support to provide increasingly intense interventions for individuals experiencing difficulty. The two approaches differ in the way instructional interventions are selected for use at each tier.

In the problem-solving approach, a team makes instructional decisions based on the individual student's strengths and weaknesses, as revealed during universal screening and progress monitoring. The team identifies areas in which the individual is struggling and then develops an intervention plan tailored to the student. While groups of students with similar profiles are grouped together for instruction, the details of the intervention vary depending on the unique needs and performance data of the groups' members. This approach has been used in schools for more than twenty years and is generally favored by practitioners.

In the standard protocol, school leaders typically decide on a select group of research-based interventions that have been proven to increase student outcomes in specific areas. For example, schools may decide that one particular program that targets basic fact knowledge will be used first for any students needing additional instruction in learning their basic facts. This approach is favored by researchers because using one standardized format helps ensure fidelity of implementation.

Summary

Response to Intervention is an integral part of comprehensive school reform. Schools will continue to improve their ability to meet the learning needs of struggling students by implementing evidence-based instructional strategies and utilizing benchmarking and universal screening as a foundation to data-based decision making. When schools follow the RtI framework, students who struggle in mathematics receive increasingly intensive interventions to supplement the research-based core instruction. In the next chapter we discuss the use of assessment to make data-based instructional decisions. In Chapter 3 we will define the key components of core mathematics instruction and describe the most effective instructional methods to support struggling students.

Chapter 2

Using Assessment to Make Instructional Decisions

At the heart of Response to Intervention is early identification of students who are at risk of academic failure. The problem-solving model provides an efficient and effective framework to assess students' academic functioning and to use the assessment data to inform and evaluate instructional practices and interventions (Deno & Mirkin, 1977). The five basic steps in the data-based problem-solving model are 1) problem identification, 2) problem analysis, 3) intervention planning, 4) plan implementation, and 5) progress monitoring and plan evaluation. Figure 2.1 gives a visual representation of these important steps developed by Rhode Island Department of Elementary and Secondary Education (2010).

The problem-solving model serves many important functions in a school. First and foremost, it provides an organizational structure that guides teams in their efforts to maximize student success. The five steps mentioned above help teams evaluate school-wide data, prioritize goals, and formulate plans to help all students. The purpose of this chapter is to provide a general overview of the problem-solving process as it relates to instructional decisions in mathematics. There are numerous, high-quality books that go into much greater detail about the technical aspects of educational assessment. Figure 2.2 gives a list of resources containing in-depth information about assessing students' understanding of mathematical skills and concepts.

One of the biggest shifts in current educational practice is the shift to using data to inform instructional decisions in the classroom setting. In the past, providing struggling students with additional support had been heavily dependent on teacher recommendations. Over the past five years, greater emphasis has been placed on using objective academic data to guide instruction and interventions in the classroom. Schools are now using universal screening, benchmarking, and progress monitoring to assess student outcomes, as well as assess the effectiveness of classroom curriculum and instruction. While schools are collecting more data, there is still a gap between collecting data and using data to inform educational decisions. By following the steps of the problem-solving model, educators can ensure that they are identifying and addressing student academic needs in the most targeted, effective way. In this chapter, we will discuss the steps of the problem-solving

Figure 2.1 Problem-Solving Model

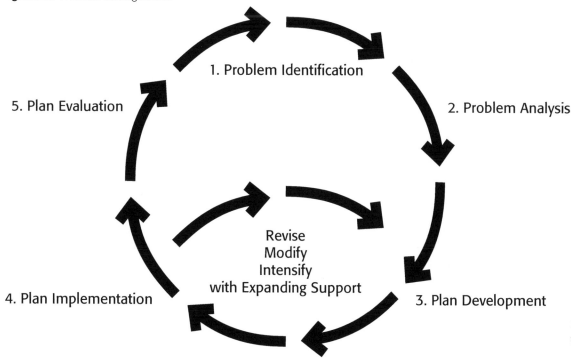

Source: Rhode Island Department of Elementary and Secondary Education. (2010). *Rhode Island Criteria and Guidance for the Identification of Specific Learning Disabilities.* Providence: Rhode Island Department of Elementary and Secondary Education. Used with permission.

model as a framework for school-based teams and individual educators to use data to guide their instruction and supplemental interventions.

Step 1: Problem Identification

What is the difference between what is expected and what is happening?

To answer this question, we must use the first step in the problem-solving process to identify both those students who are on track and those students who need additional support to be successful. This requires schools to identify local criteria for what is considered adequate performance and the cut-off for what is considered "at risk."

Universal screening provides a comprehensive "sweep" of all children in the school to identify students who need additional support in foundational skills. This sweep enables schools to analyze the effectiveness of the core curriculum and identify which students need additional support.

Screening requires an assessment that is generally inexpensive, easily administered and scored, and provides reliable data on critical skills (number sense, quantity discrimination, etc.). The skills being assessed should have high *predictive validity*, meaning the students' performance

Figure 2.2 Resources for Information About Math Assessment

Organizations

Center on Instruction (COI). www.centeroninstruction.org

COI is a website funded by the U.S. Department of Education that provides a collection of free, scientifically based resources on instruction. One resource available through the site is *Improving instruction through the use of data. Part 1: How to use your data to inform mathematics instruction* (2011). This professional development module includes a PowerPoint presentation and manual describing progress monitoring in mathematics at the elementary and secondary levels, as well as a list of additional resources.

The National Center on Response to Intervention. http://rti4success.org/progressMonitoringTools

The National Center on RtI provides information on selecting instruments for universal screening and progress monitoring. Reviews of several assessment measures are summarized in an easy-to-read "Tools Chart." This chart is continually updated, so it is an excellent resource for selecting assessment instruments.

The National Council of Teachers of Mathematics (NCTM). www.nctm.org

NCTM is the professional organization for teachers of mathematics. Its website offers a wide variety of high-quality publications on the subject of formative assessment in mathematics, as well as other resources for teaching mathematics.

Research Institute on Progress Monitoring. www.progressmonitoring.net

The Office of Special Education Progress funded the Research Institute on Progress Monitoring. The site contains multimedia presentations and technical reports on several assessment measures for mathematics.

Books

Ashlock, R. B. (2009). *Error patterns in computation: Using error patterns to help each student learn* (10th ed.). Upper Saddle River, NJ: Merrill Prentice Hall.

This text provides examples of common errors students make in operations involving whole numbers and fractions, followed by suggestions for effective intervention strategies for each error pattern.

Hosp, M. K., Hosp, J. L., & Howell, K. W. (2007). *The ABCs of CBM: A practical guide to curriculum-based measurement.* New York: Guilford Press.

This book provides in-depth information about creating and using CBM for screening and progress monitoring.

Spinelli, C. (2011). *Classroom assessment for students in special and general education* (3rd ed.). Boston: Pearson.

This text contains information on using interviews, observation, and questionnaires, and provides sample task analysis checklists.

Ysseldyke, J. E., Salvia, J., & Bolt, S. (2009). *Assessment in special and inclusive education* (11th ed.). Boston: Houghton Mifflin.

Figure 2.2 *(cont'd)* Resources for Information About Math Assessment

Websites

Math Assessments for Universal Screening and Progress Monitoring

Accelerated Math. www.renlearn.com
   This software programs allows educators to monitor individual student progress by creating assessments tailored to the student's current skill level.

AIMSweb. www.aimsweb.com
   AIMSweb provides a progress-monitoring system in the areas of reading, spelling, written expression, and mathematics. It includes a web-based data management and reporting system.

CBM Warehouse. www.jimwrightonline.com/htmdocs/interventions/
   cbmwarehouse.php
   This site is devoted to providing CBM resources to do everything from school-wide screening to individual student progress monitoring.

easyCBM. http://easycbm.com
   EasyCBM provides three forms of a screening measure for grades K–8 as well as multiple assessment measures for progress monitoring. The website provides data management, assessment measures, report generating, and training on administration and scoring.

EdCheckup. www.edcheckup.com
   This company provides a progress-monitoring system for reading, writing, and mathematics for students in grades K–8.

mClass: Math. www.wirelessgeneration.com
   mClass: Math is a set of screening and progress-monitoring measures for students in grades K–3.

Monitoring Basic Skills Progress. www.proedinc.com
   Monitoring Basic Skills Progress provides CBM assessments for computation as well as concepts and applications for students in grades 1–6.

National Center on Student Progress Monitoring. www.studentprogress.org
   Includes case studies, webinars, PowerPoint presentations, and other tools related to monitoring student progress in mathematics.

Orchard Software. www.orchardsoftware.com
   Orchard Software provides targeted instruction and progress monitoring for students from pre-K to ninth grade.

Process Assessment of the Learner (PAL-2). www.pearsonassessments.com/
   HAIWEB/Cultures/en-us/Productdetail.htm?Pid=015-8661-729
   This software can be used to diagnose math problem areas and can also be used as a progress-monitoring tool for grades K–6.

Figure 2.2 *(cont'd)* Resources for Information About Math Assessment

Slosson Diagnostic Math Screener. www.slosson.com/onlinecatalogstore_c51693
.html
This math assessment can be administered to groups or individuals. Five grade
ranges cover math content from grades 1–8.

STAR. www.renlearn.com
STAR Math is a computer-adaptive assessment of general mathematics achievement, including computation, mathematic application, and mathematics concepts for students in grades 1–12.

Vanderbilt RTI Monitor. www.RTIMonitor.com
Vanderbilt RTIMonitor.com provides assessment tools designed to frequently
monitor students' progress and provide benchmark performance in grades 1–8
in math.

Yearly Progress Pro. http://ctb.com/ctb.com/control/productFamilyViewAction?p
-products&productFamilyId=591
Yearly Progress Pro, from McGraw Hill, is a program that provides assessment
and intervention for grades 1–8 mathematics.

Creating CBM Probes and Math Worksheets

AplusMath. http://aplusmath.com/
This website provides free single-skill sheets to help students improve their
math skills. It also provides a worksheet generator.

Intervention Central. http://interventioncentral.org
Intervention Central provides an early math fluency generator and a math worksheet generator.

The Math Worksheet Site. http://themathworksheetsite.com
This website provides an online math worksheet generator.
SuperKids. http://superkids.com/aweb/tools/math
This website provides a worksheet creator.

on the subskills provides meaningful data regarding future success in that
domain. For example, a student who struggles with quantity discrimination and identifying missing numbers is at risk for future challenges in
mathematics. Typically, schools conduct school-wide or universal screening
two or three times per year. For students who are performing adequately in
their classes and on these screening measures, this frequency is sufficient.
Other students, who are struggling or who score in the at-risk range on the

universal screening, need to be monitored more frequently. This topic will be discussed in more detail later in the chapter under Plan Evaluation.

Core Program Evaluation

One of the main purposes of universal screening is to evaluate the effectiveness of the core curriculum. When schools collect data on all students, rather than analyzing student data in isolation, it is easier to identify trends in student performance across grade levels. Assuming the core curriculum is being implemented with fidelity (meaning all teachers deliver the instruction and curriculum the way they were designed), we can assess how well the curriculum teaches the requisite skills across grade levels and classes. For example, in analyzing the universal screening data for quantity discrimination at the second-grade level at School X, we can see if the curriculum effectively addresses this concept. If we find that a high percentage of students in multiple second-grade classrooms score poorly on the universal screening assessment for quantity discrimination, we could logically deduce that additional time and instruction need to be added to the core curriculum in this specific area. If a small percentage of students score poorly, we can conclude that the core curriculum is adequately covering the concept of quantity discrimination for the majority of the students. It should be noted that the appropriateness or adequacy of the core curriculum also depends on the students receiving instruction in that curriculum. Since students' background knowledge and mastery of skills will vary from year to year, it is possible that the core math curriculum adequately meets the academic needs of the students in some years but that in other years supplemental instruction or materials may need to be added to the core curriculum. By using universal screening data to assess the effectiveness of the core curriculum, school leaders can ensure that all the students are receiving quality, effective instruction in Tier 1.

Identifying Struggling Learners

The main purpose of screening all children in the school is to identify students who are performing adequately and those who are at risk for academic failure. Schools use various assessments to evaluate how students are performing academically. Some examples of universal screeners are curriculum-based measurement (CBM), statewide assessments (Illinois Standards Achievement Test, Texas Assessment of Knowledge and Skills, California Standards Test), and other informal standards-aligned assessments. While each of these assessments provides valuable information about the student's performance, it is paramount that multiple sources of data are used to determine a student's need for additional academic support. Collecting data from multiple sources allows educators to confirm that an academic issue really exists across settings and time and is not simply a single piece of data that may or may not represent the student's actual academic functioning. Two key features of a universal screening tool are sensitivity and specificity. The *sensitivity* of the

Figure 2.3 The Ideal Screen

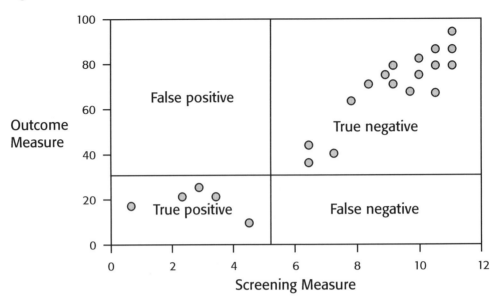

Adapted from Hosp, Hosp, & Howell, 2007.

screening tool refers to how accurately it identifies students who are at risk (true positives), while the *specificity* refers to how well the tool identifies students who are not at risk (true negatives). In Figure 2.3 an "ideal" screen is depicted by showing that all students who are at risk and all students who are not at risk are accurately identified. Additionally, no students are incorrectly identified as being at risk or not at risk. This graph in Figure 2.3 would indicate that the measure is very accurate in identifying struggling learners.

If we can reliably identify students who need additional support and those students who are performing adequately without additional support, we can be more efficient and effective in delivering targeted explicit instruction and interventions.

After educators administer the universal screening and then collect and analyze the student performance data, it is important for teachers to monitor the progress of their students throughout the year. Students who performed adequately on the screening assessment and are considered at or above benchmark only need to be monitored three times per year. Students who are identified as at risk and require supplemental support in mathematics should be monitored monthly to ensure that the interventions and additional support effectively assist them to make adequate progress toward the benchmark. Those students identified as needing "intensive" support should receive more explicit small-group support in addition to Tier 2 services; these students should be monitored at least every two weeks (ideally weekly). The general rule of thumb about how frequently to monitor student progress is this: the more severe or intensive the need, the more frequently progress should be monitored. The National Center on RTI provides information on selecting instruments for universal screening and progress monitoring (http://rti4success.org/progressMonitoringTools). Its website contains reviews of several assessment measures, which are summarized in an easy-to-read "Tools Chart." Students who are identified as struggling will need additional support. For these students, we move to the next step in the problem-solving process: problem analysis.

Step 2: Problem Analysis

What is the nature of the problem? Why is the problem occurring?

To answer these questions, qualified school personnel must analyze the student's work and possibly do additional diagnostic testing in an attempt to pinpoint the nature of the discrepancy between the student's performance and the expected level. This step in the problem-solving process is crucial because it sets the foundation for the subsequent plan that will identify the student's targeted area of need and also guide the intensity and type of intervention to be matched with that need. Once we have identified the students who performed below the expected benchmark on the school-wide assessment, we use diagnostic assessment techniques to gain in-depth information about the individual student's specific strengths, weaknesses, and instructional needs. Diagnostic assessment can include administering additional assessments, conducting error analysis, observing students while they work, or using structured interviews to gain further insight into their mathematical reasoning. The information gained during diagnostic assessment is used to guide the intervention planning.

Error analysis involves identifying consistent patterns of errors that a student makes. To conduct an error analysis, we collect three to five examples that illustrate the student's work for a particular type of problem, such as adding single-digit numbers or dividing by a one-digit divisor. These samples can be taken from the student's daily work or from responses on the universal screening or other assessment measures. We then analyze the samples, looking for patterns in the errors and identifying possible reasons for the errors, such as lack of understanding of place value or incomplete mastery of basic facts. For example, on a universal screening measure a student might have missed most of the problems involving addition of one- and two-digit numbers. It would be easy to assume that the student needs an intervention focused on adding one- and two-digit numbers. However, we can use error analysis to confirm this hypothesis or perhaps identify a reason for the errors that would suggest a different intervention. Error analysis helps pinpoint areas of confusion and allows us to select interventions that will most efficiently target the student's needs.

Student errors fall into several categories. The simplest errors involve problems with computational fluency. Basic math facts include the addition, subtraction, multiplication, and division problems formed with two single-digit numbers. Students sometimes miss math problems simply because they made an error at the basic fact level. Look at these two examples from one student's work:

$$
\begin{array}{r}
^{1} \\
39 \\
+\ 6 \\
\hline
44
\end{array}
\qquad
\begin{array}{r}
^{1} \\
87 \\
+\ 36 \\
\hline
125
\end{array}
$$

In these problems, the student correctly executed the regrouping algorithm but made an error calculating basic facts. In the first problem, she added $9 + 6$ and recorded the sum as 14. In the second problem, she added $7 + 6$ and recorded the sum as 15. Since she completed the regrouping part of the problem correctly, additional instruction in regrouping might be unnecessary. However, if the student consistently says the sum of $9 + 6$ is 14 or the sum of $7 + 6$ is 15, she may need additional work to master basic facts. On the other hand, factual errors also occur when students make careless mistakes because their attention has wandered or they are rushing through the assignment. Additional investigation may be necessary to discriminate between these two scenarios. If the problem is due to carelessness, the student can usually fix the error when asked to review the work. A student who struggles when computing basic facts needs additional practice to develop computational fluency, while a student who makes careless errors will benefit more from an intervention that teaches him to check his work or that rewards computational accuracy. Both students might make errors on the regrouping portion of the screening measure, but neither of these students needs an intervention focused on learning how to regroup in addition.

A more serious type of error occurs when students lack conceptual understanding. Consider how a different student solved the same two problems:

$$
\begin{array}{r}
39 \\
+\ \ 6 \\
\hline
315
\end{array}
\qquad
\begin{array}{r}
87 \\
+\ \ 36 \\
\hline
1113
\end{array}
$$

These errors do not involve computational fluency. This student correctly added the digits in the ones and tens columns, but recorded the sums without regrouping. Such errors reveal a lack of understanding of place value, which is a far more serious problem than a simple computational error. An intervention for this student would require instructional activities that first develop his understanding of place value followed by instructional activities to develop understanding of regrouping.

Although all these students made errors on the same problems, error analysis suggests they need very different interventions. It is common practice to mark math problems correct or incorrect, then to calculate the student's score based on the percentage of correct problems. Students can get an incorrect final answer for a variety of reasons, so it is important for teachers to tease out the type of errors the students make in order to select the appropriate intervention strategies.

While error analysis is a critical component for selecting effective interventions, a study of subtraction error patterns conducted by Riccomini (2005) found that only 59 percent of general education teachers were able to correctly identify error patterns, and even fewer teachers were able to design targeted instruction to address the error patterns they identified. These findings suggest that teachers may need additional training and practice to develop this important skill. An excellent resource for developing skill in error analysis is the book *Error Patterns in Computation: Using Error Patterns to Improve Instruction* by Robert B. Ashlock.

Students can also make procedural errors by failing to follow the correct steps (or procedures) required to solve the problem. In the following example, the student added from left to right, beginning with the tens column and ending with the ones column.

$$
\begin{array}{r}
87 \\
+\ 36 \\
\hline
114
\end{array}
$$

Procedural errors sometimes occur because the student lacks conceptual understanding. In the above example, the student may be confused about place value and so make errors because he is trying to execute an algorithm he does not truly understand. If that is the case, an appropriate intervention would focus on developing understanding of place value and later of the regrouping process. However, the student may have a solid understanding of place value and the regrouping process, but have problems with reversals. A student who occasionally tries to read from right to left may have read the above problem as 78 + 63. Such a student would not need additional instruction in place value or regrouping, but might benefit if an arrow is placed across the top of the page pointing from left to right in order to remind him which way to read the problem. Procedural errors can also occur for a variety of other reasons, such as memory deficits, visual-motor integration problems, and impulsivity. Additional investigation might be needed to determine the cause of the procedural error in order to select an appropriate intervention.

Information gleaned through error analysis can be enhanced through observation and discussion. Interviews provide valuable insight into students' mathematical reasoning and are increasingly advocated to improve mathematical instruction (Allsopp et al., 2008; Buschman, 2001; Crespo &

Figure 2.4 Questions to Evaluate Student Understanding

- Can you explain what you have done so far?
- How did you know to do that?
- Will that work every time?
- Why did you do it that way?
- How did you get your answer?
- Can you explain why that works?
- What should I do next?
- What is the next step?
- What does that that mean?
- How did you reach that conclusion?
- Does your answer make sense?
- Does your answer seem reasonable?
- How would you prove that?
- Can you convince me that your answer makes sense?
- When would we use this?
- What would be another example where we would use this?
- Can you use these blocks to show me what that means?
- Can you make a model to show that?
- Can you draw a picture to show what that means?
- How else could you show that?

Nicol, 2003; Ginsburg, Jacobs, & Lopez, 1998; Long & Ben-Hur, 1991). One interview technique involves asking the student to "think aloud" while solving the problem. Watching the student work and hearing her thinking may reveal possible misconceptions. Follow-up questions can provide further information. For example, you can ask the student why she selected a particular strategy, ask her to explain her reasoning or suggest alternative approaches, use objects or pictures to demonstrate the solution, or prove that the answer makes sense. Another interview strategy is to let the student play the role of teacher and show you how to solve the problem. Interviews provide evidence of students' mathematical reasoning. They can reveal gaps in learning, provide insight into the thinking strategies students use, and identify the strengths and weaknesses in their understanding. All this information can guide intervention planning. Figure 2.4 shows an example of interview questions that can be used to evaluate student understanding.

For more information about error analysis, interviews, observation questionnaires, and sample task analysis checklists, see the resources listed in Figure 2.2.

Problem analysis helps us develop a complete picture of a student's mathematical understanding. Obtaining this level of detailed information about why the student is struggling allows us to target our instruction or intervention to effectively and efficiently address the specific skills or concepts a student needs to develop. By pinpointing the deficit area, we can identify appropriate instructional goals and interventions that will enable the student to obtain mathematical proficiency.

Step 3: Intervention Plan Development

What is the plan? What is the goal? How will we measure student progress?

After forming a hypothesis about why the student is struggling in math, the intervention team can devise a plan that matches the intensity and type of intervention that will best meet the student's academic needs. To answer the above questions, the problem-solving team should identify strategies that have research or evidence to support their effectiveness in the target area. The two most common methods for providing interventions in an RtI framework are to use a standard protocol and to use individualized problem solving. The biggest difference between the two methods is that educators using standard protocol group students with like needs and implement a standard, research-based intervention that addresses the specific needs of that group of students, while educators using individualized problem solving consider each student individually. Both methods set goals for the students and use interventions that address the specific needs of those students. Typically students with severe academic deficits require an individualized plan and may require a variety of specialists to be involved in the decision-making process. It is also common for schools to use standard protocol to address student skill deficits by implementing supplemental interventions in small groups before referring the student for additional support. For example, any students who are struggling with their math facts at a predetermined level might automatically receive additional support by completing computer-assisted basic math fact problems (such as MathFacts in a Flash by Renaissance Learning) in the deficit area. See Figure 2.5 for a matrix one Colorado school district uses to classify standard protocol and individual problem solving.

After the student's academic needs are identified, the teacher and/or problem-solving team determine appropriate goals for the student. Many times, if the area of need is not severe, the team can work backward from the performance level that is considered adequate for future success. After determining an appropriate performance level on a given skill or concept, the team uses local or national norms to identify the level that will enable the student to close the gap between her current performance and her average performing peers. For example, the student may be scoring in the 10th percentile on addition facts. The goal should not be that the student will perform at the 90th percentile, but rather the 50th percentile if that is deemed sufficient performance to progress in the mathematics curriculum and other formal and informal assessments. See Figure 2.6 for an example of an intervention plan for a second-grade student.

Figure 2.5 Comparison of RtI Approaches

A comprehensive school-wide RtI framework includes multiple approaches to providing early intervention for students who are struggling or advanced and not sufficiently challenged. Interventions begin in the classroom at Tier 1. Students not progressing can move to Tier 2 through two options: 1) standard protocol interventions selected by the school to address multiple students' needs, or 2) the problem-solving approach, which is most effective for students with multiple skill deficiencies or complex situations.

	Standard Protocol	Problem Solving
Universal Screening	All students are assessed three times a year (fall, winter, spring) via MAP. Literacy assessment tools (DIBELS, TOWRE, SRI) are used to identify student progress against national norms for grade level.	
Tier I	All students receive high-quality standards-based core curriculum and instruction. Struggling and advanced students are provided classroom supports in general education classes and their progress is monitored.	
Tier II	Students whose universal screening and classroom (Tier I) data indicate that progress is not adequate receive targeted supplemental instruction in the area of skill deficiency. School or grade level teams review student data and recommend standard protocol interventions outside the Problem Solving Team. A minimum of four (4) data points (universal screening and classroom data) are recommended to make a standard protocol referral. 1. Students with similar needs are presented with one standard, research-validated intervention. 2. The intervention may address multiple skill sets and is delivered with fidelity.	Students whose progress in Tier I is not adequate receive supplemental instruction targeted at specific skill deficits. Students referred to the Problem Solving Team typically have more complex problems requiring analysis and consultation with a variety of building specialists. 1. A team makes instructional decisions based on an individual student's performance. The team reviews universal screening, standardized test and classroom (Tier I) data; identifies the academic problem; determines its probable cause; and then develops, implements, and monitors a plan to address the problem.

Figure 2.5 (cont) Comparison of RtI Approaches

2. Students are presented with a variety of interventions, based on their unique needs and performance data.
3. Interventions are flexible and individualized to meet a student's needs and are delivered with fidelity.
4. Individual student goals are established. Progress is monitored at least 2 times per month; results are charted and trended over time.
   a. Four to six (4–6) consecutive data points below goal line: add or change intervention.
   b. Six (6) consecutive data points above goal line: set a different goal or reassess to grade level norms.
5. The Problem Solving Team regularly reviews intervention effectiveness and progress towards goals.

3. Individual student goals are established. Progress is monitored 1–2 times per month; results are charted and trended over time.
   a. Four to six (4–6) consecutive data points below goal line: add or change intervention.
   b. Six (6) consecutive data points above goal line: set a different goal or reassess to grade level norms.
   c. Students not making progress after 4 to 6 data points at multiple interventions should be referred to the Problem Solving Team.

Tier III

Students whose progress is still insufficient in Tier II are referred to the Problem Solving Team to determine if more intensive interventions are needed. The Problem Solving Team regularly reviews intervention effectiveness and progress of all students in Tier III.

Source: Colorado Springs School District 11. Revised Sept. 2009.

Figure 2.6 Math Intervention Plan

Student's name: John Doe	Referring teacher: Mrs. Teacher

Problem statement: John is able to complete 10 correct digits per minute (in addition, sums to 18). The fall benchmark is 40 correct digits.
Specific intervention and general goal: John will practice addition facts on the computer or with a peer helper for 5 minutes daily with flashcards or using the MathFacts in a Flash program.
Length of time: 4 weeks
Days per week: 5 days/week
Number of minutes per day: 5 minutes/day
Where intervention will be provided: Classroom
Progress monitoring to determine student progress: Timed addition facts on Fridays

Step 4: Plan Implementation

Is the plan being implemented with fidelity?

After the plan has been implemented, it is critical that the fidelity of implementation is documented to ensure that the student is getting the correct intervention content, amount of time, and intensity that was determined to be the best support to address the student's specific academic needs. While there are multiple definitions and contexts for considering the fidelity of implementation, for the purposes of this book, we are referring to the level to which a specific instructional plan is implemented and executed in the way it was designed (i.e., length, duration, intensity, etc. of instructional strategies and interventions). There are many ways to ensure the intervention plan is being implemented with fidelity. Teachers or other support staff can keep a log of daily intervention group skills, time, number of students in the group, and so on. It is also possible to teach students how to monitor their own progress; in some cases, it is appropriate for the student to maintain a log showing the time spent on the specific skill if the process is supervised by a teacher. Some computer programs have developed a way to track when and what students practice when working on computer-assisted programs.

Figure 2.7 Questionnaire to Determine the Fidelity of the Intervention Plan

Did the interventionist have adequate training to implement the strategy or intervention the way it was designed?	Yes	No
Was the intervention provided in the prescribed amount of time each day/week?	Yes	No
Did the student receive the intervention for the determined length of time (e.g., 6 weeks)?	Yes	No
Was the quality of delivery consistent and documented?	Yes	No
Did the interventionist contaminate the prescribed strategy or intervention by taking content piecemeal from different programs?	Yes	No
Were students on task and engaged during the intervention time?	Yes	No
Can it be determined that the student's progress or lack of progress was directly influenced by the prescribed intervention plan?	Yes	No

Regardless of which option you choose, it is important to be consistent and diligent about keeping accurate records so that when a teacher or team analyzes the student's progress in the targeted skill or concept, there is a record of the prescribed plan being followed. Math curricula and intervention programs are designated "evidence-based" if they have produced significant increases in achievement outcomes in multiple high-quality studies. When a team selects an evidence-based intervention and implements it in the same way that it was used in the research studies—that is, implements it with fidelity—then their students should obtain similar outcomes. If the intervention is changed, then similar outcomes cannot be assumed. Therefore, if there is empirical evidence that a specific strategy or program produces certain student outcomes, it is imperative that the strategy be used consistently and in the way it was designed. Figure 2.7 provides an example of a questionnaire that could be used to assess whether an intervention was implemented with fidelity. If a student fails to make progress, the questionnaire can help the team determine whether the designated intervention plan was followed consistently. If the plan was followed consistently and the student did not progress, then the team should consider additional diagnostic assessment and/or a new intervention strategy. On the other hand, if the original plan was not followed consistently, then it would be appropriate to continue the intervention but take steps to ensure fidelity of implementation.

Inherent in a plan being implemented with fidelity are the following key aspects: 1) the implementer has adequate training in the method or program, 2) the implementer has access to the needed materials, space, and scheduled time to successfully implement the plan as designed, 3) progress is monitored frequently to assess the student's level of performance and the appropriateness of the intervention in addressing the targeted area, and 4) accurate and consistent documentation of the intervention is maintained throughout the entire plan or until the team decides to make a change.

Step 5: Plan Evaluation

Is the plan working? Is the student making adequate progress?
What do we need to maintain or change?

If we use data to identify a student's academic needs and we implement an intervention plan that specifically addresses the areas of need, then we can determine if the plan is successfully targeting the area of need and enabling the student to make adequate progress by closing the gap between the current and the expected level or benchmark. While there are many factors that must be considered when making instructional decisions, an in-depth discussion of those factors is beyond the scope of this book. Figure 2.2 lists additional resources containing information about setting criteria, cut scores, decision points, and so on.

For the purposes of this book, the plan evaluation step in the problem-solving process provides teachers and/or teams with a point at which they can evaluate their own efforts in addressing a student's targeted needs. The plan can be continued as designed (if it is determined to be working but needs to be extended), minimally revised (possibly by increasing the number of times per week), or completely changed (if the student is not responding to the designed intervention plan in its current design).

Summary

This chapter described the problem-solving model as a clear, efficient, and effective framework for applying student data and instructional programming to improve student academic outcomes. The five basic steps of the problem-solving model are 1) problem identification, 2) problem analysis, 3) intervention planning, 4) plan implementation, and 5) progress monitoring and plan evaluation. By using these steps, teachers and other school personnel can identify and target areas of student need. In the next chapter we provide an overview of evidence-based strategies and programs for use in the core mathematics curriculum and during targeted interventions.

Chapter 3

Overview of Evidence-Based Practices for Teaching Mathematics

A growing body of research describes practices that are effective for teaching mathematics in the general education classroom. Students who are mathematically proficient may succeed without the benefit of high-quality instruction, but best practice is essential for struggling learners. Consistently implementing evidence-based practices is therefore the first step in supporting at-risk students. In this chapter we will discuss recommendations for effective mathematics instruction in the core curriculum, followed by a summary of additional recommendations for supporting individuals who struggle with mathematics. Each of these recommendations will be discussed in more detail in subsequent chapters. Readers interested in an overview of the recommendations, as well as a discussion of the rationale and research supporting each recommendation, will find this chapter useful. Readers looking for suggestions about how to implement a particular intervention may find it more useful to go directly to the chapter of interest.

What Is the Core Curriculum?

Description of the Core Curriculum

Curriculum includes both the content and the process of instruction, so it defines both what is to be taught and how it is to be taught. The core curriculum is provided at Tier 1; it is the instruction *all* students receive. Anything that happens in the general education classroom is considered to be part of the core curriculum. Typically a district purchases a program for mathematics that includes textbooks and student workbooks, teachers' guides describing instructional activities, and supplemental materials. Such a program is part of the core curriculum, but the core also includes anything else that happens in Tier 1. For example, a school may expect teachers to use additional materials or activities to supplement the purchased program, or a teacher may add activities or substitute materials. The core curriculum is the total of all instruction provided to all students in the general education classroom.

Research has not yet established an optimal amount of time for core instruction in mathematics, but fifty to sixty minutes per day is generally considered appropriate at the elementary-school level. For children needing additional support, Tier 2 or Tier 3 interventions are provided in addition to the core curriculum. State and federal regulations specify that *all* students will participate in the general education core curriculum (Tier 1). The only time a child may be pulled from core instruction is if the child is receiving special education services and has an individual education plan (IEP) that explicitly states that he or she will not participate in core activities. With that single exception, all students participate during core instruction time.

Core instruction is not one-size-fits-all, however. In Tier 1, the content, process, and products are differentiated in response to students' interests, learning styles, and academic readiness. Sometimes instruction is provided in a large group setting, but at other times students work in small groups or independently. Sometimes students with similar interests or needs are placed together in homogeneous groups, while at other times heterogeneous groups are used. Flexible grouping allows teachers to match instruction to students' needs. Differentiating instruction provides extra support and practice for students who are struggling, while advanced students can work with more challenging material.

One of the cornerstones of RtI is that all students should receive high-quality instruction. This means that the materials and instructional methods used in a classroom should be supported by rigorous research—that is, they have demonstrated effectiveness in controlled experimental studies—and must be implemented with fidelity. In order for students in the district to receive the same positive results obtained in the research studies, each component of the program must be presented as it was designed and presented when the research study results were collected. While there is continuing emphasis on developing high-quality, evidence-based core programs, no single program will meet the needs of all learner populations. For example, students who are transient, come from low socioeconomic backgrounds, have a disability, or who are not native English-language speakers are at a greater risk for experiencing academic difficulties. Learning is optimized when a district selects a core curriculum that matches the learning needs of the majority of its students. Research has established that at-risk learners typically benefit from explicit instruction and hands-on instructional activities and so will benefit from a curriculum that emphasizes these approaches. When the core program is effectively matched with the student population, the majority of students will successfully learn what is taught in the classroom.

If a district uses an evidence-based curriculum that matches the needs of its students and delivers it with fidelity, at least 80 percent of the students should meet benchmarks on state proficiency tests and other screening measures, while up to 20 percent of students may need additional support. In a class of twenty-five students, this means that at least twenty should flourish in Tier 1 and about five may need additional support. If screening data indicate that more than 20 percent of students in a school are struggling, then it is time to reexamine the core curriculum. The curriculum in use may not be supported by rigorous research, may not be a good match for the student population, or may not have been implemented with fidelity. Solutions include additional training and support for teachers, more or different differentiation, and possibly changing the core curriculum.

Evidence-Based Practice for the Core Curriculum

As discussed in Chapter 1, the term "evidence-based practice" refers to instructional methods that have been found effective in multiple studies that have used rigorous scientific methodology. In 2006 the U.S. Department of Education created the National Mathematics Advisory Panel (NMAP), composed of education professionals, researchers with expertise in mathematics and mathematics instruction, and stakeholders, and charged it with reviewing the available research on mathematics instruction and identifying instructional practices effective for the core curriculum. The panel's final report, *Foundations for Success* (2008), is available at www.ed.gov/MathPanel. Its recommendations are summarized below. Many of the recommendations were incorporated in the Common Core State Standards (www.corestandars.org/), which have now been adopted by the majority of states.

Emphasize Critical Concepts

The panel's first recommendation was that the curriculum for pre-kindergarten through eighth-grade students should be streamlined to emphasize critical topics. International comparisons reveal that high-performing nations typically focus on in-depth coverage of five or six concepts at each grade level. In contrast, U.S. students have routinely covered more than twenty (Schmidt, Wang, & McKnight, 2005). To help students make optimal progress, districts need to select core instructional materials that provide focused, in-depth coverage of the topics emphasized in their state standards, minimizing the time spent on less critical content.

Teach Critical Foundations to Mastery

NMAP recommended that critical foundations should be taught to mastery by the grades indicated: "Any approach that revisits topics year after year without bringing them to closure should be avoided" (NMAP, 2008 Fact Sheet, p. 1). Many basal math programs that have been popular in the United States follow a spiral curriculum design, with the same topics taught for exposure year after year. Teachers are told not to worry if a student fails to master a particular skill or concept because it will be reintroduced later. However, some critical skills and concepts are prerequisites for more advanced mathematics, and students who fail to attain proficiency will struggle with subsequent lessons, falling further and further behind (Porter, 1989). Research evidence suggests that the most effective programs avoid introducing topics year after year without closure. When selecting programs for use in their core curriculum, districts are urged to consider a program that teaches foundational skills to mastery.

Balance Conceptual Understanding, Fluency, and Problem Solving

Historically, mathematics instruction in the United States emphasized computational and procedural fluency. Students learned rote procedures, but often lacked conceptual understanding. As a result, students who might be able to complete a worksheet quickly and accurately were often unable to apply the same skills when they encountered real-life mathematical problem situations. To improve students' mathematical competency, math educators began to emphasize the importance of developing conceptual understanding and teaching mathematics in the context of solving real problems (NCTM, 1989, 2000). This paradigm shift has had many positive effects, but unfortunately some classrooms de-emphasized computational and procedural fluency so much that students failed to become proficient with basic computation. After examining pertinent research, NMAP concluded that conceptual understanding, computational fluency, and problem-solving skills are mutually supportive and that all three are important components of high-quality instruction (NMAP, 2008). When adopting material for a core curriculum, districts should therefore select programs that balance conceptual understanding, computational and procedural fluency, and problem solving.

Use a Combination of Teacher-Centered and Student-Centered Approaches

In recent years, mathematics educators have moved toward an inquiry approach that emphasizes conceptual understanding rather than memorizing facts or teaching a particular algorithm. The teacher first engages students in a real-life problem. Rather than telling students how to solve the problem, teachers give students time to explore and work collaboratively to find a solution. The teacher's role is to facilitate student learning and create a classroom environment in which differing mathematical ideas are shared and valued (Hiebert et al., 1997).

While general education teachers are often taught to use the inquiry method exclusively, special education teachers are typically taught to use a direct or explicit instruction model of instruction, because extensive research documents the value of explicit instruction for students with disabilities and other struggling learners (for example, see NMAP, 2008; Vaughn, Gersten, & Chard, 2000). Explicit instruction is more teacher-directed. Teachers break skills into small steps and explicitly teach algorithms for solving each type of problem, first modeling a skill and then gradually fading support as students gain proficiency. Since the typical classroom contains a wide range of students, research findings suggest that the core curriculum should not rely exclusively on either instructional model. Instead, districts should seek core curriculum programs that provide a balanced approach to teaching mathematics (NMAP, 2008).

Follow the CRA Sequence

NMAP (2008) recommended that students at all grades and performance levels experience instruction that incorporates the progressive use of concrete

Figure 3.1 The Concrete-Representational-Abstract Continuum

Concrete	Representational	Abstract
• Manipulatives • Acting it out	• Pictures • Drawings • Diagrams • Number lines • Tally marks	• Words • Symbols

$1 + 1 = 2$	Number Line	$2 + 3$ $a + b$ 5^2 one half

manipulatives, representational models, and abstract symbols. Manipulatives are concrete objects that "appeal to several senses and that can be touched, moved about, rearranged, and otherwise handled by children" (Kennedy, 1986, p. 6). While manipulatives are commonly used by early childhood teachers, they are used less frequently with older students. However, researchers have demonstrated the value of beginning instruction at the concrete level even for students in middle school and high school (Butler et al., 2003; Gersten & Clarke, 2010; Witzel, Mercer, & Miller, 2003).

Once students demonstrate understanding of concepts using concrete representation, they can progress to using two-dimensional visual representations such as pictures, drawings, number lines, graphs, diagrams, and tally marks to demonstrate mathematical concepts. Abstract presentations using words and symbols to convey mathematical content are most effective after students have developed conceptual understanding using manipulatives and visual representation. This progression is known as the concrete-representational-abstract (CRA) sequence (Peterson, Mercer, & O'Shea, 1988; Sousa, 2007; Witzel, 2005). Figure 3.1 shows examples of concrete, representational, and abstract representation of mathematics.

While mathematics educators have long advocated following the CRA continuum (for example, see Van de Walle, 2004), many instructional materials rely almost exclusively on abstract representation (Bryant et al., 2008; Hodges, Carly, & Collins, 2008). Selecting materials that provide sufficient examples of concrete and pictorial representation can enhance all students' understanding.

Select High-Quality Programs

In order to help schools find high-quality instructional programs, several organizations maintain a database summarizing the research on commercially available instructional materials. The What Works Clearinghouse, a division of the Department of Education's Institute for Education Sciences (IES), assesses the rigor of evidence regarding programs, practices, and products, and provides a summary of its findings that can help educators make informed decisions (www.whatworks.ed.gov/). For basal mathematics programs, each review contains an overview of the program, a summary of research on the program, and a statement about the program's effectiveness. Another website that provides information about the strength of evidence supporting elementary and middle-school math programs is the Best Evidence Encyclopedia (www.bestevidence.org). This website, created by Johns Hopkins University School of Education's Center for Data-Driven Reform in Education and funded by IES, currently provides ratings for a variety of popular math programs. Both websites continue to update their recommendations to reflect ongoing research findings.

Interventions to Support Students Who Struggle in Mathematics

The term "intervention" is used to describe instructional activities that provide additional support for students who are struggling to master the critical competencies introduced in the core curriculum. One benefit of the RtI process is that the support allows students to move at a slower pace and spend more time practicing each skill. However, in addition to providing individualized pacing, research studies have identified other differences between the instruction recommended for the general population and strategies that support learners who struggle to master mathematics. These recommendations are summarized in two important publications: the Center on Instruction's guide, *Mathematics Instruction for Students with Learning Disabilities or Difficulty Learning Mathematics: A Guide for Teachers* (www.centeroninstruction .org/), and the What Works Clearinghouse practice guide, *Assisting Students Struggling with Mathematics: Response to Intervention (RtI) for Elementary and Middle Schools* (Gersten et al., 2009). The What Works Clearinghouse recommends screening all students, providing intensive interventions for individuals identified as at risk and monitoring their progress regularly. The

Figure 3.2 Recommendations from the WWC Practice Guide

> **Assisting Students Struggling with Mathematics:**
> **Response to Intervention (RtI) for Elementary and Middle Schools**
>
> 1. Screen all students to identify those at risk for potential mathematics difficulties and provide interventions to students identified as at risk.
> 2. Instructional materials for students receiving interventions should focus intensely on in-depth treatment of whole numbers in kindergarten through grade 5 and on rational numbers in grades 4 through 8. These materials should be selected by committee.
> 3. Instruction during the intervention should be explicit and systematic. This includes providing models of proficient problem solving, verbalization of thought processes, guided practice, corrective feedback, and frequent cumulative review.
> 4. Interventions should include instruction on solving word problems that is based on common underlying structures.
> 5. Intervention materials should include opportunities for students to work with visual representations of mathematical ideas and interventionists should be proficient in the use of visual representations of mathematical ideas.
> 6. Interventions at all grade levels should devote about 10 minutes in each session to building fluent retrieval of basic arithmetic facts.
> 7. Monitor the progress of students receiving supplemental instruction and other students who are at risk.
> 8. Include motivational strategies in Tier 2 and Tier 3 interventions.

Source: Gersten et al., 2009, p. 6.

practice guide then lists six recommendations for evidence-based interventions in mathematics (see Figure 3.2), and these recommendations form the basis for the rest of this book. We provide an overview of each recommendation in this chapter and explore each one in greater detail in subsequent chapters.

Teach Critical Content During Interventions
Focus on Whole Numbers and Rational Numbers

In the general education classroom, the core mathematics curriculum addresses the full range of mathematical content, including number sense and operations, algebra, geometry, measurement, and data analysis and probability. In response to concerns about the scope of mathematics curricula, educators have attempted to limit the range of topics covered each year, encouraging schools to provide in-depth coverage of fundamental concepts and skills. While the NCTM and NMAP recommendations were directed at the core curriculum, focusing on in-depth coverage of foundational topics is even more important for students who struggle with mathematics. The WWC practice guide recommends, "Instructional materials for students receiving interventions should focus intensely on in-depth treatment of whole numbers in kindergarten through grade five and on rational numbers in grades four through eight" (Gersten et al., 2009). This means that in the early grades, interventions provided for students receiving Tier 2 and Tier 3 support should emphasize counting, number value, place value, and operations with whole numbers. We will discuss strategies for developing proficiency with whole numbers in Chapters 7 and 8. Once students have mastered this content, the focus should shift to rational numbers, including understanding the meaning of fractions, decimals, ratios, and percents, and operations using rational numbers. In Chapter 9, we will discuss interventions for developing proficiency with rational numbers. Topics such as data analysis, measurement, and time should be de-emphasized for students receiving support in Tiers 2 and 3 until the students have mastered the foundational skills. Because of its intense focus on foundational skills, Tier 2 and 3 instruction will not necessarily align with the content being presented in the general classroom. However, since Tier 2 instruction is provided in addition to Tier 1 instruction, students receiving tiered support will still be exposed to the supplemental content when they are in the general education classroom.

Basic Facts

All students should master basic math facts involving addition, subtraction, multiplication, and division. Once students can compute fluently, they are able to direct their cognitive energy to more complicated tasks. Students who cannot identify basic facts quickly and easily must devote too much of their working memory to computation, which limits their ability to attend to other aspects of instruction. For example, during a demonstration on how to regroup when solving a multidigit subtraction problem, a student who is unable to solve basic subtraction facts automatically might have to focus so much energy on the basic computation that the new information about regrouping would be lost.

Research studies have found that students who struggle in mathematics typically lack automaticity with basic facts (Geary, 1993, 2003; Jordan, Hanich, & Kaplan, 2003; Goldman, Pellegrino, & Mertz, 1988; Hasselbring, Goin, & Bransford, 1988). Therefore, the IES practice guide recommends, "Interventions at all grade levels should devote about ten minutes in each session to building fluent retrieval of basic arithmetic facts" (Gersten et al., 2009). We describe strategies for developing fact fluency in Chapter 8.

Problem Solving

The purpose of learning mathematics is to be able to apply that knowledge to solve real-life problems. Both the National Council of Teachers of Mathematics (NCTM) and NMAP (2008) identify problem solving as one of the key components of an effective core mathematics program. Unfortunately, students who struggle with mathematics often experience extreme difficulty solving mathematical word problems (Geary, 2003; Hanich et al., 2001).

Math programs designed for use as a core curriculum in the general education setting frequently teach problem solving using a variation of Polya's (1965) four-step process: (1) understand the problem; (2) devise a plan; (3) carry out the plan; (4) look back and reflect. Students who struggle with mathematics often become stuck at step one; they do not understand the problem. Also, these students often lack strategic knowledge (Carnine, Silbert, Kame'enui, & Tarver, 2004; Swanson, 1990, 1993) and struggle to devise a plan to solve the problem.

A strong body of evidence demonstrates that teaching underlying structures can produce significant improvement in these students' problem-solving performance. Students first learn to recognize problem patterns, then to organize the information from the problem on a schematic diagram. Next, students learn a strategy for solving that type of problem. Because the effectiveness of using underlying structures to teach problem solving is well documented (see, for example, Darch, Carnine, & Gersten, 1984; Fuchs, Fuchs, Craddock et al., 2008; Jitendra et al., 1998; Xin, Jitendra, & Deatline-Buchman, 2005), it is a beneficial approach to use in all tiers. The IES practice guide recommends, "Interventions should include instruction on solving word problems that is based on common underlying structures" (Gersten et al., 2009). In Chapter 10 we provide detailed explanation and examples of how to use underlying structures to teach problem solving.

Effective Instructional Methods for Struggling Students
Explicit Instruction

For students who struggle with mathematics, studies show that learning increases when teachers use systematic, explicit instruction (Gersten et al., 2009; Jayanthi, Gersten, & Baker, 2008; NMAP, 2008). While experts recommend using a balanced approach that combines inquiry methods and explicit instruction for students in Tier 1, the Center on Instruction, the National Mathematics Advisory Panel, and the What Works Clearinghouse all recommend increasing the emphasis on explicit instruction for students receiving mathematical interventions (Gersten et al, 2009; Jayanthi, Gersten, & Baker, 2008; NMAP, 2008). This means that students receiving core instruction should experience some explicit instruction at Tier 1 before being moved to Tier 2. At higher tiers, explicit instruction should be the predominant instructional method. Although explicit instruction is not a specific mathematics strategy, it may be the most important support interventionists can provide. Chapter 5 contains detailed description of how to use explicit instruction to support students who struggle with mathematics.

Manipulatives and Visual Representation

Students who struggle with mathematics have difficulty understanding abstract symbols (Hecht, Vogi, & Torgesen, 2007). In order to develop conceptual understanding, they need to first experience mathematical concepts by dramatizing problems or using manipulatives to demonstrate them. After they have mastered a skill using manipulatives, students are ready to solve problems by using two-dimensional representations such as pictures, tally marks, and graphic representations. Finally they move to the abstract phase, fading the use of concrete and pictorial representation and relying on numbers and symbols to solve problems.

As we discussed earlier, all students benefit when instruction follows the CRA continuum. However, its systematic use is critical during interventions. Multiple studies have demonstrated that students with disabilities or who struggle with mathematics typically need about three lessons at the concrete level, each consisting of twenty problems, before they are ready to fade concrete support; they then need three twenty-problem lessons at the representational level before they develop conceptual understanding and are ready to work solely with abstract words and symbols (for example, see Butler, Miller, Crehan, Babbitt, & Pierce, 2003; Mercer & Miller, 1992; Miller, Harris, Strawser, Jones, & Mercer, 1998). Unfortunately, studies show that typical textbooks do not provide adequate concrete and representational models of mathematical problems, but instead rely primarily on abstract words and symbols (Bryant et al., 2008; Hodges, Carly, & Collins, 2008). While students who are talented in mathematics may master new concepts, skills, and procedures with minimal concrete and visual representation, the omission of these foundational activities can be devastating for students struggling to understand mathematics.

In addition, students who struggle with mathematics need to have the relationship between the concrete, representational, and abstract depictions explicitly demonstrated. The IES practice guide states, "We . . . recommend that the interventionists explicitly link visual representation with the standard symbolic representations used in mathematics" (Gersten et al., 2009, p. 31). In other words, teachers should explicitly teach concepts and operations at the concrete level, then repeat the instruction using the same language and procedural strategies at the representational and abstract levels, so that students clearly see the relationship between the various forms of representation.

The CRA sequence has been shown to be effective with elementary and secondary students. In Chapter 6 we discuss the CRA continuum in greater depth. In Chapter 7 we provide ideas for how to use the CRA continuum to develop conceptual understanding of whole numbers, and in Chapter 9 we apply the sequence to rational numbers.

Motivation

Students who struggle with mathematics often have processing problems, cognitive disabilities, problems with memory retrieval or storage, attention deficits, and other problems that make it difficult to focus on instruction or to complete assignments. In addition, many have experienced failure or frustration when they attempted mathematical tasks in the past, so they now approach mathematics with trepidation. Therefore, effective interventions must address student motivation. While a discussion of motivation may seem out of place in a mathematics book, research studies demonstrate that the planned use of motivational strategies is more important than the choice of textbook or the use of technology for improving learning outcomes (see, for example, Epstein et al., 2008; Fuchs et al., 2005; Marzano, Pickering, & Pollock, 2001). For this reason, the IES recommends that motivational strategies be included in all Tier 2 and Tier 3 interventions (Gersten et al., 2009). Because motivation is a prerequisite for all learning, we begin our discussion of interventions by addressing motivation in Chapter 4.

Summary

If American children are to become mathematically proficient, they need high-quality instruction. The core curriculum provided to all students in the general education classroom (Tier 1) should use materials and instructional approaches that have been validated through rigorous scientific study. Although research into effective approaches for teaching mathematics continues to emerge, a number of evidence-based practices have already been identified that can guide instructional decision making. The core mathematics curriculum should be streamlined to emphasize critical concepts, establish clear benchmarks that specify the grade by which students should master each concept, and emphasize conceptual understanding, computational and procedural fluency, and problem-solving skills. When selecting mathematics programs to use in their core (Tier 1) curriculum, districts will need to focus on materials that align with the standards followed by their state.

Struggling learners will be exposed to the full core curriculum in the general education classroom, but the interventions they receive through Tier 2 and Tier 3 support should focus intensely on the most critical foundational concepts and skills. These include whole numbers and rational numbers, computational fluency with basic facts, and problem solving. While all students benefit when concepts are introduced using concrete and visual representation, developing understanding at the concrete and visual levels is critical for students who struggle with mathematics. In addition, research findings consistently show that students who struggle with mathematics benefit from explicit instruction and the use of motivational strategies in Tier 2 and Tier 3. Although instructional design and motivation are not topics unique to mathematics, the strong body of evidence supporting these strategies led the What Works Clearinghouse to include them in their recommendations for supporting learners in K–8 mathematics (Gersten et al., 2009), and we therefore focus on these strategies in the next two chapters. In Chapters 6–10 we will discuss how to incorporate the other WWC recommendations when providing interventions for whole numbers and fractions.

Chapter 4

Setting the Stage: Increasing Motivation

Why Focus on Motivation?

Motivation is critical for success. Robert Sternberg, former president of the American Psychological Association, describes it as "indispensable" for learning. "Without it," he writes, "a student never even tries to learn" (Sternberg, 2005, p. 19). Unfortunately, many of the students who struggle with mathematics lack the motivation to successfully engage in mathematical activities; they dread tasks involving mathematics because they fear another experience of failure (Gersten et al., 2009). Many are struggling to overcome a variety of very real challenges that negatively impact their ability to achieve mathematical proficiency, including language deficits, processing problems, memory and attention deficits, cognitive disabilities, and problems with executive functioning, so their fear of failure may be well founded. These students may actually need to work harder than their normally achieving peers just to achieve minimal success. Students who already dislike or fear mathematics may find it hard to summon the necessary effort to succeed in mathematical tasks.

It is not surprising, therefore, that research studies find that effective interventions address motivational factors in addition to mathematical content. In fact, studies show that addressing students' motivation, especially with the use of structured rewards, has a greater impact on mathematical achievement than the choice of textbooks or the provision of computer-assisted technology (Best Evidence Encyclopedia, 2009). These findings have led experts to recommend that mathematical interventions should include a motivational component (Gersten et al., 2009; NMAP, 2008).

Motivation can be addressed indirectly through lesson design or more directly using strategies such as self-monitoring, goal-setting, praise, and rewards. We will briefly review some of the components of lesson design that can increase motivation, and then discuss direct motivational strategies in more detail.

Increasing Motivation by Creating Meaningful, Engaging Lessons

Attention is necessary for learning. When students are not attentive and engaged, they are not learning. In order to hold students' attention, math lessons must help students perceive that the information is meaningful to them. The human brain is constantly bombarded with information, and attending to the full deluge of stimuli would be overwhelming. Therefore, the brain is designed to filter incoming information and selectively focus on those stimuli that hold personal meaning. As Wolfe explains in her book, *Brain Matters: Translating Research into Classroom Practice*, "Our species has not survived by attending to and storing meaningless information" (Wolfe, 2001, p. 87). Too often students perceive mathematics lessons as containing meaningless information, and they ask, "Why do we have to learn this? When will we ever use this?" If teachers can relate mathematical content to students' previous experiences and personal interests, students are more likely to perceive the information as meaningful and relevant and so will pay closer attention. The National Council of Teachers of Mathematics (NCTM) places meaning squarely at the center of an effective mathematics program (NCTM, 2000).

Unfortunately, despite the NCTM emphasis on creating authentic connections, most textbooks only occasionally create a meaningful connection to real-world applications or relate new mathematical concepts to students' personal experience (Hodges, Cady, & Collins, 2008). To increase motivation, instructors will often need to add examples of real-world applications for mathematical content. For example, students will be more engaged in finding the diagonal of a rectangle if they realize that is the dimension used to designate the size of a television screen; they will be more interested in working with fractions if the fractions are related to the beat in their favorite music video. When the teacher can successfully combine the students' own interests with relevant mathematical content, their natural motivation is aroused.

Humans are social creatures, so activities that involve social interaction often elicit increased participation and engagement. Even when the topic is not inherently interesting, when the learning process involves social interaction students may be motivated to attend and participate because they enjoy the peer interaction. This positive emotional response can actually increase learning. Wolfe explains, "The brain is biologically programmed to attend first to information that has strong emotional content. . . . It is also programmed to remember this information longer" (Wolfe, 2001, pp. 87–88). Using games and other interactive activities can arouse emotional responses that improve long-term learning. In Chapter 8 we will describe several games that can

Figure 4.1 Evidence-Based Peer-Tutoring Programs for Mathematics

Classwide Peer Tutoring (CWPT)
CWPT combines reciprocal peer tutoring with an incentive system. It is designed to be used in grades K–6 for 30 minutes per day, 4 days a week. Each week students are pretested on that week's content and assigned to a partner and team for the week. Partners take turns tutoring and testing each other using a highly structured tutoring procedure. Students receive points for answering correctly, for correcting and practicing after an incorrect response, and for weekly test performance. Bonus points are awarded when students are observed engaging in appropriate task-related behavior. Teams earning the greatest point totals receive recognition. • For additional information, see www.promisingpractices.net/program.asp?programid=99. • The *Together We Can* manual and posters can be purchased from www.sopriswest.com.
Peer Assisted Learning Strategies (PALS)

PALS is a version of Classwide Peer Tutoring used to reinforce material previously covered by the teacher. It is designed to be implemented for 25-35 minutes 2-4 times per week. Teachers pair low- and high-performing students, and each set of partners works on activities matched to the particular problems they are experiencing. Partners change weekly so that all students have the opportunity to act as both coach and as player. Scripted lessons and materials are available for mathematics content covering kindergarten through sixth-grade skills.
 	
• For additional information, see the following websites:
  ▪ www.cec.sped.org/AM/Template.cfm?Section=Home&CAT=none&CONTENTID=5445&TEMPLATE=/CM/ContentDisplay.cfm
  ▪ www.k8accesscenter.org/training_resources/mathpeertutoring.asp
• PALS materials can be purchased from www.kc.vanderbilt.edu/pals.

be used to develop computational fluency. On its Illuminations website (http://illuminations.nctm.org/), NCTM provides many additional games that can be used in tiered interventions to increase student motivation.

Cooperative learning activities are another excellent way to incorporate social interaction into tiered interventions. Ideas for using cooperative learning activities are available at Kagan Cooperative Learning (www.KaganCoopLearn.com). One type of cooperative learning that has produced especially strong gains in mathematical proficiency is peer

Figure 4.1 *(cont)* Evidence-Based Peer-Tutoring Programs for Mathematics

Student Teams-Achievement Divisions (STAD) **(now Power Teaching: Mathematics)**
STAD is a cooperative learning strategy in which small groups of learners with different levels of ability work together to accomplish a shared goal. Students in a class are assigned to 4- or 5-member heterogeneous learning teams. After the teacher introduces the material, team members help each other master the material with the aid of worksheets, tutoring, discussions, and quizzes. At the end of the week each student is quizzed individually. Students are graded on their improvement, and teams with the highest scores and greatest improvement receive recognition for their progress. • For additional information, see the following article: www.lit.az/ijar/pdf/jes/4/JES2010(4-2).pdf. • Power Teaching: Mathematics can be purchased from www.successforall.org.
Team Accelerated Instruction: Math (TAI Math)

TAI Math combines interactive instruction by teachers with cooperative learning, individualized instruction, and an incentive system. It is designed to provide supplementary math support for students in grades 3 through 6 or older students who are not yet ready for algebra. Students work in small groups. They complete a pretest and then are placed in an individualized instruction sequence and allowed to proceed at their own pace. Within their teams, students assist one another with problems and check each others' work. Teachers provide direct instruction to small groups of students who are performing at similar levels. Students receive weekly awards based on the average performance of their teams.
 	
• For additional information, see the following websites:
  ▪ www.childtrends.org/lifecourse/programs/tai.htm
  ▪ www.promisingpractices.net/program.asp?programid=139
• TAI Math materials can be purchased from www.charlesbridge.com/school/html/tai.html.

tutoring (see the Best Evidence Encyclopedia report at www.bestevidence .org). A variety of formats for peer tutoring have been developed, all involving students working in pairs or small groups to help each other master the material. The most effective peer-tutoring programs combine highly structured cooperative learning strategies with a structured reward system. We will discuss how to create effective structured reward systems later in this chapter. See Figure 4.1 for a description of peer-tutoring programs that have shown strong evidence of effectiveness in mathematics.

Using Self-Monitoring and Goal-Setting to Increase Motivation

Self-monitoring is a strategy that involves students monitoring their own behavior and recording the results. Studies have shown that students who use self-monitoring are more engaged and more productive, have greater accuracy, and show increased awareness of their own behavior (Moxley, 1998; Rock, 2005). The IES practice guide suggests, "Allow students to chart their progress and to set goals for improvement" (Gersten et al., 2009, p. 46). Students can monitor a variety of their own behaviors, such as attention, participation, and amount of time on task, or aspects of the academic performance, such as accuracy or rate.

While successful students typically monitor their performance intuitively, students who struggle with mathematics frequently lack metacognitive awareness. Therefore, they may need to be explicitly taught to monitor their own behavior. Figure 4.2 provides a summary of self-monitoring and goal-setting. An instructional module describing self-monitoring and goal-setting, with more detailed explanations and multiple examples, can be obtained by accessing Vanderbilt University's Iris module, "SOS: Helping Students Become Independent Learners" (http://iris.peabody.vanderbilt.edu/sr/chalcycle.htm).

Effective Use of Praise

In recent years, praise has been the subject of hot debate among educators. Teachers hear a great deal of contradictory advice about whether to praise or how to praise their students. As sometimes happens with complex topics, conclusions based upon specific research studies have been overgeneralized, leading to educational recommendations far removed from the actual scientific research. Many teachers have been warned to use praise cautiously because of a mistaken belief that any form of teacher praise undermines student motivation. In fact, while certain kinds of praise do lead to self-defeating behavior, research reveals that "the right kind motivates students to learn" (Dweck, 2008, p. 34).

What is the "right kind" of praise? To answer this question, we must first examine assumptions about human intelligence. At one time intelligence was viewed as a fixed entity; people thought you were born with a certain amount of ability, and nothing you did could change that innate potential.

Figure 4.2 Self-Monitoring

Self-monitoring teaches students to develop greater metacognitive awareness by learning to assess their own behavior and track the results. Studies of self-monitoring have demonstrated a variety of benefits, including increased self-awareness, fewer disruptive behaviors, increased on-task behavior, and increased academic achievement. Self-monitoring and goal-setting are evidence-based practices recommended by the What Works Clearinghouse practice guide, *Assisting Students Struggling with Mathematics: Response to Intervention (RtI) for Elementary and Middle Schools* (Gersten et al., 2009).

Teaching Students to Monitor Their Behavior

1. **Select a behavior.** If the behavior is clearly described in specific, observable terms, students will be able to more accurately monitor their own behavior.
2. **Collect baseline data.** Monitor the frequency, duration, and/or intensity of the behavior for at least three days before the student begins to self-monitor. The baseline data are useful when determining a reasonable standard for improvement. Comparing baseline data to the students' later performance enables both teachers and students to evaluate the effectiveness of the intervention.
3. **Discuss the strategy with the student and obtain the student's agreement to participate.** Teach the student how to self-monitor and graph the results. Establish the time period when the student will monitor the behavior. Provide the student with materials for recording behavior and graphing the results, and teach the student how to use them. Provide cues as needed to help the student remember to self-monitor.
4. **Implement the agreed-upon plan.**
5. **Monitor the student's progress.** Spend time discussing the graph with the student. Celebrate improvement, and help students develop strategies to facilitate further growth.

We now know that the brain is malleable and ability can be cultivated. Learning causes physiological changes in the brain, including larger cortical neurons and more heavily branched dendrites (Wolfe, 2001). In other words, the process of learning makes you smarter. Students who believe that intelligence is fixed and unchangeable tend to seek activities that showcase their

Figure 4.3 Examples of Effective Praise

- You really worked hard on this assignment, and it shows. You stuck with it, and in the end you solved it!
- I like the way you kept working on this, even when it was difficult. Good job!
- You studied for this test, and your improvement shows it!
- You really put forth effort on this. I noticed you got straight to work and stayed focused. That's great!
- This was hard, but you really stuck with it!
- You studied hard. I noticed that you practiced your flash cards and tried the extra problems. That really worked!
- You're really staying focused on this. That's how you'll be successful in the end.
- You paid attention and now you're trying the strategy we discussed. That's great!
- You did well on this! I can tell you worked hard.

intelligence, and they avoid tasks where they might make mistakes, erroneously believing that mistakes reveal a lack of intelligence (Hong, Chiu, Dweck, Lin, & Wan, 1999; Mueller & Dweck, 1998). Studies have shown that students with this fixed view of intelligence are less likely to seek help to correct mistakes, but instead try to hide them. They report that mistakes make them feel dumb and cause them to study less and consider cheating (Hong et al., 1999; Nussbaum & Dweck, 2008). These students believe that individuals who have high ability do not need to expend effort to succeed. They fear that working hard reveals a lack of ability, so they reject tasks that require effort. When they fail, they attribute that failure to lack of ability rather than lack of effort (Blackwell, Trzesniewski, & Dweck, 2007; Marzano et al., 2001). Although students receiving tiered support through RtI have not been specifically targeted for these studies, much of the work has involved students who were identified by teachers as struggling in mathematics. Dweck concludes, "it was the most vulnerable children who were already obsessed with their intelligence and chronically worried about how smart they were" (Dweck, 2008, p. 35).

Successful students, on the other hand, tend to believe that intelligence can be developed. They view mistakes and setbacks as something that can be remedied. When they make a mistake, they study harder or try a new strategy. For these students, effort is a positive attribute integral to the learning process.

How do students develop such different mind-sets regarding the role of effort in learning? Researchers investigating this question have found that the kind of praise children receive has a profound influence on their beliefs about the role effort and dedication play in intelligence and achievement. In one study, investigators gave two groups of students various problems and then praised them. One group of children was praised for their intelligence, receiving feedback like "Wow, that's a really good score. You must be smart at this." The other group was praised for effort, hearing, "Wow, that's a really good score. You must have worked really hard" (Kamins & Dweck, 1999; Mueller & Dweck, 1998). The different forms of praise produced dramatically different results. According to one of the researchers:

> The children praised for their intelligence lost their confidence as soon as the problems got more difficult. Now, as a group, they thought they weren't smart. They also lost their enjoyment, and, as a result, their performance plummeted. On the other hand, those praised for effort maintained their confidence, their motivation and their performance. Actually, their performance improved over time. (Dweck, 2008)

In another study, students with learning disabilities in mathematics who received effort-attributional feedback (e.g., "You've been working hard") demonstrated significantly greater academic gains than students who received only performance feedback (Schunk & Cox, 1986).

Interventions designed to help students appreciate the importance of effort have improved achievement in mathematics and other areas (for example, see Aronson, Fried, & Good, 2002; Blackwell et al., 2007; Good, Aronson, & Inzlicht, 2003). When teachers praise students' effort and engagement, students often work harder and achieve more (Brophy, 1981; Marzano et al., 2001).

Effective praise emphasizes student effort and task-relevant behavior instead of focusing on ability or attributes such as pleasing the teacher or receiving external rewards. Figure 4.3 provides examples of praise statements that focus on the learning process and so can foster a growth mind-set in students.

Rewards

Rewards are increasingly prevalent in today's classrooms. Candy, trinkets, extra credit points, coupons, and pizza parties are frequently offered in an effort to motivate students. Programs in Kansas City and New York City have paid students for attendance and good grades with gift cards and cash (Kumar, 2004). A recent cover of *Time* magazine featured the question "Should schools bribe kids?" The headline then provided the answer: "A major new study reveals an uncomfortable truth—it can work (if it's done right)" (Ripley, 2010).

Research supports the use of incentives to motivate reluctant learners (for example, see Cameron, Bank, & Pierce, 2001; Epstein et al., 2008; Fuchs, Seethaler et al., 2008; Marzano, Pickering, & Pollock, 2001). Providing rewards has led to increased achievement and improved behavior without decreasing intrinsic motivation. In fact, incentive systems that are properly structured can jump-start reluctant learners' motivation. As noted above, cooperative learning programs that included a structured reward system were more effective than those that relied on cooperative learning alone (www.bestevidence.org). Students may initially work to gain the rewards, but once they begin to experience success, intrinsic motivation increases and they begin to experience satisfaction from completing the task successfully. The IES practice guide states:

> Tier 2 and Tier 3 interventions should include components that promote student effort (*engagement-contingent rewards*), persistence (*completion-contingent rewards*), and achievement (*performance-contingent rewards*). These components can include praise and rewards. Even a well-designed intervention curriculum may falter without such behavioral supports. (Gersten et al., 2009, p. 44)

However, reward systems that are poorly designed or poorly implemented are frequently ineffective and can actually be counterproductive (Deci, 1971; Lepper, Greene, & Nisbett, 1973).

What makes an incentive system effective? To answer that question, we will use a mnemonic created from the letters in the word "INCENTIVE" (Forbringer, 2007). Each letter in the mnemonic represents an element that researchers have found essential to create an effective incentive system. These elements are equally important whether developing an incentive system to use with an individual student or a large group of students. They are appropriate for use during Tier 2 and Tier 3 interventions or in the general classroom. The mnemonic is illustrated in Figure 4.4, which is explained below. The explanation is followed by a sample incentive system that could be effectively used when providing tiered support.

I = Instruction with Incentive
Is the reward paired with appropriate instructional assistance?

To be effective, the incentive must be coupled with appropriate instructional strategies. Tasks must be broken into small steps and carefully sequenced so that a student who expends the necessary effort will be able to complete the task successfully and earn the reward. When an incentive does not produce the desired results, educators sometimes say, "Rewards don't work with this child." Often the error is not with the reward system, but rather that the rewards were not accompanied by the necessary instructional support.

N = Not Negative!

Does the incentive system give rewards for positive behavior rather than taking away rewards for inappropriate behaviors?

Research and best practice both suggest that an incentive system that rewards appropriate behavior is preferable to one that punishes inappropriate behavior (Council for Exceptional Children, 2003; Kampwirth, 1988; Mandella, Nelson, & Marchand-Martella, 2003). Unfortunately, many of the incentive systems recommended online or found in classrooms are negative systems that offer a reward but then withdraw it when the child exhibits inappropriate behavior. For example, one negative system uses stoplights to indicate whether a student can participate in free time or obtain other privileges. Everyone begins the period with a green light, and as long as the student behaves, the light remains green. When the student misbehaves, the light is moved to yellow, and then to red, and the student loses the right to receive the reward. Another commonly used negative system awards points when students are doing well, but takes those points away when problems arise. The reward is dangled before the child, but then taken away if the child misbehaves. The Council for Exceptional Children (2003), the professional organization for professionals who work with individuals with disabilities, specifies that aversive procedures such as response-cost systems may be used, but only as a last resort after more positive interventions have been tried. They are not the best choice for a reward system to be used for an entire class or group of students, and they should not be selected as the motivational system to use in tiered interventions. Response-cost systems may be especially counterproductive with minority students. Research indicates that students from Arab, Asian, and Hispanic cultures respond more positively to quiet, private feedback than to more public correction such as writing names on the board or posting stoplights (Cheng, 1998; Lockwood & Secada, 1999; Walqui, 2000).

Instead of withdrawing rewards when students misbehave, effective incentive systems recognize students when they are engaged in productive behaviors. For example, students may receive bonus points, signatures, or smiley faces when they exhibit desirable behaviors such as beginning work promptly, attending to the task, or completing assignments. These tokens can be accumulated and later exchanged for rewards. Attending to students' appropriate behavior is an evidence-based practice that has been shown to increase task-relevant behavior; in fact, studies of effective classrooms have shown that effective teachers provide four times more attention to students when they are behaving appropriately than the amount of attention given to inappropriate behavior (Sprick, Garrison, & Howard, 1998). When teachers use a negative system that involves response-cost, they are forced to attend to inappropriate behaviors. Focusing attention on the child's problematic behavior can foster a negative self-concept and also reinforce inappropriate behaviors in students who find negative attention

Figure 4.4 Elements of Effective Incentive Systems

I	**Instruction with Incentive** Is the reward paired with appropriate instructional assistance?
N	**Not Negative!** Does the incentive system give rewards for positive behavior rather than taking away rewards for inappropriate behavior?
C	**Criteria** Is a baseline used to determine what the student must do to earn the reward?
E	**Easy** Is the system easy to understand and implement?
N	**Never leave a child with no reason to try!** Is the system designed so students always have a reason to keep trying?
T	**Time** Is the amount of time students must work to earn the reward realistic for their developmental levels?
I	**Individualized Incentive** Is the incentive offered something that will motivate students to put forth the necessary effort?
V	**Verbal Feedback** Is verbal feedback provided along with the reward in a way that emphasizes effort?
E	**Evaluate** If the system is not effective, re-evaluate. Have you followed all eight guidelines for effective incentive systems?

rewarding. In summary, research findings suggest that incentive systems used during interventions should be positive systems structured to reward productive behavior rather than negative systems that take away rewards for inappropriate behavior.

C = Criteria
Is a baseline used to determine what the student must do to earn the reward?

Incentive systems are most effective when they allow students to experience initial success quickly. Students must believe that they can earn the reward with a reasonable amount of effort. If they perceive the criteria as too difficult, they will rapidly lose interest. Too often students initially respond enthusiastically to a reward system, but become discouraged when their hard work does not produce immediate results. Just as a trainer working with an aspiring pole-vaulter will first set the bar low, then gradually raise it as the young athlete becomes more skillful, so too the criteria for an incentive system should be initially set low and gradually raised as students experience success. To identify effective criteria, instructors should first collect baseline data on the target behavior and use that baseline to determine how well the student must perform in order to earn a reward. For example, if baseline data show that a student typically remains on task for no more than five minutes at a time, it would be unrealistic to require her to remain on task for the whole period in order to earn a reward. Instead, an excellent first step would be to offer a reward if she remains on task for slightly more than five minutes, perhaps six or seven minutes. Students who experience initial success are likely to respond enthusiastically to the incentive system and continue to progress. Just as with the pole-vaulter, the bar can gradually be raised as students gain proficiency. Teachers who shape behavior by rewarding small improvements usually see greater success than those who require more rapid change.

E = Easy
Is the system easy to understand and implement?

An incentive system should improve behavior and increase academic engaged time, not make life more difficult. If explaining or implementing the system requires the teacher to interrupt a lesson in order to record student behavior or to pass out rewards, it can interfere with learning, and the teacher may be tempted to abandon the system. Poorly designed systems can actually create behavior problems. For example, in some systems that focus on negative behavior, when a student is caught misbehaving the teacher directs him to give back a token, move his namecard to the "unsatisfactory" column on the board, or demonstrate failure in some other public way. When this happens, many students will express their embarrassment by becoming increasingly oppositional. A child with a behavior disorder may retaliate by throwing tokens across the room, ripping things off the wall, or otherwise disrupting the classroom. Any system that takes too much time to implement or creates behavior problems in the classroom is not a useful system. The best systems are simple and easy to understand and implement.

N = Never Leave a Child with No Reason to Try!
Is the system designed so students always have a reason to keep trying?

The function of an incentive system is to motivate the most reluctant learners. If a student knows she has already lost all chance of earning the reward before the end of the period, what motivation will she have to keep trying? Conversely, if she realizes part way through the period that she has already

Figure 4.5 Suggested Rewards

No Salt, No Sugar, & No Money
Acknowledgement Menu: Incentives for Supporting Positive Behaviors
Developed by Effective Educational Practices
www.successfulschools.org

Illinois PBIS Network's
Non/Low-cost PBIS Reinforcements for Students
www.slideshare.net/aerobinson1/no-and-lowcost-student-rewards

Dunn-Rankin Reward Preference Inventory
www.docstoc.com/docs/58163762/Dunn-Rankin-Reward-Preference
  -Inventory

done enough to earn the reward, why should she continue working? For example, if the teacher tells a student that she must complete seven out of ten problems correctly in order to earn the reward, then once she has accurately completed seven problems there is little motivation to work carefully on the remaining three. On the other hand, once she has four mistakes she knows she has no chance of earning the reward and so may give up rather than keep trying.

The best systems allow students to earn a small reward for expending some effort, but a greater reward for expending greater effort. They are designed so the student will always have a reason to keep trying.

T = Time
Is the amount of time students must work to earn the reward realistic for their developmental level?

People work harder when they believe the reward they seek is almost won. Since children's sense of time differs from that of adults, students may become discouraged when expected to work for a time span that seems perfectly reasonable to adults. A reward that the student thinks cannot be attained until the distant future is less motivating than a reward the student believes can be quickly earned. Students may be given frequent points or tokens to show their progress toward earning the reward, but the reward itself should also be offered within a time period that they understand. Canter and Canter (2001) suggest that students in kindergarten and first grade should be able to earn their reward the same day; those in second and third grade may be able to work for two days to a week to attain the reward. Students in fourth through sixth grade should be able to work for one week, and students in grades seven through twelve can work for up to

Figure 4.6 Sample Elementary and Secondary Reward Menus

Reward Menu—Elementary
Piece of candy = 1 point
Sticker = 1 point
Baseball card = 2 points
Rent marker for 15 minutes = 1 point
Buy marker = 20 points
Sit in teacher's chair for one period = 3 points
Pass to visit another class for 15 minutes = 5 points
Skip one assignment = 25 points
Earn extra 15-minute recess for class = 30 points
Additional rewards will be added throughout the school year.
Reward Menu—Secondary
Piece of candy = 1 point
Borrow pen or pencil = 1 point
First pick of project partner = 3 points
Sit in teacher's chair for one period = 3 points
Bag of chips or candy bar = 5 points
Earn 5 minutes of talking time for class = 10 minutes
Pick on problem class can skip on homework = 10 points
Move your desk to a chosen location = 20 points
Homework pass = 25 points
Additional rewards will be added throughout the school year.

two weeks for a reward. However, students within any given grade differ in their maturity levels. Usually the least mature students in the class are the ones who need the incentive system the most. When deciding how long to ask students to work for a reward, consider the developmental level of the least mature students in the group.

I = Individualized Incentive
Is the incentive offered something that will motivate students to put forth the necessary effort?

If the incentive system is going to work, students must want the reward enough to work hard for it. Just because teachers or parents think a particular item or activity should be rewarding does not mean students will perceive it as rewarding (Downing, 1990; Downing, Moran, Myles, & Ormsbee, 1991; Shea & Bauer, 1987; Smith & Rivera, 1993). Children differ, and not all children will be equally motivated by any given incentive. The list of

Figure 4.7 Example of an Effective Incentive System: The Good Behavior Board Game

The Good Behavior Board Game is an incentive system that can be used with a group of students or the entire class. A detailed description of the game, with accompanying blackline masters, is provided by Cipani in *Classroom Management for All Teachers* (2008). Versions of the game have been studied and found effective with a wide variety of students (Barrish, Saunders, & Wolf, 1969; Carpenter & McKee-Higgins, 1996; Harris & Sherman, 1973; Medland & Stachnik, 1972).

The game requires a large game board posted at the front of the classroom. When students follow classroom rules, they can advance a game piece around the board until they reach a treasure box on the board. When they reach the treasure box, everyone in the class participates in a rewarding activity. Before introducing the game, the teacher must first establish clear expectations for behavior and collect baseline data on the number of rule violations that occur during a ten-minute interval. These baseline data are used to determine the criteria that will be required for students to earn an initial reward. For example, if baseline data reveal that the class averages five rule infractions every ten minutes, then an appropriate initial expectation would be for the students to show improvement by exhibiting fewer than five rule infractions during a ten-minute interval. If the class meets the expectation, they can advance their game piece. If they do not meet the expectation, then their game piece does not advance, and they must wait to try again during the next interval. As students become better at controlling their behavior, the behavioral expectations become more rigorous, until eventually students may be required to have zero infractions in order to advance their game piece. Game boards are designed so that students must demonstrate between five and ten appropriate intervals in order to reach a treasure box and earn a reward. Comparing students' baseline behavior to their performance after the intervention has been implemented allows the teacher to evaluate the effectiveness of the intervention.

potential rewards is almost limitless. Material items include food, trinkets, school supplies, or art supplies. Privileges and social rewards such as extra recess, social time with friends, selecting the assignment, using preferred art materials, being line leader, skipping a problem or assignment, or getting a positive note home can be extremely effective. Rewards can also include teacher attention or bonus points for improvement. To make sure that the incentive offered is something the students in the group find motivating, teachers can watch what the students do during free time and use those items and activities as rewards. They can also ask students what they would like to earn, or use an interest inventory to identify potential rewards. The websites listed in Figure 4.5 suggest rewards that can motivate elementary and secondary students. Although some of these lists include food-based rewards, interventionists should follow school districts' wellness policies when selecting rewards.

Figure 4.7 *(cont)* Example of an Effective Incentive System: The Good Behavior Board Game

Reward activities include a variety of privileges, such as allowing the class five or ten minutes of social conversation time, minutes to begin working on homework during class time, time for doodling, listening to music, looking at teen magazines with friends, and other activities that students in the group would find reinforcing.

The Good Behavior Board Game can be evaluated using the mnemonic formed by the letters in the word "incentive." It contains the elements research studies have determined to be essential in an effective incentive system:

- **I = Instruction with Incentive**
  This incentive system has been used successfully in a variety of subjects. To be effective, students must be capable of performing the skills required to attain the reward, or they must be taught how to perform those skills.
- **N = Not Negative**
  In this game, students move their game piece around the game board contingent upon intervals of good behavior. When they reach the treasure box, they receive a reward. Students gain rewards for appropriate behavior; they do not lose rewards for inappropriate behavior. If they fail to meet the behavioral goal for a time interval, the game piece remains where it was.
- **C = Criteria**
  The Good Behavior Board Game uses a baseline to determine what the students must do to earn the reward. This ensures that the criteria are appropriate for the students in the group.
- **E = Easy**
  The system is easy to understand and implement. It requires minimal preparation time, and game pieces can be advanced quickly with minimal disruption to the academic lesson. When students reach the treasure box, they earn the

Another option is to offer choices for rewards, such as letting students spend reward points on items from a classroom store or select from a list of choices on a reward menu. Students who need immediate gratification can purchase a small item at a small cost, while those able to delay gratification can save their points until they have enough to purchase a more desirable, higher-priced item. Offering choices is especially effective when working with a group of children who might be best motivated by a variety of incentives. See Figure 4.6 for an example of a reward menu.

V = Verbal Feedback
Is verbal feedback provided along with the reward in a way that emphasizes effort?

Whenever incentives are used, they should be paired with social reinforcement such as a smile, a thumbs-up gesture, a pat on the back, or verbal

Figure 4.7 *(cont)* Example of an Effective Incentive System: The Good Behavior Board Game

selected prize or activity, but the activity occurs at a time during the day designated by the teacher.

- **N = Never leave a child with no reason to try!**
  Students always have a reason to keep trying. Even when they fail to advance their game piece, they have another chance during the next ten-minute interval.

- **T = Timing**
  The length of time students must work is realistic. They can advance their token every ten minutes. The game board can be designed with varying numbers of spaces between treasure boxes, but typically students must advance five to ten spaces in order to earn a reward. If baseline data are used to determine the criteria for advancement, then students should be able to earn a reward every two days to a week. For younger students, the time interval is generally reduced from ten minutes to five minutes, allowing them to earn a reward in a day.

- **I = Individualized Incentive**
  In this system, the entire class receives the same reward. It is crucial, therefore, that the reward options are carefully selected to include activities and items that will be valued by all members of the group.

- **V = Verbal Feedback**
  The Good Behavior Board Game does not specify the type of verbal feedback teachers should provide with this incentive system. Teachers will need to use what they know about effective praise to help students focus on their own effort and task-relevant behavior and develop their own internal locus of control.

- **E = Evaluate**
  The game directions include suggestions for trouble-shooting that emphasize reviewing the criteria, timing, and selection of appropriate incentives.

praise. Pairing social reinforcement with incentives develops the student's ability to maintain the desired behavior after the incentive system ends (Walker & Shea, 1999).

When students begin to attribute success to their personal effort, research suggests that their achievement will increase (Marzano et al., 2001). Incentive systems are supposed to be temporary interventions designed to help motivate students. Teachers can help students move beyond the need for an incentive system by providing specific verbal feedback along with the earned reward.

E = Evaluate
If the system is not effective, reevaluate the eight guidelines for effective incentive systems.

A well-designed incentive system will be effective. If the system is not working, the problem is usually with one of the eight elements described above.

For example, the criteria may be too high, causing students to become discouraged, or the incentive offered may not be something the students truly desire. When incentive systems adhere to these research-based guidelines, they help students achieve success in tiered interventions. Figure 4.7 provides an example of an evidence-based incentive system that has been used to improve behavior and increase achievement in a variety of classroom settings; it would be an excellent choice for increasing motivation among students receiving math interventions. We use the elements described in the mnemonic to critique this incentive system.

Summary

Motivation is critical for success, but many students who require mathematical support lack motivation. Often, they have experienced so much failure that they are no longer interested in putting forth the effort needed to benefit from interventions. Research supports using motivational strategies when working with students who struggle academically.

Several strategies can increase student motivation, including connecting the lesson to real-world applications and students' interests, incorporating active participation and social interaction through games or cooperative learning activities, providing effective praise, teaching students to set goals and monitor their progress, and rewarding task-related behavior and academic performance using incentive systems that follow research-based guidelines. The use of motivational strategies when providing interventions can help all students become mathematically proficient.

Chapter 5

Explicit Instruction

Students who struggle with mathematics have a variety of learning characteristics that affect their response to instruction. Of the many instructional designs used by teachers, research studies have demonstrated that explicit instruction is the most effective with these students (Gersten et al., 2009). In this chapter we will first examine important instructional considerations for students who are not making adequate progress, then describe the critical elements of explicit instruction that help meet these students' needs, and finally discuss how explicit instruction improves students' motivation.

Instructional Considerations for Struggling Learners

Students who fail to make adequate progress in mathematics frequently have problems with memory and executive functioning (Hallahan et al., 2005). Working memory is the conscious processing of information that enables us to hold small amounts of information in conscious awareness for a short period of time. It allows us to integrate perceptual information with knowledge stored in long-term memory. For example, when a student is asked to mentally add the numbers $3 + 5 + 7$, he must process what the question is asking, retain the three numerals in working memory while drawing on his stored knowledge of the process of addition and his knowledge of basic addition facts, and use all that information to obtain a partial sum ($3 + 5 = 8$) before computing $8 + 7$ to obtain the final answer of 15. The average adult can retain about seven items in working memory (plus or minus two) for about eighteen seconds (G. A. Miller, 1956; Wolfe, 2001). You can try this for yourself with a short test. Spend about one second per digit memorizing the following list of seven numbers. Then look away and write them down, in order, from memory:

2   5   1   8   3   4   9

If you have an average memory span you probably remembered all seven, because $7 + 2$ is the typical capacity of individuals age fifteen and older

(G. A. Miller, 1956). Children have a much more limited capacity, which increases gradually as they mature. The average five-year-old can recall about two items. A seven-year-old can typically retain three items, and a nine-year-old can retain four. By age eleven, retention increases to about five items, and by age thirteen, the average individual can recall about six (Pascual-Leone, 1970).

Individuals who struggle with mathematics generally have less working memory than their normally achieving peers (Allsopp et al., 2010; Geary, 2004; Hulme & Mackenzie, 1992; Mabbott & Bisanz, 2008; Mazzocco, 2007; Swanson & Cooney, 1991; Swanson, Jerman, & Zheng, 2009). In today's diverse classrooms, the working memory capacity of students may range from only two to as many as nine items. In addition, the length of time these items can remain in consciousness varies widely among students, creating a challenge for teachers. In order for students with limited working memory to be successful, information must be introduced in small chunks, followed by sufficient practice for the information to be stored in long-term memory before another small chunk of information is introduced. Unfortunately, in many schools the standard curriculum encourages teachers to present complex problem-solving tasks and to move through content at a brisk pace, under the mistaken assumption that such an approach will offer enrichment for some students while still allowing all students to master the basic information. But look what happens when we ask students to tackle too much information at once. Test your own memory as you did before, but this time, try a list of eleven digits. Spend about one second per digit memorizing the following list of numbers, then look away and write them down, in order, from memory:

$$8 \quad 4 \quad 9 \quad 7 \quad 2 \quad 6 \quad 5 \quad 9 \quad 3 \quad 1 \quad 7$$

How did you do? If you are like most people, you probably did not do as well on this list as you did on the list of seven items. When we try to overload working memory, the result is similar to what happens when a computer becomes overloaded and all you can do is hit "control-alt-delete." Educators sometimes assume that if they press forward and cover more information, students will retain the basics and only the excess will be forgotten. In reality, when we overload working memory, students typically retain less information than they would have if we had introduced a more limited amount of information. In other words, less may be more. Instructional approaches that introduce a small amount of information, then provide time for students to actively process that information before we introduce additional information, will be more successful with learners struggling to master mathematics. If an average eleven-year-old can retain five items in working memory, then teachers who work with that age group might plan to present a problem that requires students to hold five items in working memory at one time. If the class also contains students with memory deficits, then those students will need less complex problems with more frequent opportunity for review and practice.

In addition to deficits in working memory, students who struggle with mathematics may also show deficits in long-term memory (Geary, 2003). Long-term memory can be defined as "a permanent storage of information that is facilitated by how information is stored using associations and organizational formats" (Bryant et al., 2006, p. 14). To be retained, new information is linked to existing information in long-term memory. Some individuals can rapidly form connections and retain new information with minimal rehearsal, while others struggle to connect new information to previous knowledge or need many more repetitions before the new information is successfully stored in long-term memory. In a typical classroom, some students will rapidly make connections on their own and rapidly learn new content, while other students need help forming connections and may need much more practice before the new content is fully retained. For all students, using instructional strategies that help them hook new content to prior knowledge will improve retention. For students with memory deficits, making such connections explicit is even more essential. In addition, students who need more rehearsal time to consolidate learning will benefit from a slower pace and additional practice. Introducing new content too soon disrupts the consolidation of previous learning (Wolfe, 2001).

Individuals who struggle with associations and organizational formats may also have difficulty retrieving previously stored content. This may explain why students with learning disabilities often seem to know something one day but forget it the next. Beginning a lesson by carefully reviewing relevant background information will help these individuals connect new information to prior learning and so improve long-term retention of the information.

Multiple studies have shown that students who struggle to learn mathematics, especially those with learning disabilities, are also less aware of their own cognition than are their normally achieving peers (Montague, 2006; Pressley & Afflerbach, 1995). They are less likely to recognize whether they have fully understood instruction or to notice whether their answer makes sense, so are less likely to ask for help or clarification when appropriate. As a result, the teacher must take a more active role to make sure these students have fully understood the lesson. For example, the teacher might ask students to explain the lesson in their own words or demonstrate the skill while the teacher watches.

In addition to the awareness of one's own cognition, metacognition also involves the ability to self-regulate, to select appropriate strategies and coordinate attention, working memory, inner speech, and rehearsal (Swanson, Cooney, & O'Shaughnessy, 1998). Students who struggle in this area will have difficulty selecting an appropriate strategy or following the strategy once selected. Instructional methods that present multiple strategies can be confusing for these students. These students benefit from exploring one strategy and mastering it fully before they are exposed to alternative methods. Multiple-step problems also pose a special challenge, as students may lose track of where they are, resulting in frequent errors (Wong, Harris, Graham, & Butler, 2003). Therefore, students with deficits in self-regulation will benefit from instruction that includes explicit modeling of strategies and multiple opportunities to practice, with support gradually faded as the learners gain competence.

Language-processing difficulties have a profound effect on students' ability to benefit from instruction. Instead of focusing their attention on the mathematics being introduced, students with language deficits must use working memory to process the language, thus reducing the capacity available for mathematical reasoning. For example, these students may have trouble understanding math vocabulary (e.g., factor, exponent, denominator, variable) as they listen to instruction, participate in group discussion, or read and comprehend word problems. Students for whom English is a second language or others with diminished vocabulary will suffer similar problems during instruction. These students benefit from focused instruction in which only a limited amount of information is introduced at one time, vocabulary is explicitly discussed, and teachers frequently check understanding.

Finally, students who have done poorly in the past may dread math and begin to think of themselves as mathematical failures (Gersten et al., 2009). Research indicates that students who have experienced success in the past will persevere even if they can only respond correctly about 75 percent of the time. In contrast, students who do not have a history of success need instruction broken down into smaller steps where they can respond correctly 95–99 percent of the time in order to remain engaged (Hunter, 2004). Explicit instruction, which breaks instruction into small steps, can help develop a sense of self-efficacy that will eventually enable these students to attempt more complex and challenging problems.

The Explicit Instruction Lesson

Explicit instruction is the recommended instructional method for students who struggle with mathematics (Gersten et al., 2010; NMAP, 2008). In this section we describe the key components of explicit instruction: instructional objectives, lesson introduction, review of prerequisite skills and concepts, presentation of new content, guided practice, independent practice, and lesson closure. Figure 5.1 provides a summary of the essential elements of explicit instruction and can be used as a reference as we explore each component.

In the next section we will review the similarities and differences between explicit instruction and inquiry-based instruction, and discuss ideas for integrating the two methods.

Figure 5.1 Summary of an Explicit Lesson

Lesson Introduction
• Engage: Make lesson meaningful by providing a real-life example that shows how the skill or concept is used. • Review prerequisite skills and concepts: Provide opportunity for each student to actively practice any previously mastered skills and concepts necessary for success in this lesson.
Presentation of New Content
• Explicitly model strategies and procedures. • Use a "think-aloud" to describe procedures and the rationale behind them. • Provide multiple examples. • Actively engage students by using multiple modalities and active student participation.
Guided Practice
• Students practice under direct teacher guidance and receive corrective feedback. • Every student actively demonstrates the skill or concept introduced in the lesson. • The teacher provides scaffolded support, gradually fading prompts as students gain proficiency. • Students discuss their strategies and the rationale for their decisions. • The teacher verifies that each student understands the material before assigning independent practice.
Independent Practice
• Students engage in massed practice of the skill or concept that has just been introduced. • Interleaving worked examples with independent problems has been shown to increase student learning.
Lesson Closure
• Students summarize the main points of the lesson. • Next steps are previewed.

Figure 5.2 Selecting Effective Verbs

Using Verbs That Describe Observable Behaviors

In the examples below, the verb in the first version of each objective does not describe an observable behavior. The revised version describes how students will demonstrate their understanding through behavior that is observable and easily evaluated.

- *Problematic verb:*   Understand counting to 100
  Revised version: Count out loud to 100 by ones
- *Problematic verb:*   Learn how to round whole numbers to the nearest ten
  Revised version: Round whole numbers to the nearest ten
- *Problematic verb:*   Know how to subtract fractions with like denominators
  Revised version: Subtract fractions with like denominators

Verbs That Describe Observable Behaviors		Verbs That Do Not Describe Observable Behaviors	
say	select	know	believe
write	name	realize	improve
explain	type	appreciate	recognize
draw	print	discover	understand
solve	state	learn	work on
circle	construct	realize	think about
copy	count out loud	value	increase under-
label	describe	feel	standing
define	put in order	gain familiarity	be familiar with
point to	model	with	

Instructional Objectives

Explicit instruction begins in the planning stage with a clearly defined instructional objective that describes observable learning outcomes. Having a clear vision of what the students will learn and how they will demonstrate that learning allows teachers to monitor the lesson's effectiveness and to clarify or reteach when necessary.

Effective objectives contain verbs describing observable behaviors that specify how students will demonstrate their understanding. Many published lesson plans contain objectives that state that learners will "understand" the content being presented, but do not specify how that understanding will be demonstrated. Because the teacher cannot see inside the student's head and cannot evaluate what the student understands, knows, believes, or realizes, such verbs are best avoided. Objectives specifying that

Figure 5.3 Effective Objectives Describe Learning Outcomes

In the examples below, the first version describes an instructional activity. The revised objective is preferred because it specifies the learning outcome.

- *Problematic objective:*   Read word problems with a partner and decide which information is needed to solve the problems

     Revised objective: Given word problems that contain extraneous information, students will identify which information is needed to solve the problem

- *Problematic objective:*   Complete the review sheet on page 32
     Revised objective: Solve single-digit addition problems, sum ≤ 18

- *Problematic objective:*   Practice using base ten blocks to model numbers to 1000
     Revised objective: Given a number less than 1000, model it with base ten blocks

the student will explain, construct, or model the concept can be easily evaluated. For example, an objective that states that the student "will improve understanding of 2-digit multiplication" is less precise than an objective that specifies that the student "will correctly multiply two 2-digit numbers where regrouping is required." Likewise, an objective that says the student "will gain familiarity with halves, thirds, and fourths" is harder to evaluate than an objective that specifies that the student "will correctly model ½, ⅓, or ¼ of a whole or set." Figure 5.2 provides examples of effective and ineffective verbs.

Effective objectives do not describe instructional activities, but focus on the outcomes of instruction. An effective teacher will switch methods, explain the concept differently or provide a different activity when what was planned is not working. The intended learning outcome is not changed by this adjustment in methods, however. For example, "The students will play a game to review skip counting" is a description of an instructional activity, not a learning outcome. Revising the objective to state "Students will skip count to 100 by 2's, 5's, and 10's" provides a much clearer description of the intended learning outcome. Figure 5.3 provides additional examples of revising objectives to clearly specify what students will learn.

Effective instructional objectives describe the behaviors that demonstrate learning and so help teachers monitor student understanding and make necessary adjustments to their methods of instruction without changing the instructional objective.

Lesson Introduction

Engage

Our bodies are biologically programmed to attend to and remember information that is meaningful. When students perceive a lesson as having personal relevance, they will be more attentive and efficient learners (Archer & Hughes, 2011; Wolfe, 2001). Therefore, the teacher's first task is to engage the students. Students want to know, "Why do we have to learn this?" In mathematics, regardless of the instructional method being used, making information meaningful and relevant means that new skills and concepts should be introduced in the context of solving real-life problems (NCTM, 2000). For example, students interested in baseball will be more engaged if the process of finding averages is introduced by calculating batting averages; students who enjoy cooking may understand fractions better when they are presented as a problem about measuring ingredients. Beginning a lesson on dividing using two-digit divisors by saying "Today we are going to learn about division" is far less engaging than beginning with a real-life problem like the following:

> Spring break is coming, and our family is going to drive to Florida for vacation. I'm trying to figure out how much this trip will cost, and one big expense will be gasoline. I looked on Google Maps and learned that it's 868 miles from here to our destination. My car can go 28 miles on one gallon of gasoline. Can you help me figure out how many gallons of gas I will use driving from here to Florida?

Unfortunately, most textbooks do not introduce mathematical procedures in the context of meaningful problem solving. One review of fraction lessons in middle-school textbooks found that less than 10 percent of the lessons presented new fraction concepts in a meaningful context (Hodges, Cady, & Collins, 2008). Therefore, teachers are often forced to develop their own examples to make the content meaningful. When districts adopt new textbooks, selecting materials that introduce new content in the context of solving real-life problems can boost student achievement.

Review of Prerequisite Skills and Concepts

In order to profit from the current lesson, students often must have mastered prerequisite skills and concepts. For example, before students can learn to regroup in subtraction, they should already be able to subtract without regrouping and to understand place value. Before counting by 5's, students should be able to count by 1's. Before learning to add coins, they need to recognize the coins, know their value, and be able to add. Therefore, when planning a new lesson, it is essential that the teacher make a comprehensive list of any prerequisite knowledge students would need in order to succeed in this lesson, and systematically check to make sure *each* student in the group has the necessary background knowledge before the new content is introduced.

The objective for an effective lesson will fall within Vygotsky's "zone of proximal development" (Vygotsky, 1978), that small area just beyond the student's current level of performance, but within reach when presented with guided support. If the objective is too advanced and too much new information must be introduced at one time, then the student's working memory will be flooded and little learning will occur. If the students have not mastered these prerequisites, then the missing information should be introduced in a separate lesson before proceeding with the new objectives.

During the lesson introduction, the teacher reviews these previously mastered prerequisites. This review has two objectives. It allows the teacher to evaluate each child's readiness for the upcoming lesson, and it provides valuable review for the students. As mentioned previously, many students who perform poorly in mathematics have difficulty retrieving previously learned information. Without the review, these students may spend valuable time during the lesson trying to recall prerequisite skills and so miss critical instructional input.

In explicit instruction, activating prior knowledge does not mean simply asking students, "Do you remember when we worked on this procedure last week?" Students who do not remember will seldom risk embarrassment by admitting their ignorance before their peers. It is also not sufficient to simply ask a couple of students to come to the board to do a sample problem or explain the information. Although the volunteers doing the explaining may have the necessary prerequisites, this procedure gives the teacher no information about how well the rest of the class has mastered and can recall the prerequisites. In an explicit instruction lesson, the teacher reviews prerequisites by providing a task that requires each individual in the group to demonstrate understanding. If the group is small, this review may be accomplished by having students complete a few review problems at their desks. Such a procedure can provide effective review for the students, but it will only provide useful formative assessment data for the teacher if the group is small enough that the teacher is able to monitor each student's work and verify understanding before proceeding. If the group is too large for the teacher to monitor each student's output, then it may be more effective to have students provide a more easily monitored response. For example, if the teacher wants to check students' recall of coin values, she could provide each child with a whiteboard and marker, then hold up a coin and ask students to write the coin's value on their whiteboards and hold the boards up for her to see. Knowledge of numerals could be reviewed by displaying a numeral and asking students to hold up the corresponding number of fingers. Recognition of prime and composite numbers could be evaluated by holding up a number and having students give a thumbs-up if it is a prime number and thumbs-down if it is a composite number. Procedures like these allow every child to actively participate while simultaneously allowing the teacher to gauge their understanding. Review should continue until all students are fluent with the necessary background information.

Presentation of New Content

Students struggling with mathematics benefit when new information is first clearly modeled. This is sometimes referred to as the "I do it" portion of the lesson. When a new skill or strategy is introduced, the teacher needs to explicitly model the process. The teacher demonstrates the procedure while simultaneously describing it. For example, if the students are learning to write the numeral "2," the teacher would first demonstrate how to form the numeral while simultaneously verbalizing the process. Pairing the visual demonstration with a verbal description of the process will increase retention by modeling self-talk students can use when executing the process themselves. While demonstrating how to form a "2," the teacher might say, "Start near the top, curve up to the top line, curve down to the bottom line, then straight across. That's a 2. Curve up, curve down to the bottom, then straight across."

Describing your thoughts and actions as you perform the skill is often referred to as "think-aloud." The words used in the description should be simple, clear, concise, and consistent. Since many students who have difficulty learning mathematics also have language deficits, using simple language will allow students to focus on understanding the information rather than being distracted by difficult vocabulary. Modeling multiple examples and consistently using the same words each time provides repetition that facilitates retention and helps students internalize the procedure.

In the following example, a teacher uses think-aloud to model comparison notation. Before introducing the comparison symbol, the teacher would review by having students practice identifying the larger or smaller of two numbers, which is a prerequisite for this skill. To make the symbol more meaningful to the students, she might compare it to the mouth of a hungry alligator that wants to devour the largest number it can find. Then the teacher models how to insert the symbol between two numbers. She puts the problem "8 __ 5" on the board and uses think-aloud to share her thoughts as she inserts the comparison symbol between the two numbers.

> Let's see. First I need to decide which number is bigger. I know that 8 is bigger than 5. We said that the hungry alligator wants to eat the biggest number it can find. That means the open mouth needs to point toward the 8. So I'm going to draw my symbol with the open part facing the 8, like this. (*Inserts the symbol to show that 8 > 5.*) Now the mouth is ready to eat the bigger, or greater number. I read the expression from left to right: 8 is greater than 5.

When introducing more complex procedures, teachers should provide step-by-step models, thinking aloud as they model each step (Gersten et al., 2009). Students who have deficits in metacognition have difficultly selecting and executing appropriate strategies. When presented with multiple-step problems, these students need clear, unambiguous models of each step in the complex process. The verbalization not only describes *what* to do, but also provides insight into *why* to do it.

In Figure 5.4 a teacher uses think-aloud to model an explicit strategy for subtracting two-digit numbers when regrouping is required. Prerequisites for this skill include regrouping in addition, computing basic subtraction facts, and understanding place value (decomposing numbers, expanded notation, and "making trades" to exchange 10 ones for 1 ten). Students should have demonstrated mastery of these prerequisites during previous instruction. During the lesson introduction, the teacher would review these prerequisites and engage the students in the new skill by providing a real-life application of regrouping such as the following problem:

> Mrs. Rivera came to me this morning and asked to borrow the science books on our shelf. I told her we'll be using some of them, but I would see how many extras we have available. We have 35 books on the shelf. There are 18 students in this class, so we need to keep 18. How many books do we have left over that we could let Mrs. Rivera use?

Note that although the example begins with a word problem, the focus of this lesson is on teaching students the standard algorithm for regrouping in subtraction. The word problem provides a context for teaching the algorithm. The process for solving word problems would be taught in a separate lesson, because students with memory deficits or problems with executive control often become overwhelmed when lessons introduce too much information at one time.

Explicitly modeling strategies does not mean teaching students rote procedures without developing conceptual understanding. In Chapter 3 we discussed the importance of using the concrete-representational-abstract (CRA) continuum to help students understand mathematical concepts. Students should first have hands-on experience using concrete models and then progress to pictures, tallies, or other types of illustration before being asked to execute a procedure using only abstract words and symbols. Exploring concrete models brings meaning to the abstract concepts. Students are not practicing rote procedures, but rather developing conceptual understanding of the rationale underlying these procedures. Explicit modeling is integrated into each step of the CRA continuum to help students understand and execute procedures. Using the CRA continuum to develop conceptual understanding will be discussed in more detail in Chapter 6.

During the modeling portion of the lesson, the teacher first demonstrates how good problem solvers approach a problem using multiple clear, unambiguous examples (Gersten et al., 2009, p. 22). Providing multiple examples allows the student to see a strategy applied in a variety of contexts and increases the probability that students will remember and be able to apply the strategy themselves when presented with similar problems in the future.

Figure 5.4 Modeling an Explicit Strategy for Regrouping in Subtraction

Steps for Regrouping in Subtraction
1. Show how many you have (the total).

2. Begin with the ones column. Decide: Can you subtract the ones, or do you need to regroup first? If you need to regroup,
   - Break down a ten
   - Write down how many tens are left, and how many ones you now have.
3. Subtract the ones. Record the answer.
4. Subtract the tens. Record the answer.

What the teacher says	What the teacher shows
Here's our problem. We have 35 science books in the room, and we need to keep 18 of them here so each of you can have a book. We want to know how many books we have left that we could let Mrs. Rivera use. I'm going to follow these steps to solve the problem. *Point to the steps listed above.*	35 − 18 ———
Step 1 says, "Show how many you have." Let's see. We have 35, so I need to use my base ten blocks to show 35. First I'm going to make a place to put my tens and ones. I'll draw lines and label the columns "ones" and "tens." *Draw a place-value chart.*	35 − 18 ——— **Tens** / **Ones** (empty chart)
OK. Now I need to lay out 35. I can use my base ten blocks to show 35 with 3 rods and 5 units. That's 3 tens in the tens column and 5 ones in the ones column. *Lay out 35 blocks.* Let's see. Have I finished step 1? It says, "Show how many I have." I've done that, so I'm going to check off step 1. *Put a check next to step 1 in the steps listed above.*	35 − 18 ——— **Tens** (3 rods) / **Ones** (5 units) 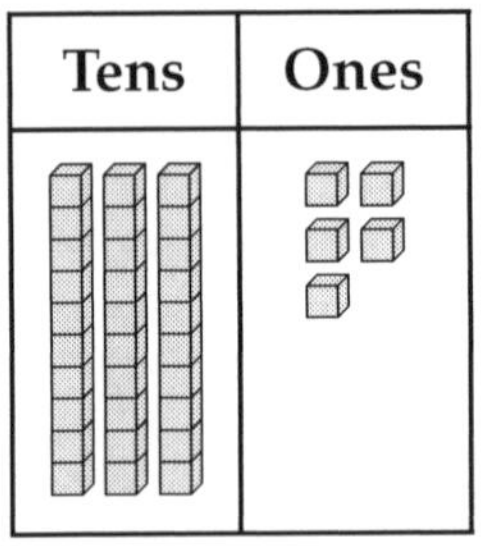
Step 2 says, "Begin with the ones column. Decide: Can you subtract the ones, or do you need to regroup first?" So I'm going to subtract the units in my ones column first. I have 5 ones, but I need to take away 8 ones. I don't have enough ones to do that, so I guess I need to regroup. It says, "If you need to regroup, break	35 − 18 ——— **Tens** (2 rods) / **Ones** (15 units) 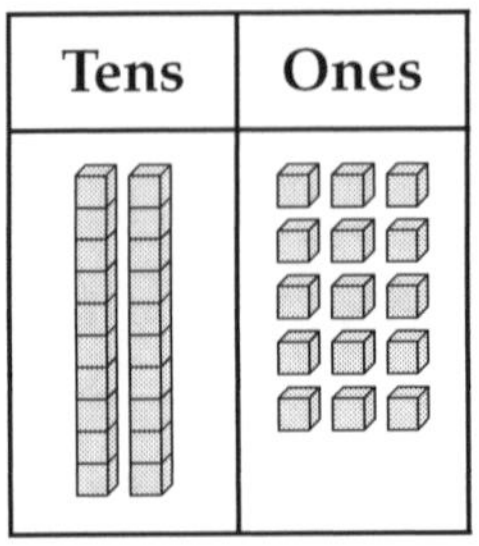

Figure 5.4 *(cont)* Modeling an Explicit Strategy for Regrouping in Subtraction

What the teacher says	What the teacher shows
down a ten." I remember from when we played Making Trades that I can break down a ten and change it to 10 ones without changing the total amount. I'm going to do that. I'm going to take one of my tens and break it apart. Now I have 10 more in the ones column. I had 5, and I've added 10 more, so now I have 15 ones. I broke down a ten and moved it to the ones, so now I can check that off. *Check off "Break down a ten" in the steps listed above.*	
Next, it says, "Write down how many tens are left, and how many ones you now have." I used to have 3 tens, but I regrouped and now I only have 2 tens, so I'll cross off the 3 and change it to say I have 2 tens. I used to have 5 ones, but now I have 15 ones, so I need to make my problem say that. All right. I've completed that step, so I can check it off. *Check off "Write down how many tens are left, and how many ones you now have" in the steps above.*	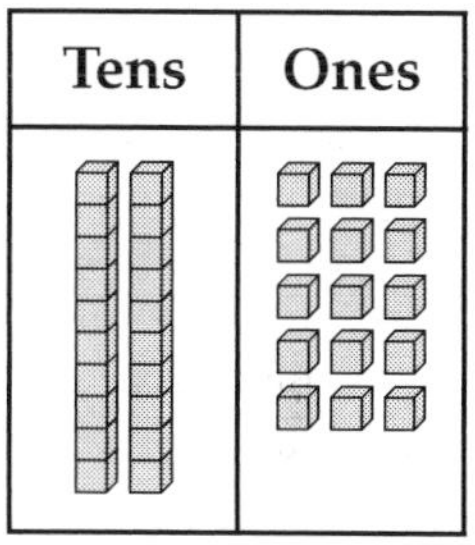
Step 3 says, "Subtract the ones, and record the answer." OK, I have 15 ones and I'm supposed to take away 8. I'm going to do that. Now I've got *(counting)* 1, 2, 3, 4, 5, 6, 7 left. That makes sense because I know that 15 – 8 = 7. I need to record the answer, so I'll write 7 in the ones column. Now I can check off step 3. *Check off step 3 above.*	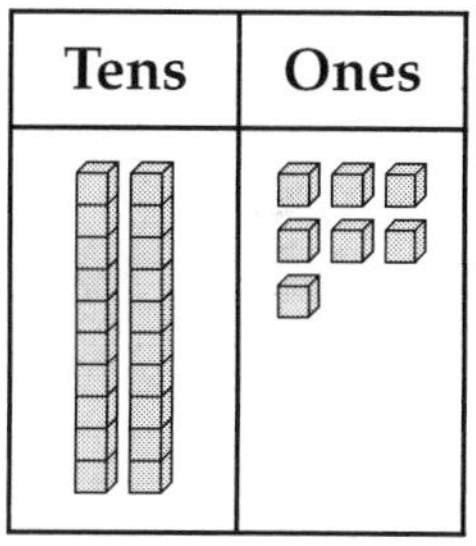
Step 4 says, "Subtract the tens and record the answer." I have 2 tens and I need to subtract 1 of them. I'm going to take one bundle of tens from the tens column. That means I have 1 ten left, so I'll write 1 in the tens column. I can check off step 4, and I'm done. *Check off step 4 above.*	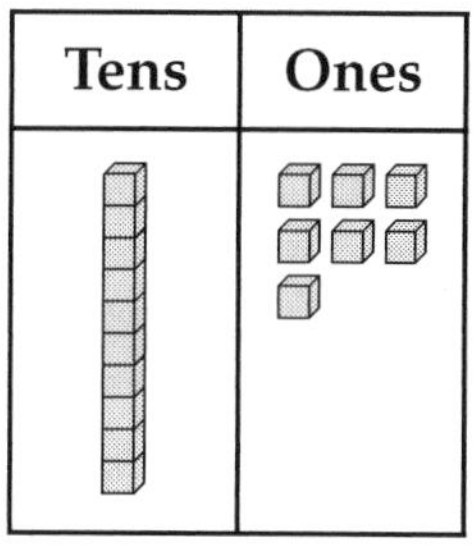
Let's look at our problem. We have 35 science books and we're using 18 of them. We have 17 left over that we can lend to Mrs. Rivera's class.	

This important feature should be included as a criterion when selecting intervention materials (Gersten et al., 2009).

After effective examples are provided, it is also helpful to model examples that include errors. Modeling incorrect use of a strategy allows the teacher to demonstrate self-monitoring, a skill that many learners with disabilities lack. The teacher can show students how to recognize whether their answer makes sense and how to correct errors. However, it is best if in the initial presentation students model the correct procedure and only the teacher models making mistakes. There will be natural opportunities for students to practice self-correction during instruction.

Modeling strategies does not mean that the teacher does all the talking and thinking while students are passive recipients. Students learn more when they actively participate. In Figure 5.4 the teacher missed multiple opportunities to involve students. Place value was identified as a prerequisite skill, so the teacher might have asked students to point out the ones column or help break down a ten. Knowledge of basic subtraction facts was also a prerequisite, so the teacher could have asked students to compute $15 - 8 = 7$ when completing step 3. During subsequent examples, the teacher could involve the students in following the strategy steps. For example, the teacher might ask the students, "What is step 1?" When students respond, "Show how many I have," the teacher could then ask, "What does that mean for this problem? How many do I have? How will I show it?" Involving students in the process helps maintain their attention, and their active participation increases learning.

Guided Practice

Guided practice has two important functions. Students practice under the teacher's guidance and receive corrective feedback that enables them to correct any misunderstandings, and teachers receive formative feedback that enables them to evaluate *each* student's understanding. The skill practiced should be the same skill that has just been modeled. It is not an extension activity; students are not asked to go beyond what was modeled, but rather to do themselves what the teacher has modeled.

In many mathematics classrooms, teachers demonstrate a few examples on the board and then students are given a worksheet or textbook assignment and asked to practice the skill on their own. This procedure is sometimes justified by saying, "Practice makes perfect." But the simple act of practicing something repeatedly does not automatically lead to perfection. Practice makes permanent. If we want to perform perfectly, we need to practice perfectly. In other words, "Perfect practice makes perfect." If students are asked to practice a skill independently before they can perform it correctly they will practice mistakes, and those mistakes can be very hard to unlearn. Anyone who has tried to help a student unlearn previous misconceptions appreciates how frustrating and time-consuming it can be for both teacher and student. In addition to having a negative impact on student learning, moving too quickly to independent practice can also negatively impact motivation. Students who have experienced failure in the past may resist activities where they anticipate another failure. They may become off-task or disruptive in an effort to avoid the task, or they may rush through an assignment because their past experience has shown that, even if they work hard, they are unlikely to experience success.

During guided practice, the teacher provides scaffolded support as needed. The teacher may provide visual prompts, such as posters or cue cards listing the steps to follow, or remind students of a critical aspect of the problem. Support also includes verbally prompting the student what to do next or asking the student process questions. Process questions require students to describe the process they are using, explain their reasoning, create an example, or prove that their answer makes sense. Students think aloud just as the teacher did during the modeling phase of the lesson. The *What Works Practice Guide* recommends:

> During guided practice, the teacher should ask students to communicate the strategies they are using to complete each step of the process and provide reasons for their decisions. In addition, the panel recommends that teachers ask students to explain their solutions. Note that not only interventionists—but fellow students—can and should communicate how they think through solving problems to the interventionist and the rest of the group. This can facilitate the development of a shared language for talking about mathematical problem solving. (Gersten et al., 2009, p. 23)

The process of articulating their reasoning helps students consolidate understanding. Figure 2.4 (page 18) provides examples of process questions that teachers can use to develop and evaluate student understanding.

Prompts are gradually faded during the guided practice portion of the lesson. How quickly the teacher fades support depends on the complexity of the task and the success of student performance. Guided practice should continue until students are able to perform successfully on their own. At the beginning of guided practice, the teacher might present a new example and ask the students to give step-by-step directions as they guide the teacher through solving the problem. The teacher would provide prompts as needed, gradually fading these prompts as the students demonstrate competence. Then the teacher would ask students to demonstrate their ability to perform the skill independently without prompts. The IES practice guide recommends, "For students to become proficient in performing mathematical processes, explicit instruction should include scaffolded practice, where the teacher plays an active role and gradually transfers the work to the students" (Gersten et al., 2009, p. 23).

In effective guided practice, every student actively responds in a way that allows the teacher to evaluate each student's level of understanding.

For the lesson presented in Figure 5.4, the teacher might ask students to solve a few problems using individual whiteboards and then hold up their answers while the teacher checks for understanding. If there are only a few students in the class, the teacher could monitor each of them as they work on problems at their desks, but with a larger group it would become difficult for a teacher using this procedure to effectively monitor each student's understanding. Small-group activities can provide effective guided practice if they are structured to ensure that every student actively participates and receives scaffolded support and corrective feedback in a timely manner. Figure 5.5 presents a variety of formats that can be used for guided practice.

Independent Practice

In explicit instruction, students practice independently only after they can perform successfully without prompts. The purpose of independent practice is to provide the student with sufficient repetition for new learning to be effectively stored in long-term memory. Students who struggle to learn new content often have deficits in working memory (Geary, 2003) and need extensive practice opportunities before they successfully consolidate new learning. Core instruction typically moves at a faster pace and provides less practice than these students need to become proficient. Independent practice involves both immediate massed practice and distributed practice.

Massed Practice

Immediately after instruction students need to solve multiple examples of similar problems, using the same strategies modeled during instruction. Practice periods are "massed," meaning that several practice periods are scheduled close together. For example, after successful guided practice, students might have several problems to complete independently before the end of the math period. They might do more examples for homework, and practice again during class the next day. Additional examples would be reviewed at the beginning of class the following day.

Problems presented during initial independent practice should include worked example solutions as well as problems for students to solve independently. Research studies have shown that students learn more when examples of worked-out problems alternate with problems students must solve independently (Pashler et al., 2007). These studies have demonstrated that asking students to solve eight practice problems independently results in less learning than if the eight problems include four completed examples that show solution steps, alternating with four problems students must solve on their own. Even though students actually solve fewer problems in the second scenario, they are more likely to solve those problems correctly and perform better on similar problems in the future. When giving students initial independent practice assignments, learning will increase if teachers provide a worked-out solution for every other problem. See Figure 5.6 for an illustration of interleaving worked example solutions and problem-solving exercises.

Figure 5.5 Guided Practice Formats

A variety of formats can be used to provide effective guided practice. The ideas described below represent a sample of the many ways teachers can structure guided practice. All of these activities allow each student to actively practice while receiving scaffolded support, and they allow the teacher to assess each student's understanding of the material and readiness for independent practice.

Manipulatives

Students can use three-dimensional objects to develop and demonstrate their understanding of many mathematical concepts. For example, when students are learning to recognize numerals, the teacher could hold up the numeral "8" and ask students to use counters to show what the numeral means. A quick glance around the room enables the teacher to evaluate student mastery. When practicing place value, students can use base ten blocks to demonstrate their understanding. For example, the teacher might write "348" on the board and ask students to represent it using their base ten blocks. All students can respond simultaneously, and the teacher can easily monitor their responses. Manipulatives allow every student to actively respond to every question, thus markedly increasing student response rates, and it is generally easy for the teacher to monitor each student's performance.

Response Cards

Response cards are cards, boards, or signs that students can use to indicate their response to teacher questions. Every student responds simultaneously to every question, ensuring continuous active student participation. When students hold up their cards, the teacher can easily gauge student understanding. With write-on response cards such as whiteboards or laminated sheets, students use erasable markers to write or draw their responses. Preprinted response cards allow students to select their response from a set of cards at their desks. Examples of preprinted cards include yes/no and true/false cards and cards showing numerals, shapes, or operation signs. Using response cards or whiteboards for guided practice has been shown to increase learning in a variety of research studies (Heward, 1996).

Interactive Remotes (Clickers)

Student response systems, or clickers, are becoming increasingly prevalent in K–12 classrooms. These hand-held remotes are similar to the ones used to poll the audience in the game show *Who Wants to Be a Millionaire*. The teacher poses a question and students use their clickers to respond. Teachers can ask multiple-choice, true/false, and sequence questions. Some types of clickers also allow students to respond using numbers or words. The responses are transmitted via radio frequency to a receiving station connected to the instructor's computer, and the aggregated responses can be displayed on a PowerPoint slide. If the graph indicates some students are confused, the teacher can review or reteach the information. Weak students are often less aware of their own cognition than are their normally achieving peers. Viewing the graphed responses helps these students gauge how well they

Figure 5.5 *(cont)* Guided Practice Formats

have understood instruction, and the ensuing discussion can provide additional clarification when needed. Clickers provide the benefit of anonymity. Because only aggregated responses are displayed, students do not know how any individual classmate responded. The anonymity allows struggling learners to actively participate without fear of embarrassment before their peers. The program's software lets teachers track individual responses, however, so the teacher can monitor how well each child has understood the lesson. These interactive remotes are available from a variety of manufacturers. Several sources for student response systems are listed below.

- eInstruction: www.eInstruction.com
- Promethean: www.prometheanworld.com/
- Qwizdom : www.qwizdom.com
- Turning Technologies: www.turningtechnologies.com

Cooperative Learning Structures
Cooperative learning activities allow students to work cooperatively with peers while practicing academic content. Learning is facilitated because students articulate their own ideas and also have the opportunity to hear their classmates' responses. Effective cooperative learning activities are structured to ensure that every student participates and each is held individually accountable for the information. Because cooperative learning activities have both an academic objective and a social skills objective, they help develop students' social interaction skills while simultaneously developing mathematical competence. The benefits of cooperative learning are well supported by research. A few structures that are especially effective for guided practice are described below.

- **Think-Pair-Share**
  Think-pair-share (Kagan, 1994) is one of the most frequently used cooperative learning structures. The teacher asks a question and gives students a minute or two to formulate their own response. Then students pair up and share those ideas with their partner. Finally, the students are given an opportunity to share their ideas with the whole class. An advantage of think-pair-share is that every student has an opportunity to speak and also hear classmates' ideas. Although the teacher may not be able to monitor each individual response, wandering around the room during the paired discussions allows the teacher to get a good idea of the level of student understanding and provide support where needed.
- **Roundrobin and Roundtable**
  In roundrobin (Kagan, 1994), students sit in a circle and take turns sharing ideas with the group. This is an excellent structure to use to generate examples, because each student has to create an individual example and also has the opportunity to hear multiple examples from peers. Roundtable (Kagan, 1994) is similar except that instead of responding orally, students sequentially write their

Figure 5.5 *(cont)* Guided Practice Formats

ideas on one sheet of paper. For example, to practice counting by 3's, the teacher might place students in small groups and give each group a 100's chart. The students would pass the chart around the group, taking turns circling the next number in the sequence. The first student in the group would circle the numeral 3, the next would circle 6, and so forth. Any student who believes a previous answer was incorrect could use her turn to make a correction in lieu of circling the next number in the sequence. Roundtable might also be used when students are asked to generate their own examples of a concept. For example, students might be asked to brainstorm ways they could represent 12. Each student in turn would write one way to represent 12. The first student might write 6 + 6, the next might draw 12 individual items, the next might show one dozen eggs, and so on. Having students work in groups allows them to support each other while the teacher walks around the room monitoring their performance and providing timely feedback.

- **Pairs Check**

   In pairs check (Kagan, 1994), pairs of students are given one copy of a worksheet containing problems similar to those modeled during the presentation portion of the lesson. The first student solves the first problem while his partner observes and coaches. Then they trade roles, and the second student solves the second problem while the first one observes and coaches. Once they have completed the first two problems, they "square up" with another pair that has just completed the same two problems. The four students compare answers. If their solutions match, they can check off those problems. The process is repeated for the next two problems on the page. If the answers differ, the students try to resolve the problem. If they cannot, they seek teacher assistance. This procedure requires students to explain their reasoning to their peers and prevents them from repeating errors without the benefit of corrective feedback.

- **Numbered Heads Together**

   Numbered heads together (Kagan, 1994) is a structure that allows students to work cooperatively to develop the best answer to a question. Students form teams and number off within their team. The teacher poses a question and teammates put their heads together to develop their best possible response. Then the teacher calls out a number and the person on each team with that number raises his or her hand to respond. The teacher can either call upon one person to respond or ask all students with that number to respond simultaneously using write-on response cards. Because only one person can answer for the team, each individual on the team must be prepared to explain the correct answer. Students who were initially confused can hear the correct answer when the team puts their heads together and must remember the answer because they may be called upon to share their group's response when the teacher calls out a number.

More ideas for using cooperative learning activities are available at Kagan Cooperative Learning: www.KaganCoopLearn.com.

Figure 5.6 Interleaving Example Solutions and Problem-Solving Exercises

Multiplication:
Use partial products to solve these problems.
Study each step in the examples given to help you solve the next problem on your own.

12	34	45	17
× 13	× 12	× 23	× 18
6		15	
20		120	
30		100	
100		800	
156		1035	

Unfortunately, most materials currently available do not provide sufficient worked-out examples for teachers to use. Until resources incorporate these research findings, teachers or teams of teachers will need to develop their own worked examples for the content they teach.

Problems presented during massed practice should also include discrimination examples that do not require use of the new skill or strategy. For example, the teacher in Figure 5.4 was teaching students to regroup in subtraction. During independent practice the teacher would include examples that require regrouping, but should also include examples that do not require regrouping. Inserting discrimination items prevents students from automatically and thoughtlessly regrouping in every problem they encounter. When students think critically about what they are doing and why they are doing it, they are better able to apply their knowledge appropriately in the future.

Distributed Practice

Once students have mastered the new content, the practice schedule moves from massed to distributed. Distributed practice involves providing short practice periods, with longer and longer time intervals between reviews. Such review increases long-term retention and also develops students' ability to retrieve previously stored content.

Current mathematical resources often fall short in this area, too. In many basal programs, students focus on one unit, then another, without the distributed practice needed for long-term retention. For example, students might complete a unit on multiplication, then move on to fractions, then to measurement, without sufficient opportunity to review the content covered in previous units. Students with memory deficits are especially harmed by insufficient distributed practice. Sometimes teachers work hard to help their students master concepts early in the year, only to watch in dismay as they miss the same problems on state achievement tests later in the year. Frequently this occurs because students did not receive sufficient distributed practice opportunities. Providing cumulative review helps students maintain knowledge over time.

Lesson Closure

How much of the explicit lesson is completed during one instructional period will vary depending on the students, the complexity of the information, and the length of the period. Sometimes you may get through the introduction, presentation of new content, and guided practice before the period ends and even have time to begin independent practice. Other days you may only get halfway through the guided practice portion of the lesson before it is time to close. However far the lesson has progressed by the end of the instructional period, it is important to summarize the learning that has occurred that day. Summarizing crystallizes key points in the students' minds. Rather than telling the students what they learned, the teacher asks the students to create the summary. The processes of selecting and articulating the important information deepens understanding and increases retention. These summaries can take many forms. The teacher might call on individual students to share their responses, ask students to share their ideas in a think-pair-share format (Kagan, 1994), or have students write or draw their ideas in a daily journal. For the subtraction lesson described in Figure 5.4, the teacher might end the lesson by saying the following:

> Today we learned how to regroup in subtraction. What does it mean to regroup? *Calls on student to answer.* How do you know you need to regroup when you're subtracting? *Calls on student to answer.* On your whiteboards, write an example of a subtraction problem that requires regrouping. *Monitors responses, then calls on a student to explain her response.* We don't always regroup every time we subtract. What kind of problem can be solved without regrouping? *Calls on a student to answer.* Think to yourself the steps we follow when we regroup, and then turn and share your ideas with your partner. *Monitors the think-pair-share, then calls on one pair to share their response with the whole class.* Now think of a real-life situation where you might need to regroup. Share your idea with your partner. *Monitors the think-pair-share, then asks one or two students to share their examples with the whole class.*

Notice that the summary is not merely a statement of the topic that was covered (regrouping in subtraction), but requires students to summarize the main points of the lesson.

How Explicit Instruction Improves Motivation

Explicit instruction has been shown to improve outcomes and help struggling students experience mastery. The following specific aspects of explicit instruction facilitate success and therefore lead to higher motivation.

1. During the lesson introduction, activating necessary background knowledge and prerequisite skills prepares learners to use that information when new content is introduced. Students are less likely to become frustrated because they have forgotten previously mastered content and are more likely to approach the lesson with a positive "can-do" attitude.
2. Introducing information in small, carefully sequenced steps minimizes frustration and allows individuals with memory deficits and cognitive processing problems to experience success.
3. Providing scaffolded support increases success. When teacher support is faded gradually, students gain confidence and are more willing to tackle similar problems on their own in the future.
4. Guided practice allows the teacher to verify student understanding before asking students to practice independently. The teacher can correct misunderstandings quickly, which helps ensure that students will be able to work successfully on their own. When students are performing successfully, the teacher can provide positive feedback, thus boosting students' confidence.
5. Frequent review increases the probability that students will retain previously mastered content. The more clearly students remember what they learn, the more confidence they will feel when approaching future mathematical tasks.

Since explicit instruction has produced strong positive results among students who have had mathematical difficulties, the IES practice guide recommends it be used in all tiered interventions (Gersten et al., 2009).

Summary

High-quality research studies have consistently demonstrated that explicit instruction can improve the mathematical achievement of students who struggle with mathematics, and it is the recommended instructional method for students receiving mathematical interventions. Research suggests that students who fail to make adequate progress in mathematics often have problems with working memory, long-term memory, and executive functioning. The typical inquiry-based lesson favored by many mathematics educators presents complex tasks that overload the memory capacity of these students and challenge their metacognitive abilities. With explicit instruction, information is presented in smaller chunks and is therefore more accessible for students with memory deficits.

The key components of explicit instruction include lesson introduction, review of prerequisite skills and concepts, presentation of new content, guided practice, independent practice, and lesson closure, which were summarized in Figure 5.1 at the beginning of the chapter. In Appendix A we provide two sample lesson plans that follow the explicit instruction model, and a form that can be used when designing an explicit instruction lesson. In the following chapters we discuss how to use concrete and visual representation to develop understanding, and we provide additional examples of explicit instruction to support learners who struggle with mathematics.

Chapter 6

Concrete and Visual Representation

Students who are successful in mathematics have a rich sense of what numbers mean and can engage in quantitative reasoning. If the teacher says the word "twelve," an individual with a robust sense of twelve will easily envision twelve objects, twelve tally marks, a dozen eggs arranged in two rows of six, a 3 × 4 array, a group of 10 + 2, the numeral 12, and so on. The ability to represent mathematical quantities in multiple ways is a critical component of quantitative reasoning. Representation allows students to organize mathematical information, describe mathematical relationships, and communicate mathematical ideas to others. According to the National Council of Teachers of Mathematics (NCTM), "representing ideas and connecting the representations to mathematics lies at the heart of understanding mathematics" (2000, p. 136). To highlight the essential role representation plays in effective mathematics instruction, NCTM developed the Representation Standard, which states:

> Instructional programs from prekindergarten through grade 12 should enable all students to—
> * Create and use representations to organize, record, and communicate mathematical ideas;
> * Select, apply, and translate among mathematical representations to solve problems;
> * Use representations to model and interpret physical, social and mathematical phenomena. (p. 67)

Representation can take a variety of forms. Students can use concrete objects to demonstrate mathematical concepts, as when they use toy blocks to model an addition problem or cut a pizza into eight equal pieces to illustrate fractional parts of a whole. They can draw pictures of those same objects or use tally marks or graphs to record quantity. Mathematical ideas can also be represented in words and symbols. The process of representing their ideas helps students construct meaning, as well as organize and clarify their thinking. Linking various representations of the same mathematical concept or procedure deepens a student's understanding of mathematics.

Research on the Concrete-Representational-Abstract Sequence

Conceptual understanding of quantity follows a developmental sequence. It begins at the concrete level when students physically act out a math problem or use manipulatives such as blocks, toothpicks, Cuisenaire rods, fraction pieces, or other three-dimensional objects to model a mathematical relationship. Manipulatives include any concrete objects that students can physically manipulate to represent a mathematical idea. These concrete representations make abstract concepts tangible. Studies show that, when students have the opportunity to use concrete materials, their mental representations are more precise and comprehensive, they have an increased understanding of mathematical ideas, they are better able to apply them to real-life situations, and they often demonstrate increased motivation and on-task behavior (Harrison & Harrison, 1986; Suydam & Higgins, 1977). As their understanding deepens, students progress to using pictorial representations such as drawings, tally marks, diagrams, graphs, charts, tables, and other two-dimensional illustrations to model mathematical concepts and procedures. They learn to connect these two- and three-dimensional representations with abstract words and symbols until finally the words and symbols are meaningful by themselves and students are able to efficiently represent mathematical concepts and procedures using just the abstract symbols. Figure 6.1 shows how the same concept could be represented using concrete, visual, and abstract representation.

When mathematical words and symbols are firmly rooted in concrete experiences, students find them meaningful. When students lack a foundation in concrete and visual representation, their attempt to perform symbolic operations often becomes a rote execution of meaningless procedures.

The progression of understanding is referred to as the concrete-representational-abstract sequence, or the CRA continuum (Peterson, Mercer, & O'Shea, 1988; Sousa, 2007; Witzel, 2005). Based on the work of Jerome Bruner in the 1960s (Bruner, 1960), the CRA continuum has been supported by mathematics educators for decades. NCTM and the National Math Advisory Panel both recommend incorporating the CRA continuum in core instructional materials at every grade level (NCTM, 1989, 2000; NMAP, 2008). It is an evidence-based practice for all grade levels that is supported by a large body of research (see, for example, Darch, Carnine, & Gersten, 1984; Fuchs, Seethaler et al., 2008; Witzel, 2005; Witzel, Mercer, & Miller, 2003; Woodward, 2006). The CRA is especially critical for students who struggle with mathematics. After an exhaustive review of the research, the authors of the IES practice guide included it as the fifth of their eight recommendations for assisting students who struggle with mathematics: "Intervention materials should include opportunities for students to work with visual representations of mathematical ideas and interventionists should be proficient in the use of visual representation of mathematical ideas" (Gersten et al., 2009, p. 6).

Figure 6.1 The Concrete-Representational-Abstract (CRA) Continuum

---

A set of matched concrete, visual, and abstract representations for introducing multiplication of whole numbers

The representations below are designed to use when teaching the following Common Core Standard:

CC.3.OA.1. Interpret products of whole numbers, e.g., interpret 5 × 7 as the total number of objects in 5 groups of 7 objects each. *For example, describe a context in which a total number of objects can be expressed as 5 × 7.*

Concrete Representation:
Use objects to represent 3 × 4. For example, lay out 3 plates, and place 4 cookies in each plate.

Visual Representation:
Use a picture to show 3 × 4. For example, draw 3 circles to represent the 3 plates, then draw 4 cookies on each plate. The student might use circles, triangles, dots, or other shapes to represent the cookies.

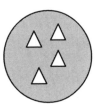 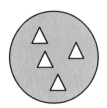 

Abstract Representation:
Represent the problem in words.

There were 3 children at my party. I gave each child 4 cookies. In all, how many cookies did I give away?

Represent the problem using numbers and symbols: 3 × 4 = 12

Struggling students need about three lessons at the concrete level, each consisting of approximately 20 problems, before they are ready to fade concrete support; they then need three lessons at the representational level before they have developed conceptual understanding and are ready to work solely with abstract words and symbols (Hudson & Miller, 2006).

To progress from one lesson to another, or to progress from one level to another level within the CRA sequence, Hudson and Miller suggest that students should be able to complete ten independent practice problems with at least 80 percent accuracy. These findings are consistent across a range of mathematical content (Butler, Miller, Crehan, Babbitt, & Pierce, 2003; Harris, Miller, & Mercer, 1995; Hudson, Peterson, Mercer, & McLeod, 1988; Mercer & Miller, 1992; Miller, Harris, Strawser, Jones, & Mercer, 1998; Miller, Mercer, & Dillon, 1992; Peterson, Mercer, & O'Shea, 1988). Although the use of manipulatives and visual representation is sometimes viewed as a technique only used with younger children, several studies demonstrate the value of continuing to incorporate concrete and visual representation with secondary students (Huntington, 1995; Maccini & Hughes, 2000; Maccini & Gagnon, 2000; Witzel, 2005).

Unfortunately, many textbooks do not make adequate use of the CRA continuum to develop mathematical reasoning (Bryant et al., 2008; Hodges, Carly, & Collins, 2008; Gersten et al., 2009); The majority of textbooks that have been examined do not use concrete or visual representation to introduce new concepts. When they do include concrete and visual representations, they fade them too quickly, providing one or two examples before focusing on abstract words and symbols. Therefore, interventionists will need to supplement commercially available materials with additional examples of concrete and visual representation.

Interventionists will also need to highlight the relationship among the various forms of representation. Case (1998, p. 1) explains that "students with good number sense can move seamlessly between the real world of quantities and the mathematical world of numbers and numerical expressions." However, students who have difficulty understanding mathematical concepts often struggle to connect the various forms of mathematical representation (Hecht, Vogi, & Torgesen, 2007). While they may appear to understand a concept when it is represented concretely or using pictures or other visual representations, these students fail to recognize how those representations relate to the same concept when presented in the form of abstract words or symbols. Increasing students' understanding of the relationship between these representations has been linked to increased understanding of mathematical concepts (Lesh, Post, & Behr, 1987). Therefore, the IES practice guide identifies this as an evidence-based practice, stating, "We also recommend that interventionists explicitly link visual representations with the standard symbolic representations used in mathematics" (Gersten et al., 2009, p. 31). In other words, interventionists should use manipulatives to introduce a concept, then show students how that concrete representation connects to the visual and abstract representations, using consistent language to highlight the relationships. In Chapter 5 we provided an example of explicitly linking concrete, visual, and abstract representations when teaching the standard algorithm for regrouping in subtraction (see Figure 5.4). Figure 6.2 presents another example of linking representational systems,

Figure 6.2 Explicitly Linking CRA

This lesson illustrates linking CRA when introducing the following Common Core Standard:

CC.3.OA.1.Interpret products of whole numbers, e.g., interpret 5 × 7 as the total number of objects in 5 groups of 7 objects each. *For example, describe a context in which a total number of objects can be expressed as 5 × 7.*

What the teacher says:	What the teacher shows:
I need your help to solve a problem. I'm going to have 3 children at my house tomorrow, and I want to give each of them 4 cookies. I need to figure out how many cookies I will need in all, so that I'll have enough to give each child 4 cookies.	
First I'm going to write my problem on the board. There will be 3 children, and each child gets 4 cookies. That is a multiplication problem. I will write it like this *(write 3 × 4).* The first number, the 3, tells how many groups I have. I have 3 groups, one for each of the 3 children. The second number, the 4, tells me there are 4 objects in each group. Each child gets 4 cookies.	$3 \times 4 =$
Concrete Representation: I have some plates here that I can use to show my problem. Each plate will represent one group. How many plates do I need? Yes, 3 plates, one for each child. *Put out 3 plates.*	

this time illustrating how a teacher could explicitly link concrete, visual, and abstract representations when teaching students to solve multiplication problems. This example focuses on the same Common Core standard used in the example provided in Figure 6.1.

In Figure 6.2, the teacher used explicit instruction to introduce multiplication. The direct model described here would be followed by multiple examples, during which the teacher would gradually fade support and allow the students to take increasing responsibility for leading the process. Once students could successfully lead the entire process, then the teacher would give students similar problems to solve independently.

Recently, Scheuermann, Deshler, and Schumaker (2009) have developed an instructional method that combines elements of explicit instruction with

Figure 6.2 *(cont)* Explicitly Linking CRA

What the teacher says:	What the teacher shows:
Now I need to put cookies on each plate. How many cookies should I put on each plate? Yes, 4. *Put 4 cookies on each plate.* Did I show 3 × 4? Good.	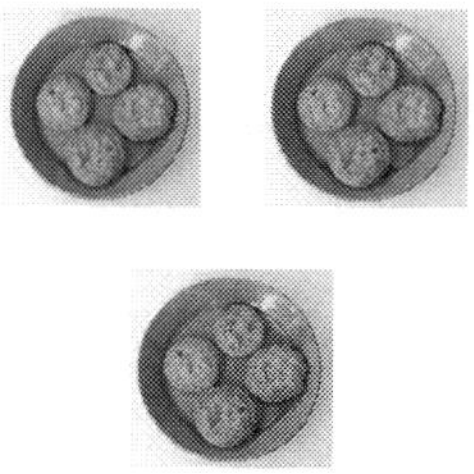
Visual Representation: I want to take notes to help me remember what I've done. I'm going to draw 3 circles on the board to represent the 3 plates. *Draw 3 circles.*	
Now I'll put cookies on each plate. My drawing doesn't have to be fancy, so I'm just going to use triangles to represent the cookies. *Draw cookies.* Let's check. Did I show 3 × 4? Does my drawing match the plates of cookies on the table? Good!	
Abstract Representation: Let's solve the problem. How can I determine how many cookies I'll need in all? Sure, I can count. Let's count together. *Count the 12 cookies with the class.* I'll need 12 cookies. I'm going to write that in my equation like this: 3 groups of 4 objects equals 12 objects. So 3 × 4 = 12. *Record the product in the equation.*	3 × 4 = 12

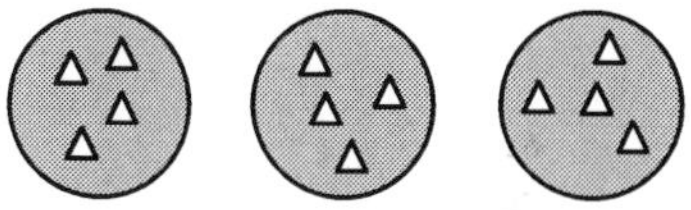

elements of inquiry-style instruction. They name their model the "explicit inquiry routine." Instead of the teacher creating the initial model, the explicit inquiry routine gives students more input in the early stages of the lesson. The teacher asks a series of carefully scaffolded questions to lead the students through the representational process, monitoring their responses in an extended guided practice activity to ensure student understanding before moving into independent practice. First, the teacher poses a mathematical problem and engages the whole class in a discussion of ways to represent that problem. The authors label this initial portion of the lesson "tell me how." The class brainstorms ways to represent the problem using concrete objects. Once students have created a successful concrete model, the teacher asks them to brainstorm ways to represent the problem using visual representation. Then the teacher moves to abstract representation, asking the group to develop a number sentence that represents the problem. After the class successfully completes the "tell me how" segment, the lesson progresses to the "tell your neighbor how" phase. Each student turns to a neighbor and explains the graphic and symbolic representations the class developed. Finally, students have an opportunity to solve the problem on their own. They are instructed to talk themselves through the process and to be prepared to explain their choices. Figure 6.3 shows the steps in the explicit inquiry routine. In their research, when this procedure was used, student learning increased (Scheuermann, Deshler, and Shumaker, 2009). The carefully scaffolded questions help students develop their own representations and make connections among concrete, representational, and abstract models. Using the explicit inquiry routine allows students to be actively involved in figuring out ways to represent mathematical concepts, but still provides enough guidance that students who typically struggle with representation can succeed.

Whether using explicit instruction or the explicit inquiry routine, when instructors clearly show students the relationship between different representations, achievement has increased. In many commercial programs, this is an area of weakness. When textbooks use concrete and visual representations, they seldom explicitly link the various forms. Materials that consistently use the CRA continuum to introduce mathematical concepts and procedures, and explicitly link the different types of representation, are likely to result in greater learning outcomes. If the available materials do not explicitly link the concrete, visual, and abstract representations, then interventionists will need to add this component to their lessons.

Virtual Manipulatives

Modern technology now provides the option of using digital "objects." These virtual manipulatives are two-dimensional renditions of traditional manipulatives. Unlike other two-dimensional representations, however, students can manipulative the virtual objects to demonstrate mathematical concepts and procedures. Virtual manipulatives therefore fall between the C and the R in the CRA continuum (Moyer, Bolyard, and Spikell, 2002). The National Library of Virtual Manipulatives (http://nlvm.usu.edu/en/nav/vlibrary.html) provides a wealth of free virtual manipulatives appropriate for use in tiered interventions. NCTM's Illuminations website (http://illuminations.nctm.org/) also includes many virtual manipulatives. The technology allows easy access to materials that may not be readily available in the classroom, and students who enjoy computer applications may be especially motivated to engage in virtual practice activities. When the application is displayed on a smartboard, the entire class can easily see the

Figure 6.3 The Explicit Inquiry Routine

Kyle and Andrew have the same number of candies. Kyle has a bowl of candies and 4 additional candies. Andrew has 14 candies.

1. **Tell me how . . .**
   - How could we represent this situation using these objects?
   - How can we represent this situation using graphic pictures?
   - Is there another way we could represent this same situation?
   - How can we represent this situation using math symbols?
2. **Tell your neighbor how . . .**
   - Now tell your neighbor how you represented the situation concretely.
   - Tell your neighbor how to represent the situation using graphic pictures.
   - Can you explain the mathematical symbols you chose to use to your neighbor?
3. **Tell yourself how . . .**

   As you illustrate and manipulate this situation by yourself, get ready to explain your choices. You may want to talk yourself through the process because I may ask you why you chose to use what you did.

Source: Scheuermann, A. M., Deshler, D. D., & Schumaker, J. B. (2009). The effects of the explicit inquiry routine on the performance of students with learning disabilities on one-variable equations. *Learning Disability Quarterly, 32*(2), 103–120.

demonstration. See Figure 6.4 for a list of websites offering activities, lessons, and games using virtual manipulatives.

Research on the use of virtual manipulatives by struggling learners is still in the early stages, but preliminary studies suggest that they are more effective than traditional lessons that do not incorporate manipulatives and that they can effectively augment instruction when combined with traditional manipulatives (Moyer, Niezgoda, & Stanley, 2005; Moyer-Packenham, Salkind, & Bolyard, 2008; Reimer & Moyer, 2005; Steen, Brooks, & Lyon, 2006; Suh & Moyer, 2007; Suh, Moyer, & Heo, 2005). Older students, who sometimes view concrete manipulatives as babyish, may respond more favorably to virtual activities. However, it has not been established that virtual manipulatives can replace three-dimensional objects to develop conceptual understanding. We recommend that students receiving tiered interventions have opportunities for hands-on experiences with actual objects before they progress to the more abstract virtual representation. Interventionists must also remember to explicitly link virtual manipulatives with the standard symbolic representations used in mathematics.

Figure 6.4 Sources for Virtual Manipulatives

National Library of Virtual Manipulatives

www.nlvm.usu.edu/en/nav/vlibrary.html

> The National Library of Virtual Manipulatives is a library of web-based virtual manipulatives that was developed at Utah State University with funding from the National Science Foundation. It contains hundreds of virtual manipulatives organized by grade level (pre-kindergarten through high school) and math content areas. Each manipulative has information for parents and teachers including instructions, suggested lessons and activities, and the relevant NCTM content standards.

Illuminations

http://illuminations.nctm.org/

> The Illuminations website, operated by the National Council of Teachers of Mathematics, contains lesson plans and materials for teaching students in pre-kindergarten through high school. The Activities tab provides a variety of virtual manipulatives. The site also offers a Dynamic Paper tool that allows you to create your own virtual manipulatives or images that can be printed or exported for use in other applications.

Math Manipulatives

www.mathplayground.com/math_manipulatives.html

> This site provides a variety of virtual manipulatives and also includes math games, math word problems, worksheets, logic puzzles, and other activities.

Learning Mathematics with Virtual Manipulatives

www.cited.org/index.aspx?page_id=151

> This website discusses the research basis for virtual manipulatives and provides links to several sources for virtual manipulatives.

Dreambox Learning Teacher Tools

www.dreambox.com/teachertools

> Dreambox offers free virtual manipulatives for pre-K through third grade. Click on the Explore icon below each tool icon to access teacher support resources.

Suggestions for Using the CRA Sequence

Here we provide a summary of suggestions for incorporating manipulatives and visual representations into lessons. In subsequent chapters we will provide more detailed discussion and examples of ways to use the CRA continuum when introducing specific mathematical content.

1. When introducing new concepts and procedures, follow the CRA continuum. Begin with concrete representation, then progress to visual representation, and then use abstract words and symbols. All three types of representation can be introduced in the same lesson, but students need several experiences with concrete representation before they are ready to discard the manipulatives and work solely at the visual level, and several more experiences before the visual representation can be faded and students are ready to rely only on abstract representation. Studies have shown that students with disabilities typically needed three lessons using manipulatives and three more using visual representation before relying solely on abstract words and symbols. Hudson and Miller (2006) suggest that students should be able to complete ten independent practice problems with 80 percent accuracy in order to progress from one level to the next.

2. Explicitly link concrete, visual, and abstract representations. Students who have difficulty understanding mathematical concepts also struggle to connect the various forms of mathematical representation. Explicitly linking the various representation systems, using consistent language across systems, has resulted in higher achievement outcomes. Figures 5.4 and 6.2 provide examples of linking representational systems.

3. When selecting manipulatives, choose items that can be used to create a clear model of the concept. Manipulatives are three-dimensional objects that can be used to represent a mathematical idea concretely. However, just because a student can manipulate an object does not mean that it can be effectively used to model a particular concept. For example, students can manipulate coins, but coins would not be an effective manipulative to teach the value of decimal tenths and hundredths, because coins do not provide a concrete model of their relative values. A penny is larger than a dime, yet its value of $.01 is less than the value of the dime. Base-ten blocks are more effective for modeling the relative values of decimal tenths and hundredths. If a flat (a 10 × 10 square block) represents one whole, then a rod (a 1 × 10 block) represents .10 and a unit (a 1 × 1 block) represents .01. The base-ten blocks provide a concrete illustration of the relative size of decimal values. Similarly, playing cards are three-dimensional objects that students can manipulate,

but they cannot be used to concretely model mathematical concepts. Playing cards may be an effective tool for increasing student engagement, but the cards present visual and abstract representations of numerical values, not concrete representation. The manipulatives students use should enable them to create a clear model of the concept they are learning.

4. Provide opportunities for students to model the same concept using a variety of different manipulatives and visual representations. The ability to represent mathematical ideas in multiple ways is a critical component of quantitative reasoning. For example, fraction circles are frequently used to model fractional parts of wholes, but students should not be limited to thinking of fractions as parts of circles. Their understanding will be enhanced if they also experience other examples, such as finding fractional parts of squares and rectangles or using fraction bars, towers, and other manipulatives. Decimal values can be modeled with a variety of manipulatives, including base-ten blocks, DigiBlocks, and metric weights. Graph paper and number lines allow students to create visual representations of decimal numbers. Using a variety of different manipulatives and visual representations to model the same concept deepens students' conceptual understanding.

5. Provide opportunities for students to translate among different representations. Students with rich number sense can fluently transition among all types of representations, but students who struggle to represent mathematical ideas may have difficulty making the same connections. For example, given the concrete representation of a mathematical expression, a student may be able to write a numerical expression to describe it. That same student may become confused when asked to reverse the process and, given the numerical expression, represent it with manipulatives. Some teachers routinely ask students to create one type of representation but neglect others. To develop a rich conceptual understanding, students need opportunities to practice converting among all representational forms. They should have opportunities to practice all of the following:
    *   Given a concrete representation, model it using pictures, graphs, and other visual representations, as well as using numbers and words.
    *   Given a visual representation, model it using concrete materials, numbers, and words.
    *   Given a numerical expression, represent it concretely and visually and explain it in words.
    *   Given a word problem, represent it using concrete representation, visual representation, and a numerical expression.

These opportunities will develop students' ability to fluently transition among representations.

6. Provide opportunities for students to explain their thinking. For example, students could share with their classmates the process they followed to obtain their answer, or explain why they selected a particular strategy, or they could explain their thoughts in a math journal or use a diagram to explain how they approached a particular problem.

Allowing students to explain their work helps consolidate their understanding. NCTM recommends that all students be provided opportunities to:
- Organize and consolidate their mathematical thinking through communication
- Communicate their mathematical thinking coherently and clearly to peers, teachers, and others
- Analyze and evaluate the mathematical thinking and strategies of others
- Use the language of mathematics to express mathematical ideas precisely (NCTM, 2000, p. 128)

7. Use manipulatives judiciously and systematically fade their use. The goal is for students to become proficient with standard symbolic representation and not remain dependent on concrete supports. If students continue to work with concrete objects, they may not develop the ability to function at the abstract level. Interventionists should systematically fade the use of manipulatives and help students transition to visual and abstract representation. Research with students with disabilities suggests that three experiences with manipulatives is usually sufficient to develop initial understanding. Students can transition from concrete to abstract representation more easily when interventionists provide scaffolded support by explicitly linking the concrete, representational, and abstract representations and using consistent language across levels.

Following these suggestions when incorporating the CRA continuum into lessons can increase success in tiered interventions.

Summary

The ability to represent mathematical quantities in multiple ways is a critical component of quantitative reasoning. Representation allows students to organize mathematical information, describe mathematical relationships, and communicate mathematical ideas to others. Conceptual understanding of quantity follows a developmental sequence, beginning at the concrete level with physical actions and three-dimensional objects. As their understanding deepens, students progress to using visual representations such as pictures and diagrams to model mathematical relationships. If these concrete and visual representations are linked to more abstract words and symbols, students eventually can use words and symbols meaningfully without needing the concrete and visual representations. The CRA continuum is an evidence-based practice for developing mathematical understanding at all grade levels.

Since available textbooks seldom provide sufficient examples or explicitly link the various forms of representation, interventionists will frequently need to add this component themselves. In the next chapter, we provide more detailed descriptions of ways to incorporate concrete and visual representation with whole numbers, and in Chapter 9 we apply the CRA continuum when introducing rational numbers.

Chapter 7

Representing Whole Numbers

The methods recommended for use in interventions differ from the methods used in the core curriculum in two important ways. First, while the core curriculum should balance the use of student-directed and teacher-directed instruction, students who struggle with mathematics benefit from the explicit presentation of carefully sequenced concepts and skills. Interventionists may need to modify instructional materials to incorporate explicit instruction methods. Second, while mathematically proficient students may master content despite limited experience with concrete and visual representation, students who struggle learn more when the CRA continuum is rigorously followed. Studies show that the CRA sequence is not adequately addressed in most commercial materials, and even those materials that incorporate multiple concrete and representational examples seldom *explicitly* link the representational systems. Therefore, the IES Practice Guide recommends that interventionists add this component to their lessons (Gersten et al., 2009). In this chapter we will focus on using explicit instruction and the CRA continuum to help students develop number sense, understand place value, and perform operations with whole numbers.

Developing Number Sense

Number sense involves the ability to count meaningfully and to understand relationships among numbers. A child whose number sense is well developed can count a set of six objects and state the total. The child can also represent the number six or recognize the quantity when it is illustrated using a variety of dot patterns or objects, knows that 6 is more than 5 and less than 7 and that it is composed of 3 and 3 and also of 2 and 4, and can identify real-world applications of six. While many students enter school with highly developed number sense, children who experience difficulty with mathematics may need intensive support to attain the same level of understanding.

In order to count meaningfully, students must master two separate skills: *rote counting* and *one-to-one correspondence*. Rote counting is the ability to state the number words in order (i.e., one, two, three, four, . . .). Young children can often recite the counting sequence from memory but cannot count meaningfully because they do not realize that each number in the sequence must represent one and only one object. When they can point to one object and say one number, then wait to say the next number until their fingers touch the next object, we say they have one-to-one correspondence. Students who lack one-to-one correspondence will not only be unable to count a group of objects or progress in mathematics, but they will also have difficulty reading, because sound-symbol relationships are based on the idea that each letter or group of letters represents one sound or word. In other words, one-to-one correspondence is a prerequisite for academic progress in both mathematics and reading.

Concrete experiences are essential for students to develop one-to-one correspondence. Activities that involve matching actual objects, such as giving one cookie to every child in the group or putting one hat on each stuffed animal, are necessary in order for students to learn to pair each object with a single number name, and each number name with a single object. Counting activities that involve large muscle movement are especially helpful, because the motor activity helps separate each item and so highlights the discrete value of the objects. For example, if the child must carry one item from the desk to a classmate and say "one," then come back and get a second item and walk to the next classmate before saying "two," the relationship between the spoken number and the physical object becomes more obvious. Students need multiple experiences like this where they move and use large muscles to match concrete objects before they will make the cognitive connection that one word is associated with just one object. Once they can count successfully when engaged in large motor activities, then they can begin to count objects that are placed more closely together and eventually transition to counting pictures and graphic representations that require minimal movement.

Counters

The concrete objects that students manipulate as they develop beginning number sense are often referred to as "counters." Any toy or small object that appeals to students can be used to help develop quantitative reasoning. Skittles, M&M's, Hershey's Kisses, gummy bears, and other types of candy can instantly capture children's attention while effectively representing mathematical concepts and procedures. Small toys such as miniature cars, bears, or dinosaurs intrigue children. Natural objects such as pebbles and shells or familiar household objects such as buttons, coins, bottle caps, poker chips, or paper clips can be equally effective. Unifex cubes or pop cubes are commercially available counters that can be snapped together, so they have the added advantage of allowing students to connect cubes when modeling larger numbers.

Counters are commonly used in elementary mathematics classrooms, and commercial programs provide excellent ideas for using counters to develop quantitative reasoning. Since most educators are familiar with these manipulatives, we will not describe their use in detail here. The big idea for interventionists is to link the concrete counters with visual and symbolic representations. Sometimes students initially model a concept or procedure with counters and then are asked to perform the skill using visual or symbolic representation but without practice that explicitly connects the various forms of representation. While normally achieving students may be able to successfully transition from one form of representation to another without the need for scaffolded support, students who have difficulty with number sense often struggle to connect the various forms of mathematical representation (Hecht, Vogi, & Torgesen, 2007) and so benefit when these connections are made explicit. For example, if students initially used M&M's to count, they could use pencil, crayon, or chalk to draw a model of their M&M's. Recording the written numeral on their drawing helps students connect the three-dimensional objects with pictorial and symbolic representations. Written numerals are at the abstract end of the CRA continuum, so students will need multiple experiences pairing these abstract representations with their concrete and pictorial equivalents before they can work meaningfully with just the abstract numerals. Students must be able to move back and forth among representations, going from concrete to representational to abstract and also from abstract to representational to concrete. Given a group of objects, students should be able to draw a picture to represent the group, represent it with tally marks, say the number name associated with that quantity, and write the numeral. Given the pictorial representation, they need to practice illustrating it with objects, tally marks, words, and numerals. When told the name of a numeral, they should be able to write it and model it concretely and pictorially. Given the numeral, we need to ask them to read it aloud and model it with objects and drawings. The ability to represent mathematical quantities in multiple ways is a critical component of quantitative reasoning, but individuals who struggle with mathematics often have extreme difficulty connecting the various types of representations. To develop a robust number sense, they must learn to move fluidly among all the representational forms.

Touchmath

Touchmath (www.touchmath.com) is a system specifically designed to help students associate written numerals with the quantities they represent. Students first learn to place counters in a set pattern on large drawings of numerals. In other words, they learn to place one counter at the top of the written numeral 1, two counters in specific locations on the numeral 2, and so on. Eventually they transition to using dots drawn on the numerals instead of actual counters, and finally the dots are faded and students mentally count the places where the dots would have been placed in order to identify the value of the numeral. The system provides very effective support that explicitly links concrete representation, visual representation, and abstract numbers. However, students sometimes become overly dependent on counting dot patterns and do not make the transition to purely abstract representation. Research with students with disabilities found that most students need about three lessons that include concrete representation, followed by three more lessons using pictorial or graphic representation, before these supports are faded and they can work meaningfully at the abstract level (Hudson & Miller, 2006). Students who have learned to use Touchmath often continue to count dots long past the seventh lesson. We recommend that Touchmath be used judiciously because students who continue to rely on counting the dot patterns are likely to have difficulty later transitioning to more efficient abstract representation.

Ten-Frames

One of the best tools to help students connect three-dimensional concrete representation to two-dimensional visual representation is the ten-frame. A ten-frame consists of an empty 2 × 5 grid onto which students place counters. See Figure 7.1.

The structure, generally attributed to Robert Wirtz (1974) and further developed by Van de Walle (1988) and Bobis (1996), is now included in many of the programs adopted for use in core instruction. A smaller 1 × 5 grid, or five-frame, is often introduced initially to help students master numbers to 5, followed by the larger 2 × 5 grid when students progress to numbers from 6 to 10. The frames can be purchased commercially or made from tagboard. In addition to the boards illustrated in Figure 7.1, manufacturers offer ten-frame trains, which are three-dimensional versions of the ten-frame grid designed to look like train cars. Students place teddy bear counters or other counters into the train's ten compartments to model quantities to ten. Teachers can make their own versions of a ten-frame train by cutting the end off an egg carton, leaving two rows of five egg cups that form the train's ten compartments. Figure 7.2 shows two versions of the ten-frame trains.

When they are first learning to model numbers with frames, students should lay the frame horizontally so that there are five boxes in the top row. They begin by placing the first counter in the upper left corner and progress from left to right across the top row, then move to the bottom row and continue placing counters from left to right, just as the eyes move when reading. Placing counters on the ten-frame in this set order helps students organize their counting and develop a mental model of each quantity. Once students master recognizing numbers when the counters are arranged in the left-to-right order described above, they should also have experiences where the counters are arranged in random order to solidify their understanding that rearranging the counters does not affect the total quantity.

In addition to using the ten-frame to model a given quantity, students can also practice adding one and then two more counters to the board and stating the new number. Students whose sense of number is still developing will recount starting from one, but as they become more proficient they learn

Figure 7.1 Ten-Frames

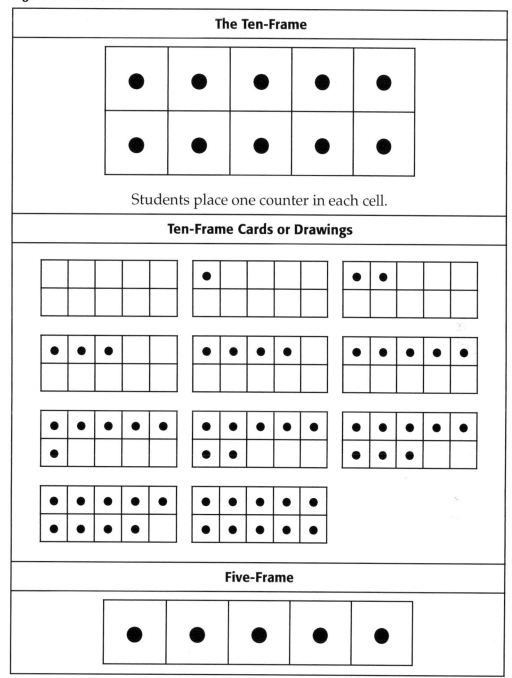

to "count on" from the last number stated. "Counting on" is a skill students will need when they begin addition. Removing the counters one by one can help students master counting backward, a skill that will help prepare them for subtraction.

The spatial organization of the ten-frame supports students' emerging number sense because the frames provide a graphic illustration of a number's relative value. Representing 8 with 5 counters on top and 3 below

Figure 7.2 Ten-Frame Trains

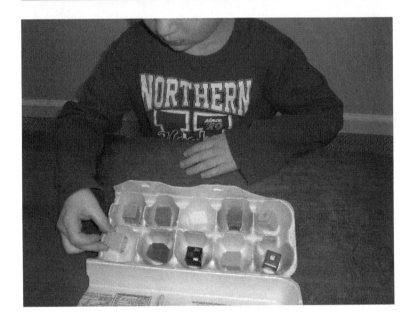

clearly shows that 8 is "5 and 3 more" and also that it is 2 less than 10. When students place a given number of counters on the frame, and then count to determine how many more counters would be needed to fill the frame, they begin to recognize combinations that make ten. By combining ten-frames, students can also model numbers larger than ten. Examples of this appear later in this chapter during the discussion of place value. After students master counting by ones, the frames can be used to model skip counting. Using multiple five-frames can help students learn to count by fives, while using multiple ten-frames provides a model for counting by tens. The frames can also be used to introduce coin values. Students can place pennies on a five-frame until all the squares are filled, and then exchange their five pennies for a nickel. In a similar manner, placing pennies on a ten-frame provides a model for the value of a dime.

Because the concrete and pictorial versions of the frames are so similar, ten-frames facilitate the transition from concrete to visual representation. At the concrete level, students directly manipulate objects when they place counters on the ten-frame board. At the visual representation level, students can draw the counters on a blank board or use pictures of ten-frame boards containing predrawn dots, like those shown in Figure 7.1. These pictures can also be made into playing cards for practicing initial counting skills and comparing numbers.

Case (1998) writes that students with good number sense "can recognize benchmark numbers and patterns, especially ones that derive from the deep structure of the number system" (p. 1). The graphic organization of the ten-frame highlights the benchmark numbers of 5 and 10 and therefore helps build number sense in learners struggling with initial mathematical concepts. Figure 7.3 lists Internet sites that offer blackline masters of ten-frame boards and numerous games and activities using ten-frames at both the concrete and representational levels.

Number Lines

In addition to using objects and pictures to model numbers, students must learn to use a number line diagram. Number lines show the relative values of all real numbers, including whole numbers like 2 and 327, which are the focus in this chapter, fractions and decimals such as ½ or 14.268, which we will discuss in Chapter 9, and negative numbers such as −4 or −1⅜. Although little research has been conducted to document their effectiveness, number lines have been frequently used with young students to develop initial counting and later to model more advanced concepts. The Common Core Standards specify that students should be able to use number lines by the end of the second grade:

> CC.2.MD.6: Represent whole numbers as lengths from 0 on a number line diagram with equally spaced points corresponding to the numbers 0, 1, 2, . . . , and represent whole-number sums and differences within 100 on a number line diagram. (National Governors Association Center for Best Practices, Council of Chief State School Officers, 2010)

Unlike counters, which show a total quantity, number lines model measurement. Whole numbers are represented as lengths, so using a number line is similar to the process of measuring with a ruler. When counting with a number line, students begin at zero and count the number of spaces as they move forward. See Figure 7.4 (p. 100).

Many students find counting spaces cognitively challenging, because what they notice is the numbers or dots on the line, not the spaces between.

Figure 7.3 Internet Resources for Ten-Frames

Winnipeg School Division Numeracy Project:
Dot Card and Ten-Frame Activities 2005–2006
(http://www.edplus.canterbury.ac.nz/literacy_numeracy/maths/num-
    documents/dot_card_and_ten_frame_package2005.pdf)
    This thirty-seven-page document provides blackline masters for cre-
    ating a ten-frame board and ten-frame cards, as well as describing an
    extensive list of games and activities to use with ten-frames. It also
    includes activities to use with dot cards.

MathSolutions
(www.mathsolutions.com)
Marilyn Burns's website provides multiple ideas for using ten-frames.
Here are three of them:

- Introduction to Ten-Frames: www.mathsolutions.com/documents/
  9781935099109_HowTo.pdf
- Life-Size Ten-Frame Game: www.mathsolutions.com/documents/
  9781935099178_G3Lesson.pdf
- Race to 20 Game: www.mathsolutions.com/documents/
  9781935099109_LessonG9.pdf

The Kentucky Center for Mathematics
(www.kentuckymathematics.org/resources/tools.asp)
    You can print large, colored five-frame and ten-frame boards using
    the templates at this site.

Open School Network
(http://teachmath.openschoolnetwork.ca/grade1/510Frames.htm)
    This site provides a variety of blackline masters showing ten-frames
    in different sizes with differing dot configurations. It also describes
    several ten-frame activities.

If they learn to focus on the dots, students will sometimes have difficulty
when they later attempt to use number lines to solve addition and subtraction
problems. For example, to model the problem 8 – 2, a student should begin at
8 and move one space to the left, touching 7. That movement represents the
first space. He then jumps back to 6, which counts as the second space. Students who follow this process obtain a correct answer of 6. Students who focus
on counting the dots might approach the same problem by placing a finger on
the 8 while counting "One," then move to the 7 and say "Two. 8 – 2 = 7." The
student might make a similar error when using a number line to model an
addition problem such as 2 + 3 by beginning at the point representing the first

Figure 7.3 *(cont)* Internet Resources for Ten-Frames

Manitoba Early Years Mathematics Activities and Games
(www.edu.gov.mb.ca/k12/cur/math/games/)
  This school website provides a variety of games for developing early
  math skills. The following games involve ten-frames:

  • How Many Counters?
  • Make Ten
  • Ten-Frame Flash
  • Twenty
  • Partners

Fuel the Brain
(www.fuelthebrain.com/Interactives/app.php?ID=29)
  In this interactive applet, base ten blocks or ten-frames flash on the
  screen for a set time limit. The student is then asked to identify what
  number was shown.

Illuminations
  • Five-frame web applet: http://illuminations.nctm.org/ActivityDetail
    .aspx?ID=74
  • Ten-frame applet: http://illuminations.nctm.org/ActivityDetail.aspx
    ?ID=75

Count Me In Too
(www.curriculumsupport.education.nsw.gov.au/countmein/children
    _butterfly_wings.html)
  This site includes many different interactive applets addressing a
  variety of math skills, including one using ten-frames called Butter-
  fly Ten-Frames.

addend, 2, and counting up from there. This incorrect process would result in
an answer of 4, which is one less than the actual sum of 2 + 3.

  Some of these difficulties can be prevented if the students' experience
with number lines follows the CRA sequence. The number line shows
abstract numbers arranged in a way that provides a diagram of their relative values, which means that it addresses the representational and abstract
levels of the CRA continuum. In order to experience this structure at the
concrete level, students can walk along a large number line taped on the
floor, counting their steps as they move. The large muscle motion helps them
focus on counting spaces. They can then progress to demonstrating bunny

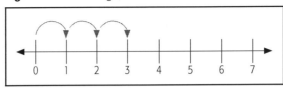

Figure 7.4 Measuring 3 on the Number Line

hops or the number of spaces a frog jumps on a smaller number line taped on the desk. By focusing on the measurement aspect of the number line, these activities help ensure that students use the structure effectively in the future.

MathLine (www.howbrite.com/) is a manipulative that adds concrete representation to the visual and abstract representation inherent in every number line. It consists of a three-dimensional number line with movable plastic rings that can be used to illustrate whole-number values. All the rings are contained within the MathLine frame, so there are no loose pieces for students to misplace, and manipulating these self-contained rings helps organize the counting process. See Figure 7.5.

The rings are white, except for multiples of 5, which are blue, and multiples of 10, which are red. To illustrate 5, the student would begin with all the rings pushed to the right end of the MathLine, then slide five rings all the way to the left. Each ring fills one space on the number line, so when the rings are pushed up against the zero mark on the left side of the device, the total value of 5 is seen just to the right of the fifth ring, as shown in Figure 7.5. To add on two more, the student would simply slide two additional rings to the left, resulting in the sum of 7 showing to the right of the seventh ring. This concrete experience combines the tactile experience of touching the rings and the kinesthetic movement of sliding the rings with the visual representation of abstract numerals arranged in order on a number line. MathLine therefore combines the complete CRA continuum in a multimodality experience that can help build conceptual understanding.

Because it highlights the benchmark numbers of 5 and 10, MathLine also provides some of the advantages of a ten-frame. For example, since the fifth ring is colored blue, students can easily see that the quantity 7 is "5 and 2 more." The tenth ring is red, so students can also see that 7 is "3 less than 10." In addition, the colored rings facilitate skip counting by 5 and 10 and are also helpful when teaching students to round to the nearest ten. The company's website offers video clips that illustrate using MathLine to enrich students' understanding of counting and rounding whole numbers and decimals, as well as performing operations with whole numbers.

When students have the opportunity to represent their thinking using a variety of different manipulatives, their understanding deepens. Allowing students to work with both counters and number lines will help them develop a richer understanding of mathematical concepts and procedures.

Figure 7.5 MathLine

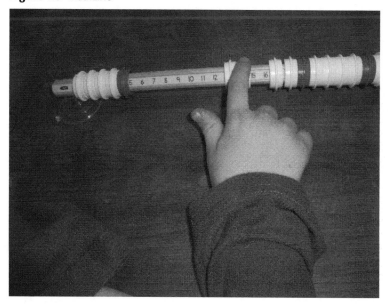

Place Value

In order to work meaningfully with quantities larger than ten, students need to develop an understanding of place value in the base-ten system. Where a digit is placed within a number tells its place value. When we write the numeral 12, the digit 1 represents one group of ten, and the 2 indicates 2 additional units. Nothing in the number word "twelve" suggests to a young child that it is equivalent to 10 plus 2, so American teachers must devote a great deal of instructional time to helping students understand place value.

Ten-Frames

In addition to developing initial counting skills, the ten-frames pictured in Figure 7.2 can be used to help students develop initial place-value concepts. With one ten-frame students can model numbers 1 to 10, but by combining several ten-frames they can model larger numbers, as shown in Figure 7.6.

For example, to model the number 12, students would use one completely filled-in ten-frame and one ten-frame that contains two single counters, as shown in Figure 7.6. Together, the frames create a clear, simple representation of 1 ten plus 2 ones. If students have previously used ten-frames to model quantities to ten, then using the ten-frame with larger numbers helps connect the new information to their existing knowledge. Because the ten-frames provide such a clear model of the value of each digit in a two-digit number, they help build students' initial understanding of place value and the base-ten number system.

Figure 7.6 Using Ten-Frames to Model Larger Numbers

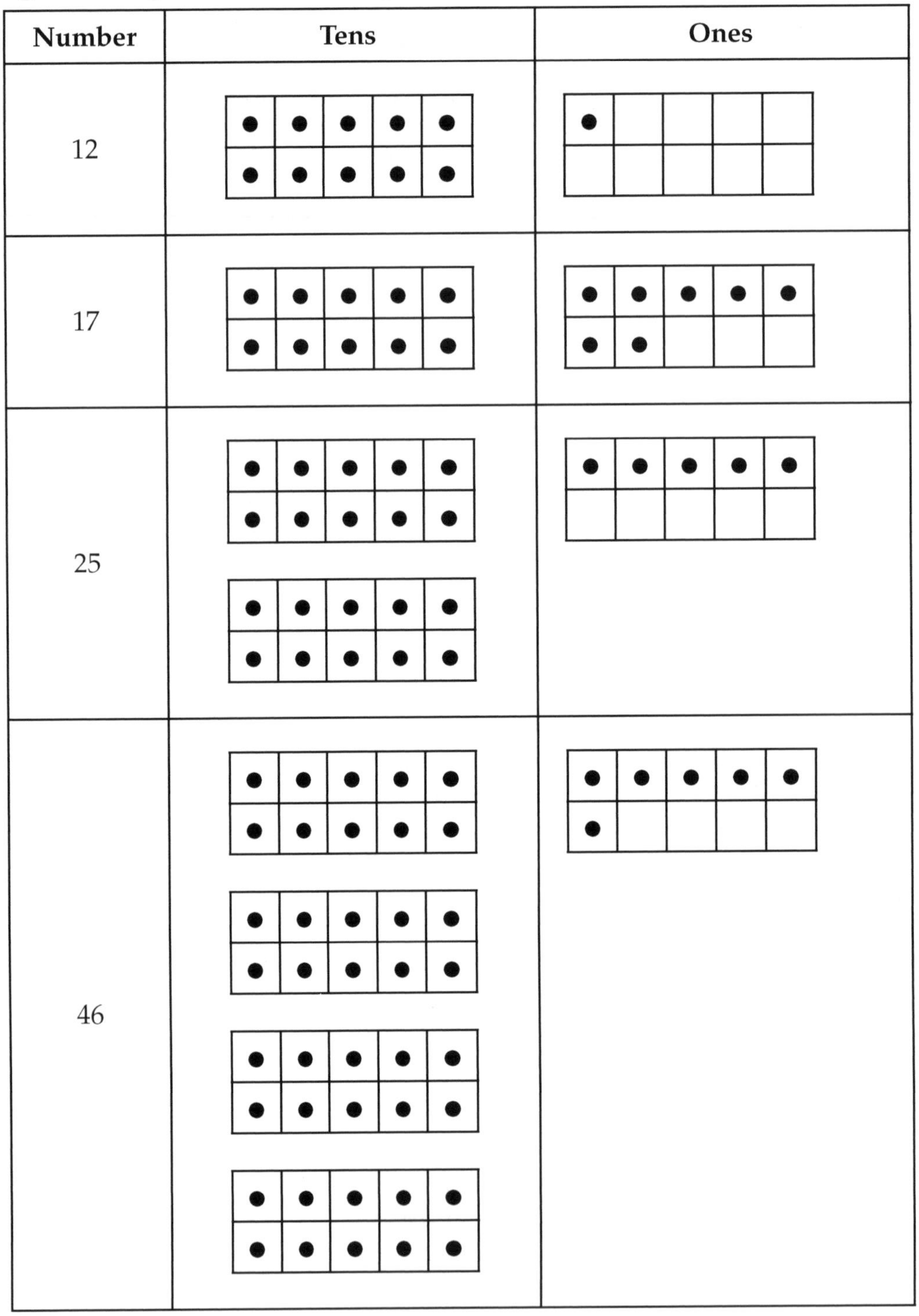

Number	Tens	Ones
12		
17		
25		
46		

Base-Ten Blocks

Once students master using ten-frames to model numbers to 99, they are ready to transition to base-ten blocks, which can be used to model ones, tens, hundreds, and thousands. The blocks consist of individual units (1 × 1 cm. cubes), "rods" or "longs" composed of ten unit cubes, "flats" formed from 100-unit cubes arranged in a 10 × 10 array, and a large cube containing ten flats which represents 1000. See Figure 7.7.

The pieces are proportional, which means that a rod is ten times larger than a unit, and a flat is ten times larger than a rod. Base-ten blocks therefore provide an excellent model of the relative values of different numbers. Students can use base-ten blocks to model any number. Figure 7.8 shows how base-ten blocks would be used to model the number 345.

Using blocks to demonstrate the value of two- and three-digit numbers, and then writing the numbers in expanded notation format (300 + 40 + 5), helps students develop a more complete understanding of the quantities involved in two- and three-digit numbers. To further solidify their understanding, students can arrange the blocks on a place-value mat, a paper or plastic mat divided into columns, with each column labeled with a different place value. Students working with numbers to 99 can use a two-column mat that is labeled "ones" and "tens," and more columns can be added when students progress to larger numbers. Figure 7.9 shows a place-value mat with blocks representing the number 234.

When students use abstract numbers to express larger quantities, the column position indicates the place value. Place-value mats help students transition from concrete blocks to abstract numbers because the mats provide a two-dimensional graphic representation that forces learners to organize the blocks in the same order they will use when writing numbers. Initially, students place actual blocks on the mats. When they are ready to progress to the visual representation level, they can simply draw the blocks on the mat. Explicitly linking the blocks on the mat with the abstract symbols in both expanded notation and standard formats will help students understand place value within the base-ten number system.

To solidify their understanding of place value, students can play the Making Trades game described in Figure 7.10. Players take turns rolling a die, collecting the designated number of unit cubes, and placing their cubes on a place-value mat. When they have accumulated ten or more units, they "make a trade" and exchange ten units for a rod, which they place on the mat in the tens column. The first player to accumulate ten rods exchanges them for a flat, places the flat in the hundreds column of the place-value mat, and wins the game. Playing the Making Trades game helps students understand expanded notation and the critical role of place value; it also lays the groundwork for future lessons involving the standard algorithm for regrouping in addition. The game can also be played in reverse: students begin with a flat and take away units and rods. In this version, the first player to run out of blocks is the winner. When the game is played in

Figure 7.7 Base-Ten Blocks

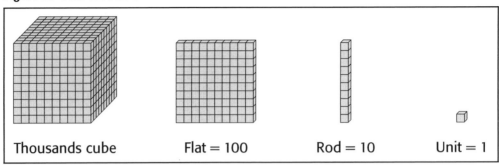

Thousands cube   Flat = 100   Rod = 10   Unit = 1

Figure 7.8 Representing 345 with Base-Ten Blocks

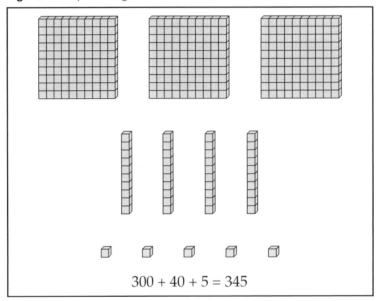

$$300 + 40 + 5 = 345$$

Figure 7.9 Representing 234 on a Place-Value Mat

Hundreds	Tens	Ones
200	30	4

Figure 7.10 Making Trades/Race for a Flat

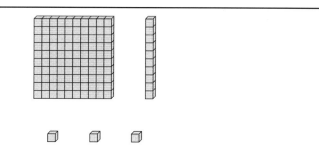

Materials: Base ten-blocks and die for each group; place-value mat for each player

Players: 2–5

Object: Be the first player to get a flat

Rules:
1. Take turns rolling the die. The player with the lowest number goes first.
2. Player #1 rolls the die, then takes that number of units and places them in the units column on her place-value mat.
3. Play continues in clockwise rotation.
4. Whenever a player has accumulated 10 units, he trades them for a rod.
5. The first player to accumulate 10 rods trades them for a flat and wins the game.

Variations:
1. To make the game go faster, students can use two dice or race to be the first to collect 5 rods instead of racing for a flat.
2. To explicitly connect the game to the regrouping algorithm, at each turn have students record the number problem that represents what they did with the blocks.
3. To practice subtraction, students can begin with a flat and race down. The first player to get rid of all pieces is the winner.

reverse, students are practicing the type of regrouping that will be required later in order to subtract multidigit numbers.

Base-ten blocks made from wood, plastic, and compressed foam are available from most teacher supply stores. Instructors can also make their own base-ten blocks from mount board, poster board, or foam sheets. Flats, rods, and units can be cut using templates or a die-cut machine. In addition to the many books and programs that use base-ten blocks to help students

Figure 7.11 Internet Resources for Base-Ten Blocks

Templates for making base-ten blocks:
- http://mason.gmu.edu/~mmankus/Handson/b10blocks.htm
- http://lrt.ednet.ns.ca/PD/BLM_Ess11/table_of_contents.htm
- http://olc.spsd.sk.ca/de/math1-3/p-printables.html

Online games using base-ten blocks:
- Representing numbers with base-ten blocks: http://nlvm.usu.edu/en/nav/frames_asid_152_g_2_t_1.html?from=grade_g_2.html
- Addition with base-ten blocks: http://nlvm.usu.edu/en/nav/frames_asid_154_g_2_t_1.html?from=grade_g_2.html
- Subtraction with base-ten blocks: http://nlvm.usu.edu/en/nav/frames_asid_155_g_1_t_1.html
- Using base-ten blocks to represent, add, subtract, multiply, and divide numbers: http://ulm.edu/~esmith/nctmregional/blocks.htm
- Decimals with base-ten blocks: http://nlvm.usu.edu/en/nav/frames_asid_264_g_2_t_1.html?from=grade_g_2.html

YouTube videos demonstrating the use of base-ten blocks:
Place value:
- www.youtube.com/watch?v=2msVlhBtppo&feature=relmfu
- www.youtube.com/watch?v=fnZihe8BsWs&feature=relmfu
- www.youtube.com/watch?v=Djp3IFYN1pQ&feature=relmfu

Making Trades:
- www.youtube.com/watch?v=bFU8tJsC6W8&feature=relmfu

understand place value, a multitude of free resources are available on the Internet. They include templates for making base-ten blocks, ideas for using blocks to develop initial number sense, applets for games featuring virtual base-ten blocks, and also ways to use base-ten blocks when performing operations with whole numbers, which we will address later in this chapter. Figure 7.11 provides a variety of Internet resources for base-ten blocks.

DigiBlocks

Another manipulative that can help students understand place value is called the "DigiBlock" (www.digi-block.com/). DigiBlocks use small rectangular blocks to represent individual units, or "ones." These small blocks can be packed into a holder designed to contain ten individual blocks. When students put a lid onto the holder, they create a ten-block that is analogous to the rod used in base-ten blocks. The block of 10 looks just like the single Digi-Block, except that it is ten times the size of the smaller block. See Figure 7.12.

Figure 7.11 *(cont)* Internet Resources for Base-Ten Blocks

Addition:
- www.youtube.com/watch?v=_qWKbS_vHkE&feature=relmfu
- www.youtube.com/watch?v=1DSgG994vqI&feature=related
- www.youtube.com/watch?v=VkCd5SQoRe4&feature=related

Subtraction:
- www.youtube.com/watch?v=o1CfyICcEfo
- www.youtube.com/watch?v=vYS7dNxw5R8
- www.youtube.com/watch?v=5IhpHmsMsNY&feature=related

Multiplication:
- www.youtube.com/watch?v=38nfYbygQwY
- www.youtube.com/watch?v=vEotY8X_jzE&feature=related
- www.youtube.com/watch?v=fnZihe8BsWs&feature=related

Division:
- www.youtube.com/watch?v=Qmkp-ZoMcxM&feature=related
- www.youtube.com/watch?v=cG3NPpEiM6k&feature=related
- www.youtube.com/watch?v=XE7F7rFwB64&feature=related

Decimals
- www.youtube.com/watch?v=WFXMkD5ICKI&feature=related
- www.youtube.com/watch?v=WFXMkD5ICKI

The ten-block holders can be grouped together into an even larger holder to form a bundle of 100, which is comparable to the flat used in base-ten blocks. The company also offers an enormous holder designed to contain ten blocks of one hundred, or 1,000 individual blocks. This large holder is about one and a half feet tall and weighs about eighteen pounds, so it provides a powerful model of the relative size of 1,000. The holders that contain individual blocks can be secured onto a place-value board, called a "counter" by the manufacturer, and then individual blocks can be inserted into the holders to model place value. In Figure 7.13 we show a student using a DigiBlock counter to model tens and ones; larger counters are available that can model larger numbers.

What sets DigiBlocks apart from other base-ten manipulatives is their ability to dynamically model the regrouping process. Students can insert up to nine blocks into the holder when it is secured in the ones column, but adding a tenth block releases a spring and causes the entire container to slide down the ramp. This provides a dramatic reminder that a maximum of nine units can be placed in the ones column. When the tenth block is added, the

Figure 7.12 DigiBlocks

holder containing a complete group of ten must be transferred from the ones column to the tens column. A similar process occurs when students attempt to place a tenth bundle in the tens column; the holder with its complete group of one hundred must be moved to the hundreds column.

To help students link the concrete blocks with abstract symbols, the holder includes a whiteboard where students can write the abstract number that represents the blocks in each column. Flip cards are also provided so that, instead of writing the numbers, students can simply display the appropriate value, as the student has done in Figure 7.13. The flip cards contain only the single digits 0–9, so they cue students that a "trade" is needed before recording larger numbers. DigiBlocks also offer miniature blocks that represent decimal tenths. Ten of the small blocks are equal in size to one single unit block, so students have a clear model of the relative size of decimal tenths compared to the value of a whole number. Students generally enjoy playing with DigiBlocks, and their active engagement facilitates learning.

Building a Solid Foundation

In addition to ten-frames, base-ten blocks, and DigiBlocks, numerous other objects can be used to model place value. Popsicle sticks, coffee stirrers, or straws can be bundled together to show a group of ten. When students

Figure 7.13 DigiBlock Counter

physically count ten sticks and bundle them into a group of ten, the relationship between a single unit and a group of ten becomes meaningful. Similarly, gathering ten groups of ten into a bundle of one hundred clearly illustrates the relative values of ones, tens, and hundreds. Pop cubes, plastic links, or paper clips can be connected to form a chain of ten or one hundred. Any of the counters students have used to develop initial number sense can be placed in small containers to create groups of ten and larger containers to form groups of one hundred. Providing students with opportunities to represent the same concepts with a variety of different materials will help solidify their understanding of place value.

Base-ten blocks and other manipulatives are commonly included in materials designed for use in the core curriculum, and most programs contain excellent ideas for using them to model place value and expanded notation. In their eagerness to help students master more advanced concepts, teachers sometimes skip over these activities. However, research has demonstrated the value of ensuring that students use concrete and pictorial representations to model their understanding of numbers and the base-ten system. Spending time modeling expanded notation with base-ten blocks and other manipulatives will actually save time later, because students with a robust sense of place value will experience fewer difficulties when they encounter more advanced operations with larger numbers. For example, consider the following addition error, which is commonly made by students who struggle with mathematics:

$$
\begin{array}{r}
74 \\
+\ \ 56 \\
\hline
1210
\end{array}
\qquad
\begin{array}{r}
67 \\
+\ \ 18 \\
\hline
715
\end{array}
$$

A student who records all the digits without regrouping does not understand the important role of place value in the base-ten number system. Errors such as these can be prevented if students have sufficient opportunities to experience concrete and visual representation of two- and three-digit numbers, to use place-value mats, and to express numbers in expanded form before they tackle advanced operations. When mathematical words and symbols are firmly rooted in experiences with concrete and visual representation, students find them meaningful. When students lack a foundation in concrete and visual representation, their attempts to perform symbolic operations may become a rote execution of meaningless procedures.

Addition and Subtraction

The Common Core Standards state that by the end of first grade, students should be able to add and subtract within twenty:

> 1.OA.1. Use addition and subtraction within 20 to solve word problems involving situations of adding to, taking from, putting together, taking apart, and comparing, with unknowns in all positions, e.g., by using objects, drawings, and equations with a symbol for the unknown number to represent the problem. (National Governors Association Center for Best Practices and Council of Chief State School Officers, 2010)

Developing Conceptual Understanding

Addition and subtraction problems are a natural extension of the counting activities used to develop initial number sense. For example, when students are learning to count, they often model a number by combining pop cubes or unifex cubes. If their pop cube "train" contains cubes of different colors, they have created an addition problem. Although students who are still learning to count are not ready to use a plus sign or an equals sign, engaging them in discussions about the many ways to model a given number will help prepare them for more formal work with addition later. We might ask a group of students to find different ways to combine two different colors to form a six-cube train, and then compare their solutions. One student might create a train with two red cubes and four yellow cubes, while another selects three red and three yellow cubes, and still another uses one yellow and five red cubes. Discussing the combinations that can be used to model any given number helps students recognize that a whole can be composed of various parts, and understanding part-whole relationships is the basis of addition. These discussions also build a foundation for understanding subtraction. If the train has six cubes, and they know that four of them are yellow and the rest are red, then students can count to determine that there are two red cubes. Decomposing numbers prepares them for later work with subtraction.

Once students are proficient at counting, they are ready to begin more formal addition. We can introduce formal notation and model how to write a complete mathematical equation by saying something like, "Melissa used five yellow cubes and then added one red cube to make her train have six cubes. Here is a way we can write that: $5 + 1 = 6$." As always, we begin with concrete representation, pair the concrete objects with pictures, tally marks, and other visual representations, and then pair these visual models with abstract numbers and symbols. Figure 7.14 contains an example of a lesson designed to explicitly connect the various types of representation when introducing basic addition.

In this lesson, the teacher begins at the concrete level by asking students to place goldfish crackers on a picture of a fishbowl. Since these crackers come in various colors, students can use them to create addition facts to describe different color combinations of fish within the bowl. At the representational level, students draw pictures to illustrate their concrete models. Note that in this example, the teacher includes the abstract symbols from the beginning. All three forms of representation are used together in this introductory lesson, but that does not mean that after this lesson students will be ready to eliminate concrete models. Research suggests that students who struggle with mathematics will typically need at least two more experiences using concrete representation to model simple addition problems before they are ready to discard manipulatives and work solely with pictures and numbers, and three more experiences where visual representation continues to be included before they will be ready to rely only on abstract words and symbols. Some students will progress rapidly through the CRA sequence, and others will need more extended practice at each level. When a student can solve a simple problem independently and also provide an explanation of what was done and why it was done that way, then that individual is ready to fade the supports and to focus on abstract representation.

As we discussed previously, numerical understanding involves the ability to use multiple models to represent the same problem or procedure. We therefore need to provide opportunities for students to use a variety of manipulatives to model each skill, and make sure they can transition fluidly among the different forms of representation. Given a word problem, can the student model it with objects or pictures, and write the associated number sentence? Given a concrete model of an addition problem, can he draw pictures or use tallies to model the same problem? Can he write the number sentence and suggest a story to go with the model? Note that the

Figure 7.14 Explicit Instruction in Addition

Teacher says:	Teacher shows:
Give each student a laminated picture of a fish bowl, a handful of colored goldfish crackers, paper, and crayons. Teacher has the same materials for demonstration. This is my fishbowl. I have 3 red fish in my bowl and 2 yellow fish. How could we show my fishbowl using these objects? *Elicit answers. Students place 3 red goldfish and 2 yellow goldfish on their mats, while the teacher does the same on the demonstration mat.* Let's check. Do I have 3 red fish? Do I have 2 yellow fish? Good. Check your mat and see if you have 3 red fish and 2 yellow fish.	
I'm going to use numbers to write the problem here on the board. I have 3 red fish, so I'll write a 3. *Write 3.* I have some more fish, so I'm going to write a plus sign. *Write +.* How many yellow fish do I have? Yes, 2. So what should I write to show that I have 2 yellow fish? Yes, I'll write the number 2. *Write 2.* That says three plus two, which is how many fish I have in my bowl.	$3 + 2$
Now, I wonder how many fish I have in all. Who has an idea how we could figure that out? Yes, we could count them. Count with me. When I touch each fish, we'll say the number. Ready? One, two, three, four, five. Five fish in all. Everybody, count and see if you have 5 fish in your fishbowl.	
I want to show that I have 5 fish on my number sentence on the board. First, I'm going to write this symbol.	$3 + 2 = 5$

problems provided at this level are very simple addition problems designed to help students develop the basic concept that addition involves joining two or more sets. We use story problems because students will attend and retain information better when they perceive it as meaningful and relevant (Archer & Hughes, 2011; Wolfe, 2001). However, students who struggle with mathematics typically have extreme difficulty solving story problems due to language deficits that interfere with their ability to process the problem. When introducing addition and subtraction, the purpose of the story

Figure 7.14 *(cont)* Explicit Instruction in Addition

Teacher says:	Teacher shows:
Write =. This is an equal sign. It means that I've got the same amount on this side *(point to the 3 + 2)* as I have over here. We just counted and found that I have 5 fish, so I'm going to write a 5 here. *Write 5.* So 3 plus 2 equals 5.	
How could we show my fishbowl using the paper and crayons? Yes, we could draw them. First, let's draw a fishbowl. I'll draw a circle on the board to represent my fishbowl. You draw a fishbowl on your paper. Now, how many fish do we need to show in the bowl? Yes, 5 fish. First I'm going to draw my fish, and then I'll color them. One, two three, four, five. My fish look a little funny, but that's OK. Do I have 5 fish? Good. How should I color them? OK, I'll use my red crayon for 3 fish, and the yellow crayon for 2 fish. *Color the fish.* Now it's your turn. You draw the 3 red fish and 2 yellow fish in your fishbowl.	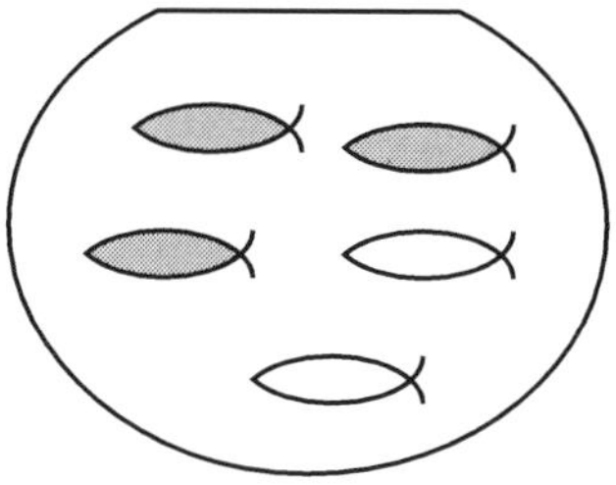
Let's check. Does my drawing match my fishbowl? Are there 3 red fish and 2 yellow fish in the drawing? Good. I'm going to write the number sentence next to my drawing. I have 3 red fish and 2 yellow fish, so I'll write 3 + 2. *Write.* How many fish do I have in all? Yes, I have 5 fish in all, so I'll write "equals 5." *Write = 5.* Let's read the number sentence together, everybody! Three plus two equals five. Very good! Now it's your turn. You write the number sentence on your paper to show how many fish are in your bowl. *Monitor student work.*	$3 + 2 = 5$

problems is to provide a context for the operation, so the problems selected should be simple and straightforward. We do not want the child frustrated by the language of the problem or confused by complex distractors. Strategies for teaching problem solving and dealing with more complex problem scenarios will be discussed much more thoroughly in Chapter 10.

Once students can successfully add two addends and explain the process, they can progress to adding three whole numbers whose sum is less than or equal to twenty. They can also learn strategies for solving addition fact problems such as "counting on" or using combinations that equal ten.

Figure 7.15 Modeling Subtraction

Important Terms
• Minuend: Original quantity from which an amount will be subtracted. • Subtrahend: Quantity to be removed. • Difference: The quantity remaining after subtraction (answer). $$\begin{array}{rl} 8 & \leftarrow \quad \text{minuend} \\ -\,5 & \leftarrow \quad \text{subtrahend} \\ \hline 3 & \leftarrow \quad \text{difference} \end{array}$$
Representing a Subtraction Problem
★ ★ ★ ★ ★ ✗ ✗ ✗ 1. Model the minuend. 2. Remove or cross out the number of items stated in the subtrahend. 3. What is left is the difference.

For example, if the child knows that $8 + 2 = 10$, she can use that knowledge to solve the problem $8 + 3$ by first solving $8 + 2$ and then adding on one more (National Governors Association Center for Best Practices and Council of Chief State School Officers, 2010). In the next chapter, we will provide a detailed description of strategies for solving basic math fact problems.

The lesson presented in Figure 7.14, using goldfish crackers to introduce addition problems, could easily be adapted to introduce formal notation for subtraction. Instead of adding goldfish crackers, we would begin the story with a group of goldfish in the bowl and then remove some and count the number remaining. Note that to model subtraction problems, we display only the minuend. In other words, we represent the top number if the problem is written vertically or the first number when the problem is written horizontally. See Figure 7.15.

In an addition problem we model both parts, and then combine those parts to find the total. In a subtraction problem we only model the total, then remove or cross some out and count to determine the difference. If students try to use counters to model both the minuend and subtrahend in a subtraction problem, they have actually illustrated an addition problem.

Subtraction is the inverse of addition, and emphasizing this relationship can help students understand and solve subtraction problems. For example, if students see a pile of three counters and another pile of five counters, they can determine that there are eight counters in all. If we cover the pile of five counters and leave the rest exposed, then ask students to determine how many counters are hidden, we have created a subtraction problem: $8 - 5 = 3$. Although we can solve this problem by beginning at eight and counting down, children often approach it as an addition problem and count up from five to eight. Counting up is a very effective strategy for solving subtraction problems that builds on students' previous experiences with addition. When students recognize that they can count up or count down to obtain the solution, they begin to understand the relationship between addition and subtraction and enhance their ability to reason numerically.

Another way to model the relationship between addition and subtraction is with dominoes. Counting the dots on each side of the domino creates an addition problem, while hiding one side illustrates the related subtraction problem. Dominoes also provide an excellent example of the commutative property of addition. For example, a domino with five dots on the left and three dots on the right represents the addition fact $5 + 3 = 8$. Flipping it around, it shows the related fact $3 + 5 = 8$. The total number of dots on the domino does not change, so students can clearly see that changing the order of the addends does not affect the sum.

At the visual level, the connection between addition and subtraction is graphically illustrated by the "number bonds" used in Singapore Math. Singapore's consistently excellent results in the Trends in International Mathematics and Science Study (TIMSS) place it among the best in the world in math achievement. The number bonds used in the Singapore Math program to illustrate part-whole relationships provide a clear visual representation of the connection among the numbers in a fact family, as shown in Figure 7.16.

Figure 7.16 Number Bonds

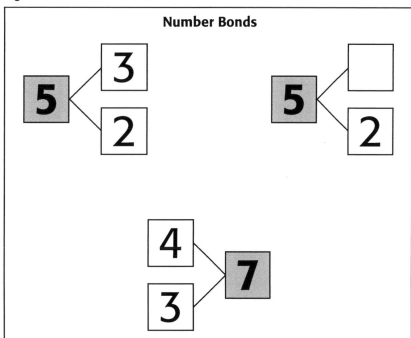

Students can use the number bonds to determine that 6 + 2 = 8 and 2 + 6 = 8, and also that 8 − 2 = 6 and 8 − 6 = 2. Composing and decomposing numbers this way increases students' number sense and develops computational fluency. For more information on number bonds, see www.kids-activities-learning-games.com/support-files/singaporemathbonds.pdf. The process of connecting addition and subtraction is explored further in the next chapter.

Whether we are working with addition or subtraction, when we introduce operations we need to make sure students develop an accurate understanding of the meaning of the equal sign in formal notation. Equality is a relationship, not an operation. The "equal" sign is the mathematical symbol placed between objects, numbers, or sets that have the same value, but when students first encounter this symbol, they often interpret it to mean "find the answer." This misinterpretation will cause difficulty when learners are asked to tackle equations presented in an unfamiliar order, such as 9 = 4 + 5, or 12 − ? = 8. Understanding equivalence is also essential for students' later work with algebraic equations. To develop this important concept, we can have students create a concrete model with a pan balance. In Figure 7.17 we show a student adding more counters to the right pan to make the scales level.

Providing multiple opportunities for students to use a balance to model equivalence will help them understand the concept of equality. The pan balance also provides an effective model for solving problems with missing middle addends (e.g., 2 + ? = 5), which students often find especially challenging. A simple line drawing of a pan balance, like the one shown in Figure 7.17, will help students make the transition from concrete to visual representation, and drawing an "equals" sign below the balance will connect the abstract symbol to the visual model. Explicitly linking the concrete and visual representations with the abstract symbol will help students understand that the set on the left of the equals sign must be the same value as the set on the right.

Developing Computational Fluency with Basic Facts

Computational fluency is the ability to compute accurately, quickly, and effortlessly. Therefore, developing computational fluency has been identified in the IES practice guide as a priority for mathematical interventions (Gersten et al., 2009). We devote the entire next chapter to strategies to help students compute accurately, quickly, and effortlessly. While automaticity with basic facts facilitates mathematical progress, students can continue to engage in mathematical problem-solving activities and build conceptual understanding of operations long before they master the basic facts. In the rest of this chapter we discuss procedures for enhancing students' conceptual understanding of addition and subtraction of larger numbers, as well as developing concepts and strategies for multiplication and division. We recommend

Figure 7.17 Pan Balance

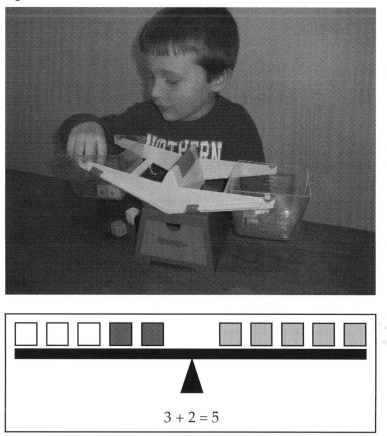

$$3 + 2 = 5$$

that the topics that follow be addressed concurrently with the ongoing practice with basic facts that will be discussed in the next chapter.

Multi-Digit Addition and Subtraction

Once students understand place value and can solve addition and subtraction fact problems, they are ready to tackle problems involving larger numbers. Typically students first learn to add a one-digit number to a two-digit number and subtract a one-digit number from a two-digit number, then add and subtract two-digit numbers, first without regrouping, then with regrouping, and gradually progress to solving problems that contain larger numbers. The Common Core Standards stipulate that by the end of second grade, students should be able to perform the following addition and subtraction skills:

CC.3.NBT.7: Add and subtract within 1000, using concrete models or drawings and strategies based on place value, properties of operations, and/or the relationship between addition and subtraction; relate the strategy to a written method. (National Governors Association Center for Best Practices and Council of Chief State School Officers, 2010)

Figure 7.18 Alternative Algorithm for Addition

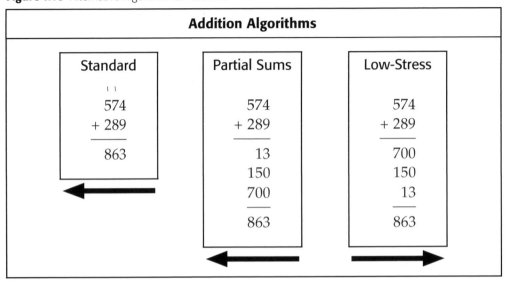

Students can begin working with multidigit addition at the concrete level by modeling a problem with concrete objects, then counting to determine the answer. This is an excellent introductory activity because it develops initial understanding without requiring any written computation. Eventually, however, students must learn to use an algorithm so they can solve these multidigit addition problems without the aid of concrete or visual representation. An algorithm is a set of step-by-step procedures for solving a problem, and there is more than one algorithm that leads to the correct solution of an addition problem. Historically, students were taught only one way to add multidigit numbers, i.e., working from right to left and "carrying" or regrouping from one column to the next as necessary. This is the standard algorithm, and it is the way most teachers learned to add. Students sometimes struggle with this algorithm because it approaches problems in a very piecemeal fashion. For example, a 7 in the tens column is really seven tens, or seventy, while a 7 in the hundreds column represents 700. In the standard algorithm, digits are manipulated in a discrete fashion that may cause students to forget their place value, resulting in some of the errors frequently observed among students who struggle with regrouping. Students may also confuse the right to left progression required to correctly execute the standard algorithm with the left to right progression used in reading. In an effort to prevent some of these problems, many math programs now teach students to use one of the alternative algorithms shown in Figure 7.18 before they introduce the standard algorithm.

To teach the alternative low-stress or partial sums algorithms, we begin at the concrete level by having students use blocks to represent each addend. Manipulating the blocks emphasizes the place value of each digit. Teachers also need to be careful that their language reflects place value so that students maintain conceptual understanding of what they are doing. For example, instead of referring to the 7 in the tens column as "seven," we should call it "seven tens" or "seventy" and encourage students to do the same. The alternative algorithms allow students to work from right to left or left to right. To solve the problem from left to right, students first add and record the total value of the hundreds (500 + 200 = 700), then the tens (70 + 80 = 150), then the ones (9 + 4 = 13). To find the total, they simply add the partial sums. The addition problem can also be worked from right to left by first adding and recording all the ones, then the tens, and then the hundreds, and finally combining these subtotals to determine the grand total. Either way, no regrouping is required. These algorithms are simple and effective, and for students who are functioning far below grade level, interventionists may elect to teach these algorithms exclusively. Students working in the core curriculum are expected to master multiple algorithms, but for students who are behind academically, the time required to master additional algorithms for addition might be more profitably devoted to working on different skills. If the decision is made to introduce multiple algorithms, allow students sufficient time to master one algorithm and solidify their understanding before introducing a second algorithm.

When we introduce the standard algorithm, we again begin at the concrete level. It is helpful to first let students solve problems that do not require regrouping. Ten-frames, base-ten blocks, and DigiBlocks all provide effective models for the standard algorithm, and letting students use a familiar manipulative will help them connect the new algorithm to their previous experiences with place value. The purpose of using concrete representation is to give meaning to the abstract algorithm, but this goal can be accomplished only if we explicitly connect each step in the algorithm with the concrete manipulation. Therefore, when we model the standard algorithm, we need to perform each step first with blocks, then with the written numbers, so students see the relationship between the concrete representation and the paper-and-pencil activity. Once students can successfully execute the standard algorithm to solve problems that do not require regrouping, then they are ready to tackle regrouping problems. Because regrouping requires students to have a solid understanding of place value, it is beneficial to review expanded notation and the "Making Trades" game described in Figure 7.10. Use the same language of "making trades" to introduce regrouping in the addition algorithm. Figure 7.19 shows how a teacher used base-ten blocks to model regrouping with the standard algorithm.

When students can explain the procedure using concrete manipulatives, the blocks can be faded while they continue to use drawings to model their work. Once they can effectively explain the procedure using the visual representations, they are ready to solve addition problems using just the abstract numbers.

The procedure for introducing multidigit subtraction is similar to that suggested for introducing addition. We recommend using the standard algorithm

Figure 7.19 Using Base-Ten Blocks to Model Regrouping in Addition with the Standard Algorithm

Skill: Two-digit addition with regrouping

Prerequisite Skills:
- Addition of basic facts 0 to 18
- Single-digit and multidigit addition without regrouping
- Two-digit plus one-digit addition with regrouping
- Adding three single-digit numbers
- Place value concepts

Modeling Using Base-Ten Blocks:

Teacher says:	Teacher shows:
Here is our problem. Our class has collected 35 cans for the recycling drive. Mrs. Smith's class collected 27 seven cans. We want to know how many cans we have collected altogether. To figure this out, we are going to add these two numbers together.	$\begin{array}{r} 35 \\ + 27 \\ \hline \end{array}$
These are the steps I am going to follow to solve this problem. *Have the following steps listed on the board and point to them.* 1. Put out blocks for each number. 2. Add the ones. If you have ten or more, make a trade. 3. Record the ones in the ones column and any traded ten in the tens column. 4. Add the tens. 5. Record. 6. Does your answer make sense? Yes/No	
Now I am going to lay out blocks to show 35. That is 3 tens in the tens column and 5 ones in the ones column. *Lay out blocks.*	$\begin{array}{r} 35 \\ + 27 \\ \hline \end{array}$

Figure 7.19 (cont) Using Base-Ten Blocks to Model Regrouping in Addition with the Standard Algorithm

Teacher says:	Teacher shows:
Now I need to lay out blocks for our second number. Our second number is 27. That is 2 tens in the tens column and 7 ones in the ones column. *Lay out blocks.* Have I finished step 1? Yes. Let's check it off our list. *Check off step 1.*	$\begin{array}{r} 35 \\ + 27 \\ \hline \end{array}$
Step 2 says, "Add the ones. If you have 10 or more, make a trade." Do you remember when we played Making Trades? I remember from our game that when we have 10 ones or 10 units, we need to trade them for a ten or a rod. So if we have more than 10 ones now, we will need to make a trade. Let's count the ones together. *Count.* We have 12 ones. Twelve is more than 10 and we cannot have that many in the ones column. We need to make a trade. I am going to trade 10 of our units for a rod and put the rod in the tens column. *Count 10 units and trade them for a rod. Place the rod in the tens column.* Now we have completed step 2. *Check off step 2.*	$\begin{array}{r} 35 \\ + 27 \\ \hline \end{array}$
Step 3 says, "Record the ones in the ones column and any traded ten in the tens column." Let's count our ones together. Good, we have 2 units, so I am going to write 2 in the ones column of my number problem. *Record a 2 in the ones column.* We also made a trade and added another rod to our tens column, so I need to make our problem say that. I am going to write a 1 above the numbers in our tens column. This makes sense because I know that 5 plus 7 equals 12. *Write a 1 over the numbers in the tens column. Check off step 3.* Step 4 says, "Add the tens." We have 3 numbers to add in our tens column now that we made a trade. We need to add 1 plus 3 plus 2. Let's count our rods together to see how many tens we have. Good, we have 6 tens. *Check off step 4.*	$\begin{array}{r} {}^{1} \\ 35 \\ + 27 \\ \hline 2 \end{array}$

Figure 7.19 *(cont)* Using Base-Ten Blocks to Model Regrouping in Addition with the Standard Algorithm

Teacher says:	Teacher shows:
Step 5 says to record. I am going to record a 6 in our tens column to show that we have 6 tens. *Record the 6 in the tens column and then check off step 5.* Let's look at our problem to see if our answer makes sense. Our class collected 35 cans for the recycling drive, and Mrs. Smith's class collected 27. We decided that the two classes together collected 62 cans. Our answer makes sense because when we are adding two numbers together, we should always have an answer that is bigger than the two numbers we started with. *Circle "Yes" next to step 6.*	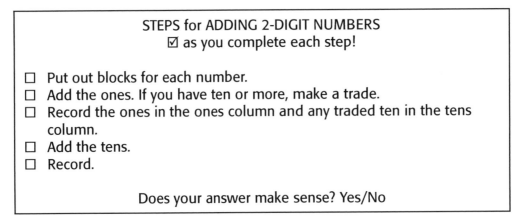

Provide students with the following laminated checklist to you when they complete problems on their own:

> **STEPS for ADDING 2-DIGIT NUMBERS**
> ☑ **as you complete each step!**
>
> ☐ Put out blocks for each number.
> ☐ Add the ones. If you have ten or more, make a trade.
> ☐ Record the ones in the ones column and any traded ten in the tens column.
> ☐ Add the tens.
> ☐ Record.
>
> **Does your answer make sense? Yes/No**

for subtraction, because learners with a history of mathematical difficulty often find alternative subtraction algorithms prohibitively confusing. First, allow students to use blocks to solve problems without including any written notation. To introduce the formal algorithm, pair each step with the concrete representation so students understand the rationale for each action. Again the decision about whether to use ten-frames, base-ten blocks, DigiBlocks, or some other manipulative should be based on which manipulative will most effectively help students connect the new procedure with their existing understanding of place value. Remind students that, when modeling subtraction problems, we lay out blocks to represent only the minuend, or top number in the problem, because if we laid out both the minuend and subtrahend, we would actually be modeling an addition problem. Before introducing problems that require regrouping, have students again play Making Trades, the game that was described in Figure 7.10, but this time, in order to model the regrouping process in subtraction, students should start with a flat and remove blocks until they have none left. Figure 7.20 shows how a teacher modeled the standard subtraction algorithm with ten-frames. In Chapter 5 we provided an example of how to model an explicit strategy, and that example used base-ten blocks to teach the standard algorithm for regrouping in subtraction (see Figure 5.4, p. 66). In Figure 7.21 we provide another, similar example using base-ten blocks to introduce the standard algorithm. In each lesson, the teacher explicitly connects the various forms of representation so that students can see the purpose of each step in the algorithm.

After the regrouping algorithm has been introduced, some students over-generalize and try to regroup in every column in every problem, whether it is appropriate or not. Mixing problems so that some require regrouping and others do not, and some require trades only in the ones column and others only in the tens, will encourage students to think more carefully about what they are doing. They need practice deciding whether to regroup or not, and they need practice explaining and justifying their decisions.

Because subtracting across zeroes requires special procedures that can confuse students, it is best to avoid zeroes during students' initial experiences with regrouping. Once students can execute the standard algorithm independently using concrete, pictorial, and abstract representation and can explain what they are doing and why they are doing it, then problems with zeroes can be introduced and the double trade modeled. When students can explain what they are doing with the models, then the teacher can fade the concrete supports and have students work exclusively with abstract numbers.

Multiplication and Division

Developing Conceptual Understanding of Multiplication

The Common Core Standards introduce the concept of multiplication in third grade. Multiplication problems contain two numbers, or factors. One factor indicates the number of equally sized groups or sets that are present, and the other factor tells the size of each group. For example, in the problem $3 \times 4 = 12$, there are three groups, and each group contains four members. The total number of objects, twelve, is referred to as the product. Figure 7.22 shows a variety of models that can help students understand the multiplicative process, including equal groups, arrays, repeated addition with number lines, and area models.

The top illustration depicts equal groups. In a multiplication fact, the first factor is traditionally used to indicate the number of groups, while the second factor tells the number of members in each group. In Figure 7.22, we model 3×4 with three groups containing four objects per group. A simple representational strategy is to give students paper plates to show the groups, and let them place counters on the plates to represent the members in each

Figure 7.20 Using Ten-Frames to Model Regrouping in Subtraction

Steps for Regrouping in Subtraction
1. Show how many you have (the total).
2. Begin with the ones column. Decide: Can you subtract the ones, or do you need to regroup first? If you need to regroup:
• Break down a ten.
• Write down how many tens are left, and how many ones you now have.
3. Subtract the ones. Record the answer.
4. Subtract the tens. Record the answer.
5. Check to see if my answer makes sense.

Teacher says:	Teacher shows:
Here's our problem. We have 35 science books in the room, and we need to keep 18 of them here so each of you can have a book. We want to know how many books we have left that we could let Mrs. Rivera use. I'm going to follow these steps to solve the problem. *Point to steps listed above.*	35 − 18 ——
Step 1 says: "Show how many I have." Let's see. We have 35, so I need to use my ten-frames to show 35. First I'm going to make a place to put my tens and ones. I'll draw lines and label the columns 'ones' and 'tens.' *Draw a place-value chart.*	35 − 18 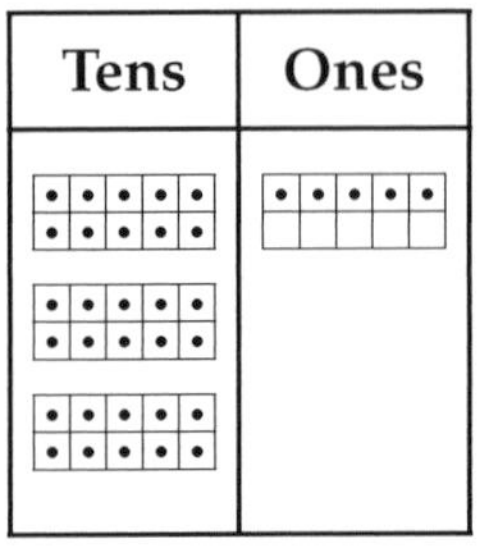 ——
OK. Now I need to show 35. That's ten, twenty, thirty-five. I need three full ten-frames in my tens column and one that only has 5 in it in the ones column. *Lay out ten-frames.* Let's see. Have I finished step 1? It says, "Show how many you have." I've done that, so I'm going to check off step 1. *Put a check next to 1 in the steps listed above.*	35 − 18 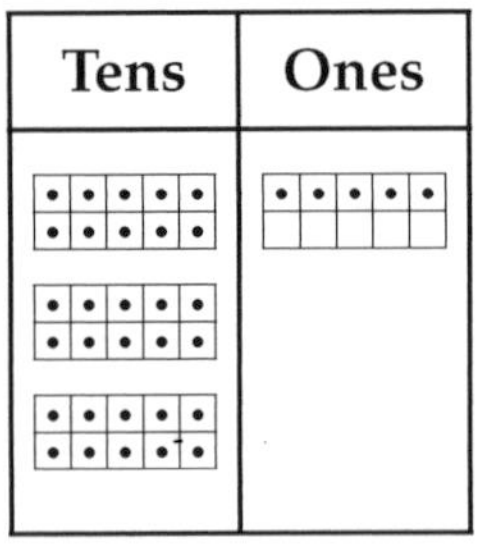 ——
Step 2 says, "Look at the ones column. Decide: Can you subtract the ones, or do you need to regroup first?" Let's look at my ones column. I have 5 ones, but I need to take away 8 ones. I don't have enough ones to do that, so I guess I need to regroup. It says, "If you need to regroup, break down a ten." I remember from when	35 − 18 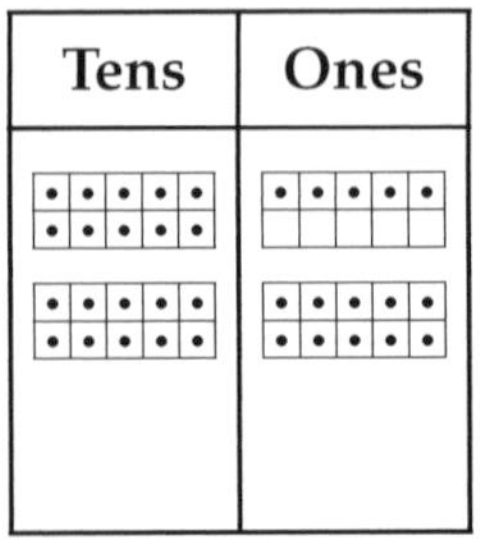 ——

Figure 7.20 *(cont)* Using Ten-Frames to Model Regrouping in Subtraction

Teacher says:	Teacher shows:
we played Making Trades that I can break down a ten and change it to 10 ones without changing the total amount. I'm going to do that. I'll take one of my tens and break it apart. Now I have 10 more in the ones column. I had 5, and I've added 10 more, so now I have 15 ones. I broke down a ten, so I can check off that part of step 2. *Check off 'Break down a ten' in the steps listed above.*	
Next it says, "Write down how many tens are left, and how many ones you now have." I used to have 3 tens, but I regrouped and now I only have 2 tens, so I'll cross off the 3 and change it say I have 2 tens. *Write.* I started with 5 ones, but after I broke down the ten I ended up with 15 in the ones column, so I need to make my problem say that. *Write.* I've completed that part of step 2, so I can check it off. *Check off "Write down how many tens are left, and how many ones you now have" in the steps listed above.*	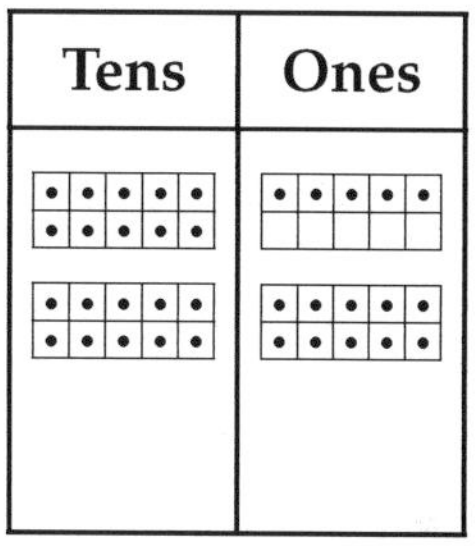
Step 3 says, "Subtract the ones, and record the answer." OK. I have 15 ones and I need to take away 8. I'm going to do that. Now I've got *(counting)* 1, 2, 3, 4, 5, 6, 7 left. That makes sense because I know that 15 − 8 = 7. I need to record the answer, so I'll write 7 in the ones column. Now I can check off step 3. *Check off step 3 above.*	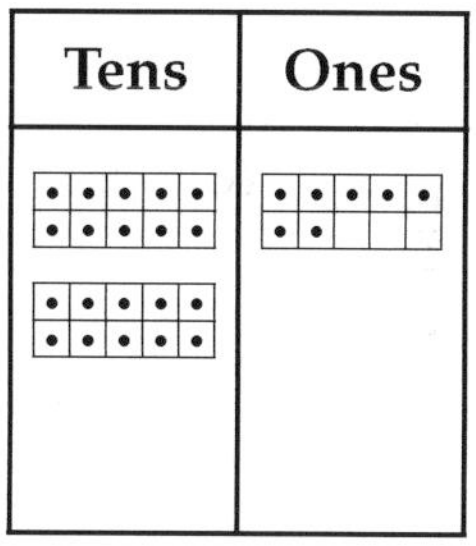
Step 4 says, "Subtract the tens and record the answer." I have 2 tens and I need to subtract 1 of them. I'm going to take one ten-frame from the tens column. I can check off step 4. *Check off step 4 above.*	
Let's look at our problem. We have 35 science books and we're using 18 of them. We have 17 left over that we can lend to Mrs. River's class. Does that make sense? I think it does, because 18 is about half of 35, so if we use about half, we should have about half left. 17 is just about half. I can check off step 5, and I'm done. *Checks off step 5.*	

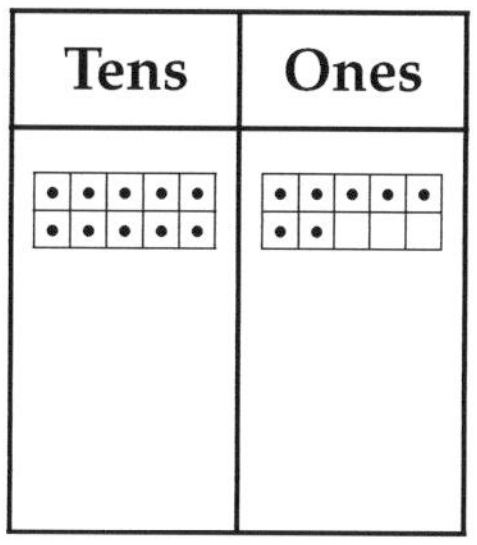

Figure 7.21 Using Base-Ten Blocks to Model Regrouping in Subtraction

Prerequisite Skills:
- Addition and subtraction of basic facts 0 to 18
- Single-digit and multidigit addition and subtraction without regrouping
- Place value concepts

Modeling Using Base-Ten Blocks:

Teacher says:	Teacher shows:

Here is our problem. Our class had 32 days of school between fall break and winter break. Nineteen of those days have passed. We want to know how many more days are left until winter break. To figure this out, we are going to complete this subtraction problem.
 	
These are the steps I am going to follow to solve this problem.
Have the following steps listed on the board and point to them.
 	
1. Show how many you have (the total).
2. Begin with the ones column. Decide: Can you subtract the ones, or do you need to regroup first? If you need to regroup,
   • Break down a ten.
   • Write down how many tens are left, and how many ones you have now.
3. Subtract the ones, and record the answer.
4. Subtract the tens, and record the answer.
5. Does your answer make sense? Yes/No
 	
Step 1 says, "Show how many you have (the total)." Let's look at our problem. We have 32, so we need to use our base-ten blocks to show 32. First, I am going to make a place to put my tens and ones. I will draw the lines for a chart and label the columns "Tens" and "Ones." *Draw a place-value chart.*
	32
	$-\,19$
	—————
	
	32
	$-\,19$
	—————
	<table><tr><td>**Tens**</td><td>**Ones**</td></tr><tr><td></td><td></td></tr></table>

Figure 7.21 *(cont)* Using Base-Ten Blocks to Model Regrouping in Subtraction

Teacher says:	Teacher shows:
Now I am going to lay out blocks to show 32. That is 3 tens in the tens column and 2 ones in the ones column. *Lay out blocks.* OK, have I placed blocks to show the total number we have? Yes. That means we have finished step 1, so I am going to put a check mark next to step 1. *Check off step 1.*	32 − 19 — Tens / Ones table showing 3 tens and 2 ones 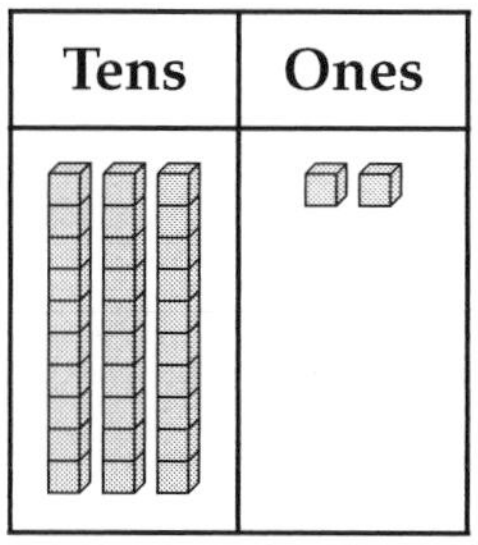
Step 2 says, "Begin with the ones column. Decide: Can you subtract the ones, or do you need to regroup first?" So let's look at our ones column. We have 2 ones, but we need to subtract 9. I do not have enough ones to do that, so I need to regroup. The step says, "If you need to regroup, break down a ten." Do you remember when we played Making Trades? I remember from the game that I can break down a ten or a rod, and change it to ten ones or ten units, without changing the total amount. I am going to do that now. I am going to take one of my tens and trade it for ten ones. *Trade blocks.* Now I have 1 less in the tens column and 10 more in the ones column. I had 3 tens; now I have 2. I had 2 ones; now I have 12. We have completed the first part of step 2, so let's check that off our list. *Check off "Break down a ten" in step 2.*	32 − 19 — Tens / Ones table showing 2 tens and 12 ones 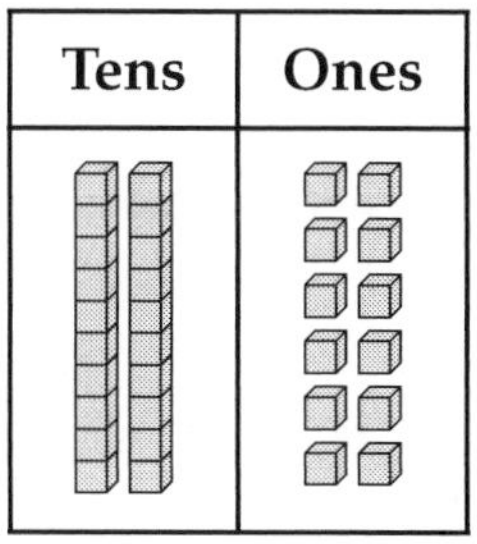
Next, step 2 tells us to "write down how many tens are left, and how many ones you have now." We had 3 tens, but now we only have 2. I am going to cross off the 3 and change it so that our problem tells us that we have 2 tens now. Now let's look at our ones. I used to have 2 ones, but now I have 12. I am going to make our problem say that. Have we completed the second half of step 2? We wrote down how many tens and ones we have now, so yes. Let's check that off the list. *Check off the remainder of step 2.*	2 1 / 3̶2 − 19 — Tens / Ones table showing 2 tens and 12 ones 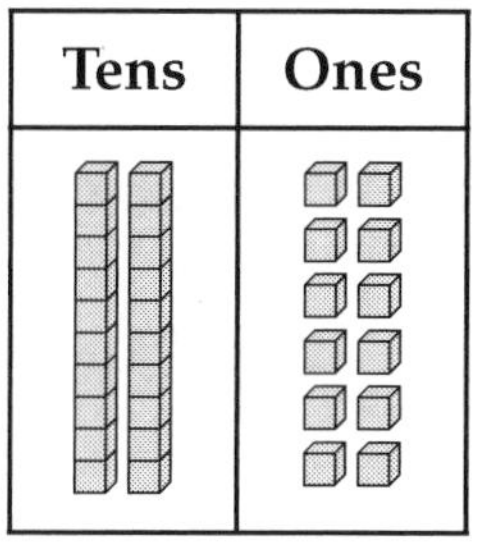

Figure 7.21 *(cont)* Using Base-Ten Blocks to Model Regrouping in Subtraction

Teacher says:	Teacher shows:
Step 3 says, "Subtract the ones, and record the answer." Let's look at our ones column. We have 12 ones, and we are supposed to take away 9. I am going to do that now. *Take away 9 ones.* Now I have *(count)* 1, 2, 3 left. That makes sense because we know that 12 minus 9 is 3. I need to record that on our problem, so I am going to write a 3 in the ones column. Now we can check of step 3. *Check off step 3.*	$\begin{array}{r} \overset{2}{\cancel{3}}\overset{1}{2} \\ -\ 19 \\ \hline 3 \end{array}$ 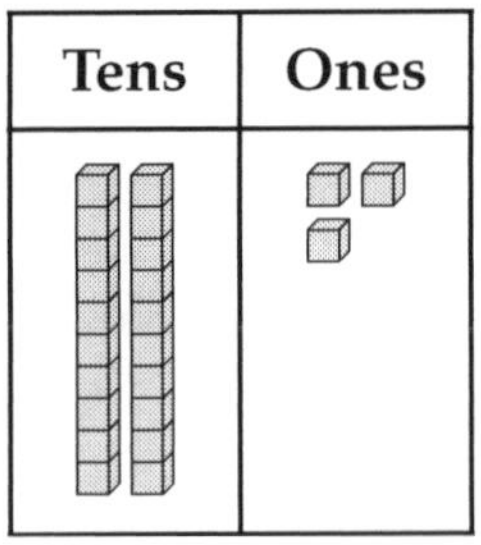
Step 4 says, "Subtract the tens, and record the answer." Let's look at the tens column. We have 2 tens, and we need to take away one of them. I am going to take away 1 ten now. *Take away a rod.* Now I have 1 ten left. I am going to record this by writing a 1 in the tens column. Can we check off step 4? Yes. *Check off step 4.* Let's look at our problem to see if our answer makes sense. Our class had 32 days between fall break and winter break. We have completed 19 of those days and wanted to know how many we have left. We know that our number should have gotten smaller because we are subtracting. We started with 32 and took away 19. Our answer was 13. That does make sense because 13 is less than 32. Let's circle yes, our answer does make sense. Circle "Yes" on the list of steps. Together we decided that we have 13 days left until winter break.	$\begin{array}{r} \overset{2}{\cancel{3}}\overset{1}{2} \\ -\ 19 \\ \hline 13 \end{array}$ 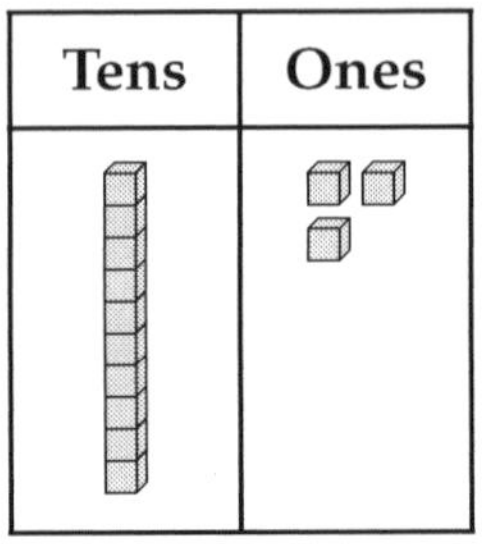

Provide students with the following laminated checklist:

STEPS for SUBTRACTING 2-DIGIT NUMBERS
☑ as you complete each step!

1. Show how many you have (the total).
2. Start in the ones column.
   Decide: Can you subtract the ones, or do you need to regroup first?
   If you need to regroup:
   • Break down a ten.
   • Write how many tens are left, and how many ones you have now.
3. Subtract the ones, and record the answer.
4. Subtract the tens, and record the answer.

Does the answer make sense? Yes/No

Figure 7.22 Representing Multiplication

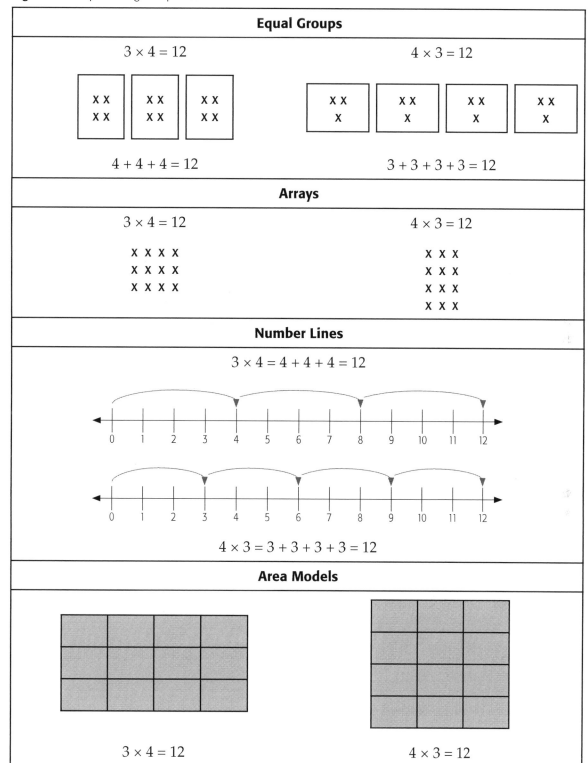

group. Coffee stirrers or craft sticks in paper cups can also help students develop a concrete understanding of basic multiplication. The commutative property tells us that the order of the factors does not affect the product; both 3×4 and 4×3 result in a product of twelve. However, the order does make a difference in the models we use to represent multiplication facts, as shown in the two drawings of equal groups presented in Figure 7.22. When we represent 3×4, we draw three groups and put four members in each group, while the illustration of 4×3 shows four groups with three members in each group. The product is the same, but the drawings look different. Students who are struggling to develop basic conceptual understanding will need to spend time exploring and discussing this relationship.

As students become more comfortable representing multiplication with equal groups, interventionists can enrich their conceptual understanding by introducing additional models. The second illustration in Figure 7.22 shows the same fact problem, 3×4, modeled with an array. Here the factors are represented by objects or pictures of objects organized in rows and columns. We will use the first factor to designate the number of rows in the array, and the second factor to indicate the number of columns in each row, although some authors reverse this order. Arrays provide an excellent introduction to the commutative property, because by flipping the array, the same drawing can illustrate the related fact, which graphically shows that reversing the order of the factors still yields the same product.

The third illustration in Figure 7.22 uses a number line to model multiplication as repeated addition. The multiplication fact, 3×4, is shown as three groups of four, or $4 + 4 + 4$, and the related fact, 4×3 is modeled with four groups of three, or $3 + 3 + 3 + 3$. Earlier in this chapter we described how Mathline can be used to connect concrete, visual, and abstract models of numbers (see Figure 7.5, p. 101). Mathline is also an excellent tool to model multiplication facts. To show 3×4, students would begin with all the rings pushed to the right so that the zero is exposed, and then create three groups, each containing four rings. When students push all three groups to the left, they will see the product, twelve, displayed to the right of the rings.

The Common Core Standards state that third-grade students should be able to represent multiplication problems using equal groups, arrays, and measurement models. In fourth grade, they add area models to their representational repertoire. An area model is similar to an array, except that it uses square units placed side by side, rather than discrete objects, to form the rows and columns. In an area model, the factors form the length and width of a rectangle, and the area of the rectangle represents the product, as shown in the fourth illustration in Figure 7.22. Figure 7.23 describes a simple activity that can help students use arrays and area models to represent multiplication fact problems, explicitly connecting these two representations with their previous experiences using equal groups to represent multiplication facts. Explicitly linking different representations will enrich students' conceptual understanding of multiplication.

Figure 7.23 Linking Multiplication Models

1. Materials: Give each student a blank 4 × 6 index card, a ruler, 24 counters, 6 paper plates, and scissors.
2. Show students how to use the ruler to measure one-inch segments along the length and width of the card and then draw the lines to create the 4 × 6 model shown below. (Students who have not mastered measuring to the nearest inch may need assistance with this step.) Have them count the number of rows and columns and write the associated multiplication fact: 4 × 6 = 24.

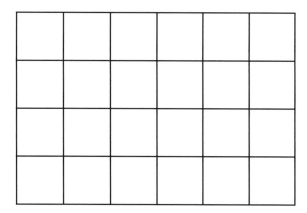

3. Have them turn the card sideways and write the multiplication fact: 6 × 4 = 24. Discuss how this is the same and different from the first fact they wrote.
4. Let them place one counter in each square to create a 4 × 6 array. Discuss how the array and area models are the same and how they are different.
5. To help students connect these models to their previous experiences using equal groups to represent multiplication facts, let them use the paper plates and counters to model the two facts, 4 × 6 = 24 and 6 × 4 = 24. Discuss how these models are the same and how they are different.
6. The 4 × 6 index card can also help students understand how different factors can be combined to form the same product. Have students cut their index cards along the grid lines to create 24 squares, each 1 inch by 1 inch. Challenge them to rearrange the 24 squares into different rectangles with areas of 24 square units. Discovering that 24 square units can be organized into rectangles with dimensions of 1 × 24, 24 × 1, 2 × 12, 12 × 2, 4 × 6, 6 × 4, 3 × 8, and 8 × 3 provides an excellent introduction to the concept of factors in composite numbers.

Understanding Division

Division is the inverse of multiplication, and students who understand the relationship between the two operations can use their knowledge of multiplication to solve division problems. Division can be interpreted two different ways: as *partitive* division or as *measurement* division. In partitive division, the divisor indicates the number of groups, and students must find the solution, or quotient, to determine how many items are in each group. For example, if the problem 12 ÷ 4 is interpreted as a partitive division problem, then students would divide twelve items into four equal groups and determine that there are three items in each group. In measurement division, the divisor represents the size of each group, so students solve the problem to determine how many equal-sized groups they can form. To solve the problem 12 ÷ 4 as a measurement problem, students would begin with twelve items and measure out four at a time until they ran out of items. Repeated subtraction is a form of measurement division. Figure 7.24 shows examples of partitive and measurement division.

Although students need to be able to solve both partitive and measurement division problems, students who are easily confused or frustrated will benefit if they have the opportunity to become comfortable with one problem format before tackling problems involving the second type of division. Textbooks often mix the two types of problems, so interventionists need to select examples carefully to avoid confusion.

Students can represent division problems with the same models they used previously for multiplication, and seeing how the models are connected will help them understand the relationship between the two operations. Groups and arrays illustrate both partitive and measurement division problems. To model the problem 15 ÷ 3 as partitive division, give students fifteen counters and three paper plates, and let them distribute the counters equally among the plates. They can use the same materials to model 15 ÷ 3 as a measurement problem by placing three counters on each plate until they run out of counters. They will find that it takes five plates to use all the counters. The same problem can be modeled as an array by distributing the fifteen counters evenly in three rows. The quotient is the number of columns they created, i.e., five. The third model used for multiplication, the number line, is best used to model measurement division problems, as shown in the example in Figure 7.24. Students need many experiences using concrete and visual models of multiplication and division to develop a sound conceptual understanding of these operations. When they can use models effectively and explain their work, then the concrete and visual supports can be faded and they can begin working with purely abstract representation.

Students who are mathematically proficient have a solid conceptual understanding of the operations and can also compute products and quotients quickly and easily. Automaticity with basic facts makes it easier to solve multidigit multiplication and division problems, because instead of having to think about the computation, students who have mastered the facts can devote their full attention to the problem-solving process. Computational

Figure 7.24 Partitive and Measurement Division

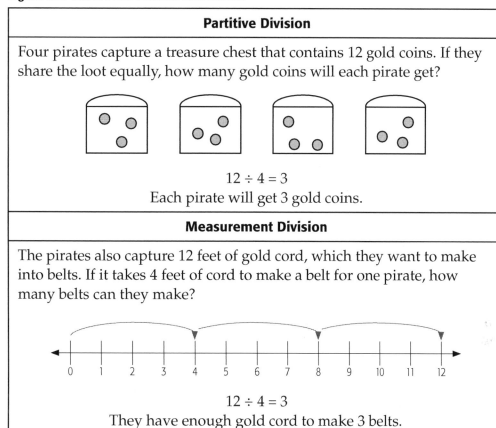

Partitive Division
Four pirates capture a treasure chest that contains 12 gold coins. If they share the loot equally, how many gold coins will each pirate get?

$12 \div 4 = 3$
Each pirate will get 3 gold coins.

Measurement Division
The pirates also capture 12 feet of gold cord, which they want to make into belts. If it takes 4 feet of cord to make a belt for one pirate, how many belts can they make?

$12 \div 4 = 3$
They have enough gold cord to make 3 belts.

fluency with multiplication and division facts is also beneficial later when students begin reducing fractions and determining common denominators, as well as when performing multiplication and division operations with fractions and decimals. We devote Chapter 8 to strategies for developing computational fluency with basic facts. However, lack of computational fluency does not preclude a student from beginning to work with multidigit multiplication and division. Students who have not mastered the facts will need additional supports, such as a fact chart, to help with computation, but they can still begin learning multiplication and division algorithms while they continue to review basic facts. The IES practice guide recommends that interventionists devote about ten minutes of each intervention session to developing computational fluency and then spend the rest of the period working on other skills (Gersten et al., 2009).

Multidigit Multiplication

Students in the core curriculum are exposed to multiple algorithms for solving multidigit multiplication problems. See Figure 7.25 for examples of different algorithms for multiplication. Students who require tiered support in mathematics need to be able to use at least one algorithm to solve multidigit multiplication problems efficiently. Whether these students should learn

Figure 7.25 Alternative Algorithms for Multiplication

Standard Algorithm	Repeated Addition Algorithm	Low-Stress or Partial Product Algorithms	
12 × 7 ——— 84	12 × 7 ——— 12 12 12 12 12 12 12 ——— 84	12 × 7 ——— 14 70 — 84	74 × 89 ——— 70 14 — 84

additional algorithms for multiplication or spend that time mastering other content is a decision best made on a case-by-case basis.

Whichever algorithm we introduce, research findings show that students benefit when instruction follows the CRA sequence (Gersten et al., 2009). Most current math programs use models to introduce multidigit multiplication, but few explicitly link these representations to the abstract representations, which is the evidence-based strategy recommended in the IES practice guide for students receiving mathematical support (Gersten et al., 2009). Helping students make meaningful connections between visual models and abstract algorithms is the focus of this section.

The Common Core Standards specify that in fourth grade, students should be able to:

> CC.4.NBT.5. Multiply a whole number of up to four digits by a one-digit whole number, and multiply two two-digit numbers, using strategies based on place value and the properties of operations. Illustrate and explain the calculation by using equations, rectangular arrays, and/or area models. (National Governors Association Center for Best Practices and Council of Chief State School Officers, 2010)

The two types of models mentioned in these standard, rectangular arrays and area models, illustrate different algorithms. To build conceptual understanding, we need to be very careful that the visual models we select match the abstract representation we use. Rectangular arrays show multiplication as repeated addition, as shown in Figure 7.26. Because arrays emphasize the connection between multiplication and addition, they provide an excellent initial model when we first introduce multidigit multiplication.

Figure 7.26 Rectangular Arrays Illustrate
Multiplication as Repeated Addition

$$5 \times 12 = 12 + 12 + 12 + 12 + 12 = 60$$

X X X X X X X X X X X X
X X X X X X X X X X X X
X X X X X X X X X X X X
X X X X X X X X X X X X
X X X X X X X X X X X X

Figure 7.27 Area Models Illustrate the Partial Products Algorithm

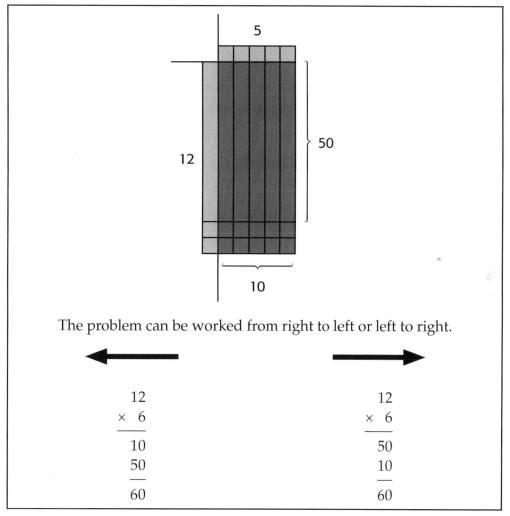

The problem can be worked from right to left or left to right.

12	12
× 6	× 6
10	50
50	10
60	60

However, arrays do not provide an effective illustration of the other algorithms students are expected to master. The second type of visual representation mentioned in the standard, the area model, matches the process used in the low-stress/partial products algorithms, as illustrated in Figure 7.27, and so can be introduced in conjunction with that algorithm.

The low-stress/partial products algorithm for multiplication is similar to the low-stress/partial sums algorithm previously described for addition. Just as in the addition version, students can approach the problem from left to right or right to left. To multiply a one-digit number times a three-digit number, they could work from left to right by first recording the total value of the hundreds, then the tens, then the ones, or they could approach the problem from right to left by first recording the total value of the ones, then the tens, then the hundreds. Once they have recorded the value of each column, they add these subtotals to find the product. No regrouping is required. In Figure 7.28 we provide an example of an explicit instruction lesson that connects the low-stress algorithm to an area model.

Students need a solid understanding of place value to successfully execute this process, so it is beneficial to review place value before introducing area models or the low-stress/partial products algorithm. To emphasize place value when using the algorithm, the teacher in the example is careful to refer to each digit using its place-value designation. When she talks about multiplying the digits in the tens column in step 4, she says, "We have 3 tens on the horizontal axis and 2 tens on the vertical axis. Three tens equals 30, and 2 tens equals 20. We know that 30 times 20 equals 600. We need to show this by placing 6 hundreds or 6 flats on the model." Because the digits 3 and 2 are in the tens column, she does not refer to them as "3" or "2" but as "3 tens" or "30" and "2 tens" or "20." Careful attention to place-value language will make it easier for students to correctly execute this algorithm.

By the end of fifth grade, students should be able to "fluently multiply multi-digit whole numbers using the standard algorithm" (National Governors Association Center for Best Practices and Council of Chief State School Officers, 2010). Neither arrays nor area models accurately mirror the steps in the standard algorithm; instead, we need a format similar to that introduced when modeling the standard algorithms for addition and subtraction, where students arrange blocks on place-value mats in the same sequence used in the algorithm. Figure 7.29 shows how a teacher can effectively model the standard algorithm by carefully linking each step to the concrete representation so that the steps are meaningful.

Too often, students are taught to use arrays and area models to illustrate multidigit problems but have no experience using a model that accurately reflects the procedures used when they follow the standard algorithm. Without the opportunity to experience this algorithm at the concrete and representational levels, students do not make meaningful connections. Their lack of understanding is evident in the errors they make. Consider the example below. The correct solution to the problem 13×45 is written first, followed by an example of a common student error.

Figure 7.28 Using Area Models to Introduce Multidigit Multiplication

Skill: Multiplication of a two-digit number by a two-digit number using an area model	

Prerequisites:
- The concept of addition and basic facts; addition of four or more one-digit numbers
- The concept of multiplication and basic facts
- Multiplying by multiples of ten in the range 10–90
- Properties of multiplication
- Place-value concepts
- Vertical and horizontal lines (vocabulary used)

Teacher says:	Teacher shows:
Here is our problem for today. There are 27 students in our class. Each student brings in a box of 35 crayons. We want to know the total number of crayons we have. To figure this out, we are going to multiply. Our problem is 35 times 27. We are going to use the area model to solve the problem. These are the steps that we are going to follow: 1. Draw the axis lines. 2. Write the first factor above the horizontal axis line. Draw or model that number of blocks on the top of the horizontal axis. 3. Write the second factor on the left side of the vertical axis. Draw or model that number of blocks on the left side of the vertical axis. 4. Begin with the largest blocks possible in the upper left corner and fill in to form a rectangle. Record the number of blocks under the multiplication problem. 5. Add to find the answer. 6. Does the answer make sense? Yes or no.	$$\begin{array}{r} 35 \\ \times\ 27 \\ \hline \end{array}$$

Figure 7.28 *(cont)*   Using Area Models to Introduce Multidigit Multiplication

Teacher says:	Teacher shows:
Step 1 says, "Draw the axis lines." I am going to draw one vertical line and one horizontal line. Each line is called an axis. Watch. This is my horizontal line. *Draw line.* This is my vertical line. *Draw line.* Make sure that your lines cross like this. *Point to upper left corner of axis.* Okay, have we completed step 1? Yes. Let's check it off our list. *Check off step 1.*	$\begin{array}{r} 35 \\ \times\ 27 \\ \hline \end{array}$
Step 2 says, "Write the first factor above the horizontal axis line. Draw or model that number of blocks on the top of the horizontal line." I am going to write the first factor above the horizontal line. The first factor is 35. Now I am going to place 35 blocks above the line to represent the number 35. How can we represent 35? Yes, let's use 3 tens and 5 ones. *Place blocks on the line.* Now, let's count them to make sure we have 35. Ten, 20, 30, 31, 32, 33, 34, 35. Have we completed step 2? Good, let's check it off. *Check off step 2.*	$\begin{array}{r} 35 \\ \times\ 27 \\ \hline \end{array}$ 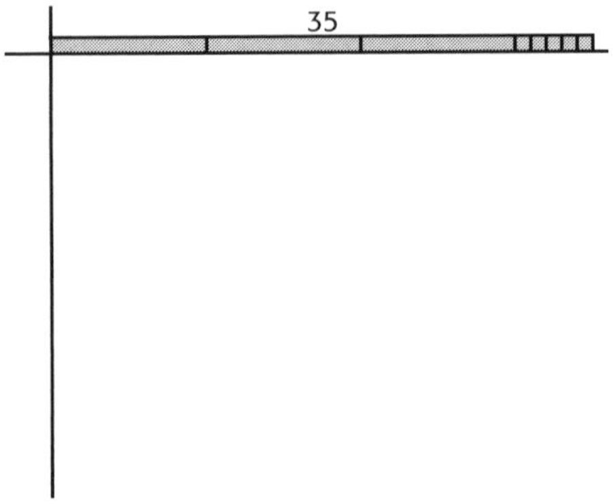
Step 3 says, "Write the second factor on the left side of the vertical axis. Draw or model that number of blocks on the left side of the vertical axis." The second factor is 27. I am going to write 27 on the left side of the vertical line. Now I am going to place 27 blocks on the line to represent the number. How can we show 27? Yes, 2 tens and 7 ones. *Place blocks on the line.* Now, let's count them together to make sure we have 27. Ten, 20, 21, 22, 23, 24, 25, 26, 27. Good, step 3 is done, so I am going to check if off. *Check off step 3.*	$\begin{array}{r} 35 \\ \times\ 27 \\ \hline \end{array}$ 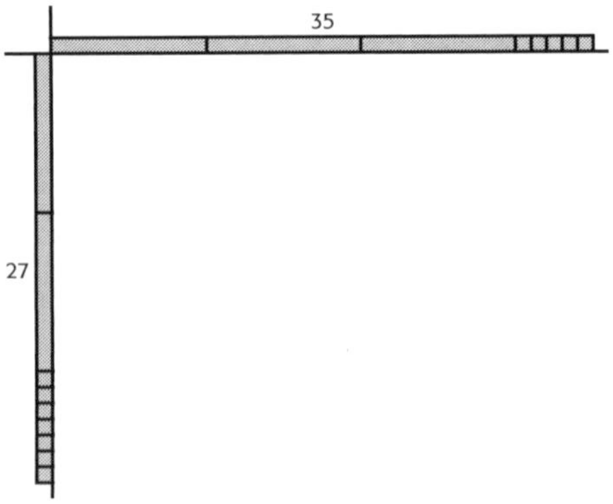

Figure 7.28 *(cont)*   Using Area Models to Introduce Multidigit Multiplication

Teacher says:	Teacher shows:
Step 4 says to begin with the largest blocks possible in the upper left corner to fill in the model to form a rectangle. We are going to use blue blocks to fill in the rectangle so we do not confuse the blocks that represent the factors with the blocks that represent the product. We need to make sure that we form a complete rectangle that touches or matches up with all of the yellow blocks. OK, let's decide what our biggest block is. Can we use any flats as part of our rectangle? Yes, we can. We have 3 tens on the horizontal axis and 2 tens on the vertical axis. Three tens equals 30, and 2 tens equals 20. We know that 30 times 20 equals 600. We need to show this by placing 6 hundreds or 6 flats on the model. *Place the 6 flats.* Now we need to record this in numbers under our problem. *Write 600 under the problem.*	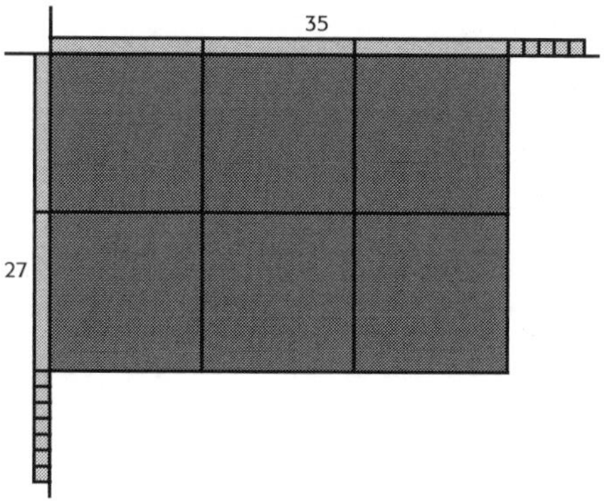
Now, we cannot use any more flats, so let's see how many rods we can use. On the horizontal axis, we have 5 units left, and we can multiply those by the 2 tens on the vertical axis. Two tens equals 20. That means we need to multiply 5 times 20. We know that 5 times 20 is 100, so we can place 10 rods to represent this. *Place 10 rods.* We need to record that we added 100 more blocks to the rectangle, so let's write that in numbers under the problem. *Write 100 under the problem.*	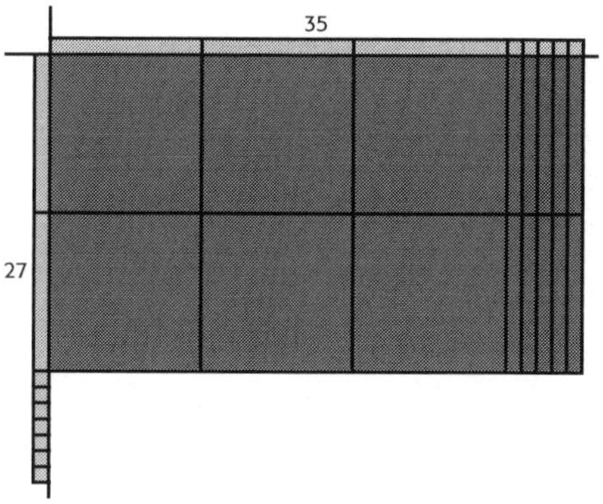

Figure 7.28 *(cont)*   Using Area Models to Introduce Multidigit Multiplication

Teacher says:	Teacher shows:
We also have 7 units on the vertical axis that we can multiply by the 3 tens on the horizontal axis. Three tens equals 30. That means we need to show blocks to represent 7 times 30. We know that 7 times 30 equals 210, so we can place 21 rods on the rectangle [**this seems confusing, since it's clearly not a rectangle yet in the diagram**] to show this. *Place 21 rods.* We need to record this in numbers on the problem. How many blocks did we add? That's right, 210. I am going to write that under the problem. *Write 210.*	$$\begin{array}{r} 35 \\ \times\ 27 \\ \hline 600 \\ 100 \\ 210 \end{array}$$ 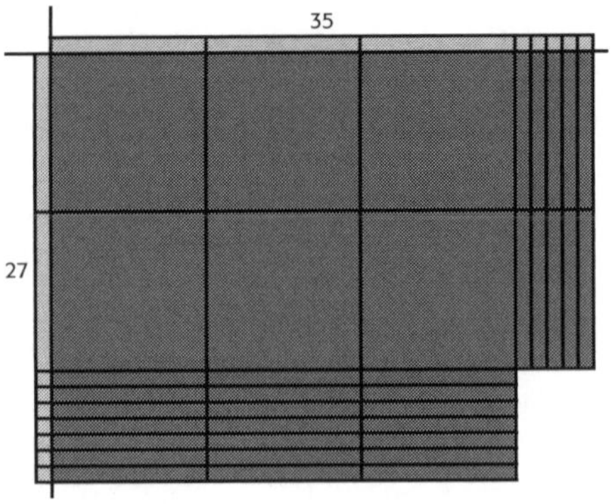
Okay, we cannot use any more rods, so we need to move onto units. On the horizontal axis, we have 5 units. On the vertical axis, we have 7 units. That means we need to multiply 5 times 7. What is 5 times 7? Good, 35. That means we need to add 35 units to complete the rectangle. *Place 35 units.* We also need to record this on the problem. I am going to write 35 under the problem. *Write 35.* OK, is our rectangle complete? Yes! Let's check step 4 off our list. *Check off step 4.*	$$\begin{array}{r} 35 \\ \times\ 27 \\ \hline 600 \\ 100 \\ 210 \\ 35 \end{array}$$ 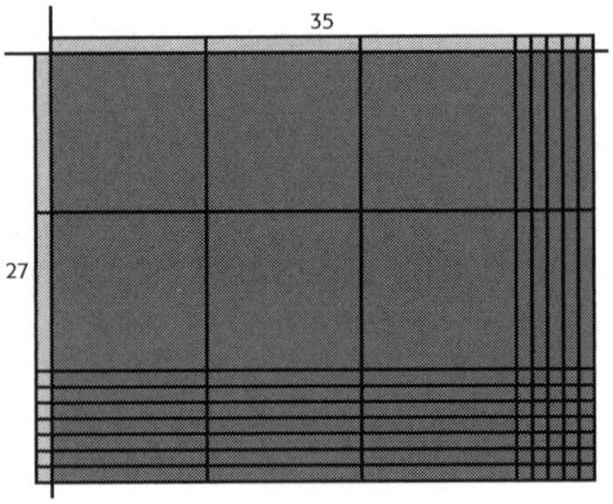
Step 5 says to add to find the product, or the answer, to our multiplication problem. So let's add together all four of the numbers that we recorded. *Draw an addition sign and an equals bar under the four recorded numbers.* OK, let's add the ones column first. $0 + 0 + 0 + 5$ equals what? Five, good. Let's record a 5 in the ones column. *Write 5.* Now,	$$\begin{array}{r} 35 \\ \times\ 27 \\ \hline 600 \\ 100 \\ 210 \\ +\ 35 \\ \hline 945 \end{array}$$ 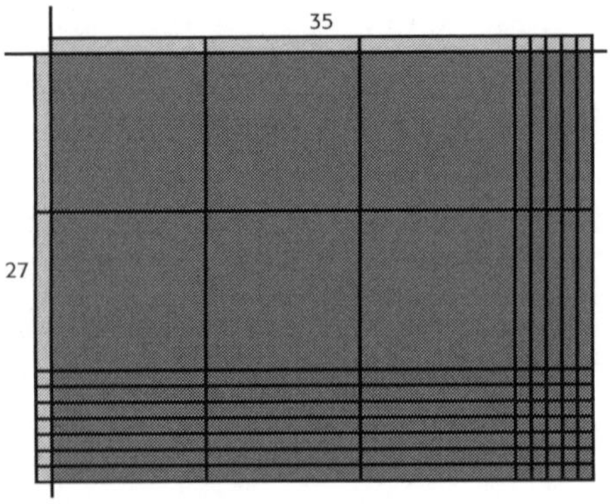

Figure 7.28 *(cont)*   Using Area Models to Introduce Multidigit Multiplication

Teacher says:	Teacher shows:
let's add the tens column. $0 + 0 + 1 + 3$ equals what? Four. Let's record a 4 in the tens column. *Write 4.* Now let's add the hundreds column. $6 + 1 + 2$ equals what? Yes, 9. Let's record a 9 in the hundreds column. *Write 9.* Our answer is 945. We added to find our answer, so step 5 is complete. Let's check it off. *Check off step 5.* The last step asks if our answer makes sense. Let's look back at the original problem. We had 27 students. Each student brought in a box of 35. That means we have 945 crayons. This makes sense because our answer got bigger. Our blocks show us how we multiplied the groups to get this answer. Does this make sense? Let's circle yes and check off step 6. *Circle "Yes" and check off step 6.*	

Provide students with the following laminated checklist to use when they complete problems independently:

STEPS for MULTIPLYING TWO 2-DIGIT NUMBERS
☑ as you complete each step!

☐ Draw the axis lines.
☐ Write the first factor above the horizontal axis line. Draw or model that number of blocks on the top of the horizontal axis.
☐ Write the second factor on the left side of the vertical axis. Draw or model that number of blocks on the left side of the vertical axis.
☐ Begin with the largest blocks possible in the upper left corner and fill in to form a rectangle. Record the number of blocks under the multiplication problem.
☐ Add to find the answer.
☐ Does the answer make sense? Yes/No

Figure 7.29 Modeling the Standard Algorithm for Multiplication

Steps for Regrouping in Multiplication

1. Show how many you have.
2. Multiply ones. *Regroup if needed.*
3. Record.
4. Multiply bottom ones times top tens.
5. *Add regrouped tens*, and record.

Prerequisites: Students can solve multiplication fact problems and multiply a one-digit number times a two-digit number without regrouping. They can regroup in addition and have recently played the Making Trades game again to review place value.

Teacher says:	**Teacher shows:**
I bought 3 packs of gum at the store last night. I opened this one, and you can see that there are 14 sticks of gum in the pack. I'd like to figure out how much gum I have altogether in the three packs. How could I figure that out? Yes, I could add 14 + 14 + 14. Is there another way to solve this? Yes, I could multiply. I'll write the multiplication problem on the board.	$\begin{array}{r} 14 \\ \times\ 3 \\ \hline \end{array}$
What are the steps we follow when we multiply? I'm going to write them on the board as you say them. *Write the steps listed <u>at right</u>.* OK, let's see what happens when we try to use these steps with this problem.	1. Show how many you have. 2. Multiply ones. 3. Record. 4. Multiply bottom ones times top tens. 5. Record.
Step 1 says, "Show how many you have." I have 14, so I need to use my base-ten blocks to show 14. First I'm going to make a place to put my tens and ones. I'll draw lines and label the columns "Tens" and "Ones." *Draw a place-value chart.* Now I need to lay out 14. I can use my base-ten blocks to show 14 with 1 rod and 4 units. That's 1 ten in the tens column and 4 ones in the ones column. *Lay out 14 blocks.* Have I finished step 1? It says, "Show how many you have." I've done that, so I'm going to check off step 1. *Put a check next to step 1.*	$\begin{array}{r} 14 \\ \times\ 3 \\ \hline \end{array}$ <table><tr><td>**Tens**</td><td>**Ones**</td></tr><tr><td></td><td></td></tr></table>

Figure 7.29 *(cont)* Modeling the Standard Algorithm for Multiplication

Teacher says:	Teacher shows:
Step 2 says, "Multiply ones." So I'm going to multiply 3 × 4. *Point to numbers in problem.* What's 3 × 4, everyone? 12. Good. I'll put 12 ones in the ones column. Uh-oh! Can I put 12 ones in the ones column? What do we do when we have too many ones? Yes, we can make a trade, like we did when we played Making Trades. So I'll trade 10 units for a rod and put that rod in the tens column. That step isn't in the directions. Let's add it. *Write "Regroup if needed" next to step 2, as shown <u>above</u>.* OK, now I can check off step 2. *Check off step 2.*	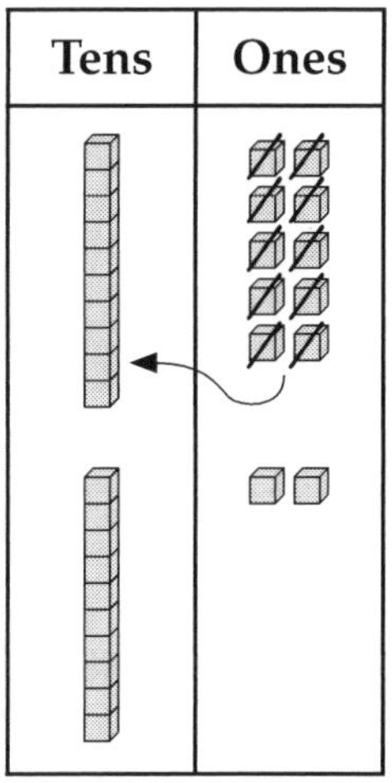
Step 3 says, "Record." I have 2 ones, so I will record that in the ones column. *Write 2.* I added 1 rod to the tens column, so I'm going to record that as a little number above the tens column. *Write 1.* I've completed that step, so I can check it off. *Check off step 3.*	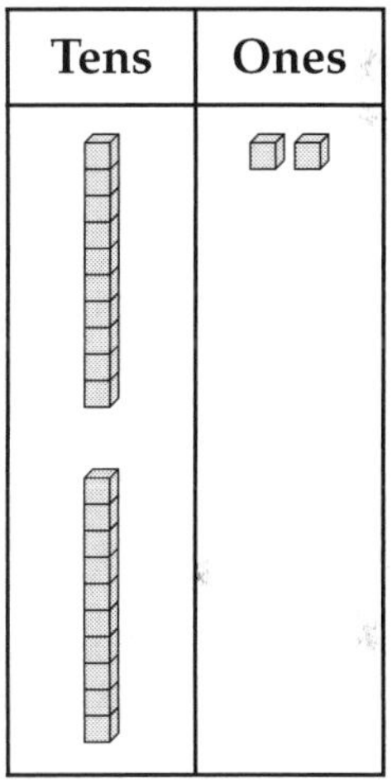
Here's where it gets a little tricky. Step 4 says, "Multiply bottom ones times top tens." That means I need to multiply 3 × 1. *Point to numbers.* But in the place-value chart I have 2 tens, not 1 ten. Why? Right, that was the regrouped ten. It's not part of the number I had at the beginning; it's part of the answer. That's why I wrote it so tiny in the number problem. I don't have 24 pieces of gum; I have 14. I'll push that extra rod to the side for now and come back to it later. So I'm going to multiply 3 ones times 1 ten, which gives me 30. Instead of my 1 original ten, I need 3 tens (plus that extra ten I pushed to the side). I've multiplied the bottom ones times the top tens, so I can check off step 3. *Check off step 3 above.*	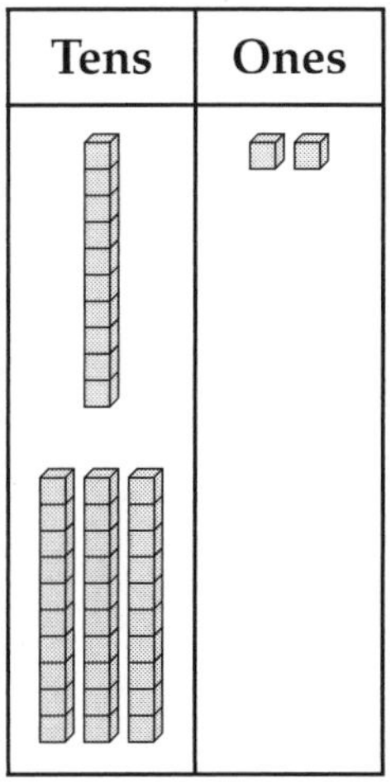

Figure 7.29 *(cont)* Modeling the Standard Algorithm for Multiplication

Teacher says:	Teacher shows:
The last step is to record the tens. But I've got that regrouped ten to deal with. That step isn't in the directions, so I'm going to add it. *Write "Add regrouped tens."* Before I can record my final answer, I have to *add* the regrouped ten to the 3 tens I got when I multiplied. So 3 + 1 = 4. I have 4 tens in all. Now I can record my answer. *Write 4 in the tens column.* Let's look at our problem. There are 14 sticks of gum in one pack. I bought 3 packs of gum, so I have 42 sticks of gum in all!	$\begin{array}{r} \overset{1}{14} \\ \times\ 3 \\ \hline 42 \end{array}$ 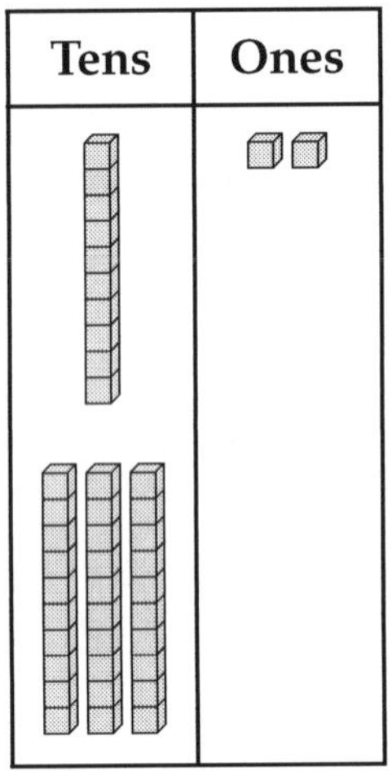

$$\begin{array}{r} 45 \\ \times\ 13 \\ \hline 135 \\ 450 \\ \hline 585 \end{array} \qquad \begin{array}{r} 45 \\ \times\ 13 \\ \hline 135 \\ 45 \\ \hline 180 \end{array}$$

In the second problem, the student omitted the zero that belongs in the second row of the partial product. When students learn to execute the algorithm as a rote procedure, they are often taught that they must add a zero as a "place holder." Students who have a solid foundation in concrete experience know that this zero has meaning; the 1 in the factor 13 represents "1 ten," and we record a zero because the product is a multiple of ten. Students are less likely to make this type of mistake if they began at the concrete level, using rods to represent numbers in the tens column and matching their concrete models to each step in the standard algorithm.

For students who have difficulty keeping the rows and columns aligned when recording their answers in the traditional format, another alternative algorithm called "lattice multiplication" may be useful. With this algorithm, students create boxes in which they record the partial products, and these boxes help keep the columns organized. Another advantage of this method is that students do not need to regroup when recording partial products, although they do regroup when combining the partial products to obtain the final product. Figure 7.30 shows how to solve a problem using the lattice method.

Students write the factors along the top and right edges of the form, record partial products inside the boxes, and write the product along the

Figure 7.30 Lattice Multiplication

- Make the boxes.
  - Along the top of your paper, draw a box for each digit in the first factor.
  - If the second factor contains more than one digit, add another row of boxes for each extra digit.
  - Draw diagonal lines in the boxes, extending beyond the boxes on the left side.
- Write the first factor along the top of the boxes, placing one digit above each box. Write the second factor along the right side of the boxes, placing one digit to the right of each box.
- Multiply each digit in the first factor by each digit in the second factor. Record the answer by writing one numeral in each half of the boxes.
- Add the numbers diagonally, regrouping if necessary. Record the answers along the bottom and left sides of the boxes.

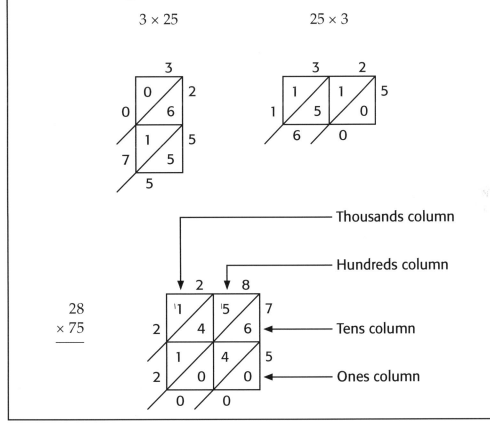

left side and below the bottom edge of the boxes. Place-value columns run diagonally, with the ones columns in the lower right corner, and progress across the boxes to the upper left corner. To model lattice multiplication, interventionists can use a format similar to that described in Figure 7.30 for introducing the standard algorithm. To make their place-value mats more accurately match the columns in the lattice, students can tip the mats on a diagonal when modeling lattice multiplication.

Multidigit Division

The instructional sequence for introducing multidigit division parallels the expectations for solving multidigit multiplication. According to the Common Core Standards, at the fourth-grade level students should be able to divide up to four digits by a one-digit divisor, using equations, rectangular arrays, and/or area models to explain their calculations. These are the same models used to represent multiplication, and connecting multidigit division to students' previous experiences with multiplication can enhance and solidify their conceptual understanding of both operations. In fifth grade students progress to solving problems containing two-digit divisors, and by the end of sixth grade they should be able to fluently divide multidigit numbers using the standard algorithm (National Governors Association Center for Best Practices and Council of Chief State School Officers, 2010). Although the Common Core Standards specifically mention using rectangular arrays and/or area models, the steps used to develop these models do not match the steps used to execute the standard algorithm in division, just as they do not match the standard algorithm for multiplication. We recommend using an "equal groups" model, similar to that presented for partitive division in Figure 7.24, for use with basic division facts, to introduce the standard algorithm. Using the same model to introduce multidigit division connects the new information to students' previous experience dividing single-digit numbers. Just as they did when modeling division of basic facts, students can use paper plates or mats to represent the divisor and base-ten blocks to model the dividend. Starting with the largest blocks, they distribute blocks evenly until no additional equal groups can be created. After students execute a step with the blocks, they should stop and record their work using the standard algorithm format. If they have blocks left over, they can make a trade for the next sized blocks, evenly distribute all the blocks of that size, and record the results. The process is repeated until all the blocks are evenly distributed. Figure 7.31 provides a detailed example of how this procedure can be used to introduce the standard algorithm for division.

One reason that students sometimes struggle with the standard algorithm is that it forces them to approach division in a piecemeal fashion, recording one small portion of the dividend at a time. For example, in the problem modeled in Figure 7.31, the teacher has students divide 312 baseball cards into two groups. The teacher models the problem with base-ten blocks by placing one flat in each group, and then records this step by writing 1

Figure 7.31 Modeling the Standard Algorithm for Division

Teacher says:	Teacher shows:

My uncle just gave his collection of baseball cards to my brother and me. There are 312 cards in the collection. Here's my question. If my brother and I split the cards evenly, how many cards will we each get?
I'm going to write the problem here on the board. *Write.*
 	
These are the steps I am going to follow to solve this problem.
Have the following steps listed on the board and point to them.
 	
1. Represent the total (dividend) with base-ten blocks.
2. Draw boxes to represent the number of groups (divisor).
3. Divide the blocks evenly among the groups.
   • If you have hundreds, begin with them. Share them equally (put an equal number of flats in each group). Record.
   • If there are flats left over, trade them for rods (tens). Share all the rods equally. Record.
   • If there are rods left over, trade them for ones (units). Share all the ones equally. Record.
 	
Step 1 says, "Represent the total (dividend)." We have 312 baseball cards. I'm going to use my base-ten blocks to represent 312. What blocks will I need? Yes, 3 hundreds, 1 ten, and 2 ones. *Put out blocks.* I've finished step 1, and I'm going to check it off. *Check off step 1.*
 	
Step 2 says, "Draw boxes to represent the number of groups (divisor)." In this example, the divisor is 2. So I'm going to draw 2 boxes. *Draw 2 boxes.* I've finished step 2, and I can check it off. *Check off step 2.*
	$2\overline{)312}$

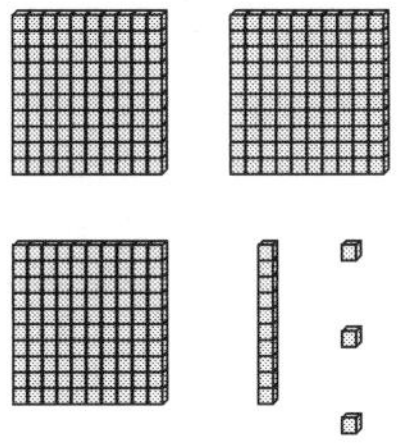

Figure 7.31 *(cont)* Modeling the Standard Algorithm for Division

Teacher says:	Teacher shows:
Step 3 says, "Divide the blocks evenly among the groups. If you have hundreds, begin with them." We have 3 hundreds, so each group gets one flat. *Moves one flat into each box.*	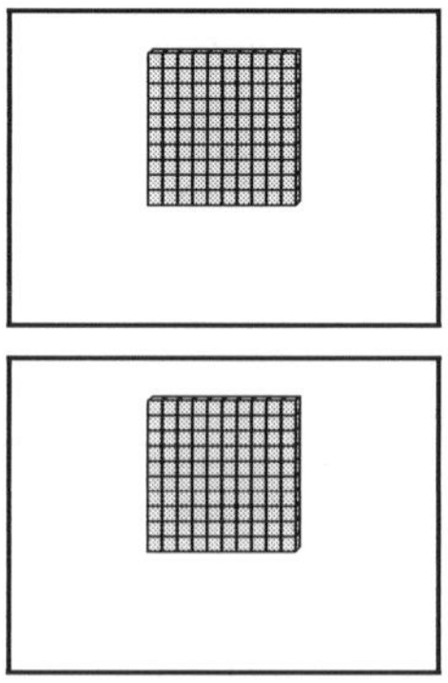
Then it says, "Record." We record our partial answer of one flat per group in the space above the problem. *Write 1.* Then we multiply that one flat times our two groups to show that we have used 2 of the 3 flats we had at the beginning. We have 1 flat left over. *Write.* OK, we've finished with that part. We can check it off.	$$\begin{array}{r} 1 \\ 2\overline{)312} \\ 2 \\ \hline 1 \end{array}$$
The next step says, "If there are flats left over, trade them for rods (tens)." In this problem we had 1 flat left over, so we'll trade it for 10 rods. We had one rod at the beginning, so now we have 11 rods. Let's share our 11 rods equally. *Put rods into boxes.* That means each group gets 5 rods, and there is 1 rod left over.	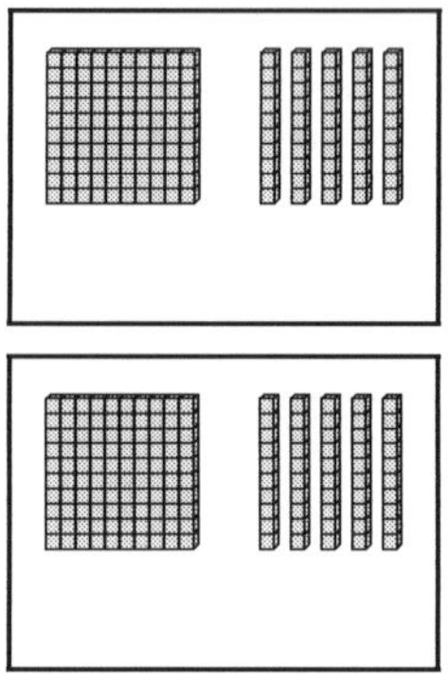

in the quotient. Although this 1 represents a flat with a value of 100, in the standard algorithm we only write the first part of the number, and the zeroes are omitted. The next step is to multiply this partial quotient times the divisor. In this example the divisor is 2, and the teacher records the product as 2. In reality, she multiplied one flat representing 100 baseball cards times two siblings and so has now distributed 200 of the baseball cards. In her explanation the teacher clarifies the value of each recorded digit, but the algorithm itself uses a shortcut method of recording that is very abstract because it omits the zeroes. To make the process more transparent, some programs teach an alternative recording method that retains the zeroes, with the result

Figure 7.31 *(cont)* Modeling the Standard Algorithm for Division

Teacher says:	Teacher shows:
Now I need to record. We record the 5 rods in the answer space. *Record.* Then we multiply those 5 rods times the 2 groups to show that we have used 10 rods. That leaves one rod left over. *Write.* OK, we've finished with that part. We can check it off.	15 2)312 2 — 11 10 — 1
The last step says, "If there are rods left over, trade them for ones (units)." We had 1 rod left over, so I'll trade that for 10 ones. If we combine that with the 2 ones we had at the beginning, then we have 12 ones. Now we need to share all the ones equally, and then record. If I share 12 ones equally among 2 groups, how many will each group get? Yes, exactly 6. This time there is nothing left over. *Put ones into boxes.*	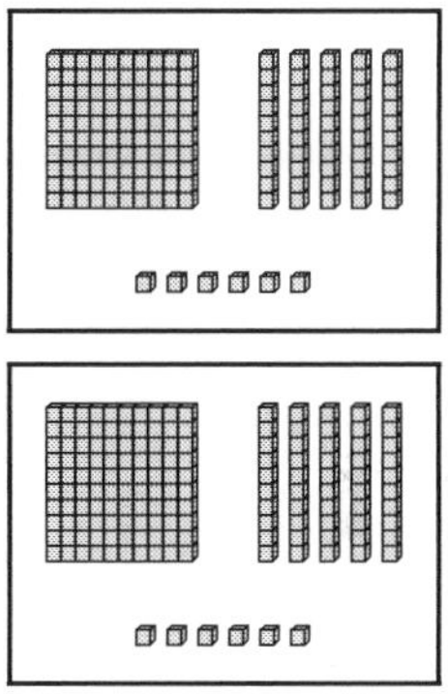
Now I need to record. We record the 6 ones in the answer space. *Record.* Then we multiply those 6 ones times the 2 groups to show that we have used 12 rods. That leaves none left over. *Write.* Let's look at the answer. 156. That means that if my brother and I divide the baseball card collection equally, we'll each get 156 baseball cards!	156 2)312 2 — 11 10 — 12 12 — 0

that the written record more obviously reflects each number's value. Instead of recording the first partial quotient as 1, students using the alternative algorithm would write its entire value of 100, as illustrated in the two versions shown in Figure 7.32.

In these algorithms, the partial quotients can be recorded in a pyramid fashion above the problem, as shown in the first alternative example, or to the right of the problem, as shown in the second example. Both versions retain the zeroes, so the numbers students write clearly indicate the actual value. Because these partial quotient algorithms employ a more holistic approach, students may find them easier to understand and remember. The

Figure 7.32 Alternative Algorithms for Division

Standard Algorithm	Alternative #1	Alternative #2
	6	
	50	
	100	
156	2)312	2)312
2)312	200	200 | 100
2		
11	112	112
10	100	100 | 50
12	12	12
12	12	12 | 6
0	0	0
		156

"equal groups" method described in Figure 7.31 for use with the standard algorithm is equally effective when modeling these alternative algorithms.

While studies have documented the value of linking concrete and visual representation to introduce abstract algorithms, research has not identified a particular model or algorithm that is most effective. We have described several possible algorithms and suggested ways to create concrete and visual models of each algorithm, but many other options exist. Whichever algorithm interventionists select, the point is to select a concrete or visual model that matches the algorithm used and then explicitly link each step in the procedure with the physical model so that students understand the meaning underlying each step in the algorithm. When students can explain the meaning of each step, then they are ready for instructors to fade the concrete and visual supports and focus on developing procedural fluency with abstract representation.

Summary

Research studies have documented the value of using explicit instruction and following the CRA continuum when introducing numbers and operations. According to the IES practice guide, "A major goal of interventions should be to systematically teach students how to develop visual representations and how to transition these representations to standard symbolic representations used in problem solving" (Gersten et al., 2009). In other words, we need to use the concrete and visual representation initially to help students develop conceptual and procedural understanding, but we must carefully link these representations to standard abstract notation and then systemically fade the supports and allow students to become proficient solving problems using standard symbolic representation.

In this chapter we provided suggestions for developing students' conceptual understanding by providing explicit strategies and systematically linking concrete and visual representations to the abstract algorithms used when computing whole numbers. In the next chapter we focus on strategies to help students develop computational fluency, because students who are proficient in mathematics not only understand what they are doing, but can also solve problems efficiently.

Chapter 8

Developing Computational Fluency with Basic Facts

NCTM (2000) standards stress the importance of computational fluency, which is generally considered to mean that students can compute each fact in three seconds or less. Basic facts include the 100 addition facts formed by combining two single-digit addends, the 100 related subtraction facts, the 100 multiplication facts formed by two single-digit factors, and their related division facts. Because zero cannot be used as a divisor, there are only 90 division facts. See Figure 8.1.

NCTM's emphasis on mastering basic facts highlights the important role of computational fluency in developing mathematical proficiency. Students who know the basic facts automatically are able to focus their attention on problem solving and higher-level computational procedures. In contrast, students who do not know the basic facts from memory must focus their attention on computation and so have less cognitive capacity available for more complex tasks. As Van de Walle explains,

> Fluency with basic facts allows for ease of computation, especially mental computations, and, therefore, aids in the ability to reason numerically in every number-related area. Although calculators and tedious counting are available for students who do not have command of the facts, reliance on these methods for simple number combinations is a serious handicap to mathematical growth. (2004, p. 156)

Researchers in the 1980s determined that students with learning disabilities struggle with automaticity (Fleischner, Garnett, & Shepherd, 1982; Hasselbring, Goin, & Bransford, 1988). Studies found that, by age twelve, the average student with a learning disability can recall only one-third as many facts as non-disabled peers (Hasselbring et al., 1988). Although they could compute accurately, the individuals with learning disabilities still relied on counting fingers or tally marks rather than responding to a fact problem automatically. Further research has extended these findings beyond students with disabilities to all students who struggle with mathematics. Individuals who fail to demonstrate mathematical proficiency and who will therefore require tiered interventions typically lack automaticity with basic

Figure 8.1 Basic Facts

100 Basic Addition Facts										
+	0	1	2	3	4	5	6	7	8	9
0	0	1	2	3	4	5	6	7	8	9
1	1	2	3	4	5	6	7	8	9	10
2	2	3	4	5	6	7	8	9	10	11
3	3	4	5	6	7	8	9	10	11	12
4	4	5	6	7	8	9	10	11	12	13
5	5	6	7	8	9	10	11	12	13	14
6	6	7	8	9	10	11	12	13	14	15
7	7	8	9	10	11	12	13	14	15	16
8	8	9	10	11	12	13	14	15	16	17
9	9	10	11	12	13	14	15	16	17	18

100 Basic Subtraction Facts										
−	0	1	2	3	4	5	6	7	8	9
0	0	1	2	3	4	5	6	7	8	9
1	1	2	3	4	5	6	7	8	9	10
2	2	3	4	5	6	7	8	9	10	11
3	3	4	5	6	7	8	9	10	11	12
4	4	5	6	7	8	9	10	11	12	13
5	5	6	7	8	9	10	11	12	13	14
6	6	7	8	9	10	11	12	13	14	15
7	7	8	9	10	11	12	13	14	15	16
8	8	9	10	11	12	13	14	15	16	17
9	9	10	11	12	13	14	15	16	17	18

100 Basic Multiplication Facts										
×	0	1	2	3	4	5	6	7	8	9
0	0	0	0	0	0	0	0	0	0	0
1	0	1	2	3	4	5	6	7	8	9
2	0	2	4	6	8	10	12	14	16	18
3	0	3	6	9	12	15	18	21	24	27
4	0	4	8	12	16	20	24	28	32	36
5	0	5	10	15	20	25	30	35	40	45
6	0	6	12	18	24	30	36	42	48	54
7	0	7	14	21	28	35	42	49	56	63
8	0	8	16	24	32	40	48	56	64	72
9	0	9	18	27	36	45	54	63	72	81

90 Basic Division Facts										
÷	0	1	2	3	4	5	6	7	8	9
1	0	1	2	3	4	5	6	7	8	9
2	0	2	4	6	8	10	12	14	16	18
3	0	3	6	9	12	15	18	21	24	27
4	0	4	8	12	16	20	24	28	32	36
5	0	5	10	15	20	25	30	35	40	45
6	0	6	12	18	24	30	36	42	48	54
7	0	7	14	21	28	35	42	49	56	63
8	0	8	16	24	32	40	48	56	64	72
9	0	9	18	27	36	45	54	63	72	81

facts. These students consistently demonstrate extremely slow fact retrieval (Geary, 1993, 2004; Goldman, Pellegrino, & Mertz, 1988; Jordan, Hanich, & Kaplan, 2003; Pellegrino & Goldman, 1987). In addition to negatively impacting students' problem-solving ability, lack of competence with basic facts has been shown to negatively affect students' attitudes toward mathematics, including decreased self-efficacy and increased anxiety (Miller, 1996; Tucker, Singleton, & Weaver, 2002). Because automaticity is essential for mathematical proficiency, the IES practice guide recommends, "Interventions at all grade levels should devote about ten minutes in each session to building fluent retrieval of basic arithmetic facts" (Gersten et al., 2009).

Conceptual Understanding and Computational Fluency

Meaningful problem solving requires students to have a strong understanding of number relationships and basic operations. Students with a solid conceptual foundation understand that addition involves joining quantities, while subtraction means taking away or comparing quantities. Multiplication is repeated addition, while its inverse, division, involves repeated subtraction. Students who score in the proficient range on universal screening measures can explain these big ideas and transition fluently among different representational forms. Given a number problem, they can represent it using objects, pictures, or words. Given a word problem, they can express it in numbers, act it out, or illustrate it graphically. In Chapter 7 we discussed using the concrete-representational-abstract teaching sequence to help students develop conceptual understanding of basic operations.

Once students understand the underlying concepts, they are ready to begin working on computational fluency. Fluency is the ability to find an answer quickly and effortlessly, either because the answer is memorized or because the individual has developed an efficient strategy for calculating the answer. To develop fluency, students need to focus on just a few facts at a time. Activities that require students to synthesize information, select from multiple strategies, or work with a variety of facts simultaneously can provide excellent practice for students who already have a solid mathematical foundation, but for individuals who struggle to understand the content, such activities can be overwhelming. Many of the materials and activities that are intended to develop computational fluency actually present too many unfamiliar facts simultaneously to foster fluent retrieval. Research into cognitive capacity has determined that the average adult can hold seven items, plus or minus two, in working memory at one time (Miller, 1956). The instructional implications of cognitive capacity were discussed in Chapter 5. Capacity increases with age, so while the average five-year-old can retain only two facts at one time, the average second-grade student can be expected to retain about three items in working memory at a time, and by the time students reach fourth grade, they can typically maintain about four items at one time (Pascual-Leone, 1970). If we apply this brain research to developing computational fluency, addition and subtraction fact practice presented in the common core curriculum should focus on no more than three facts at a time, because that is the cognitive capacity of average second-grade students. Practice activities for multiplication and division facts should focus on no more than four facts at a time, because that is the cognitive capacity of the average fourth-graders who are learning these facts. Individuals who struggle with mathematics often have less working memory capacity than their normally achieving peers (Bryant et al., 2006; Hallahan, Lloyd, Kauffman, Weiss, & Martinez, 2005), so the IES Practice Guide recommends that interventionists working with these students focus on only one or two unfamiliar facts at a time. The two unknown facts can be interspersed with review of known facts, so that a student might practice five or even ten facts at a time, but only two of these should be facts that the student cannot yet compute fluently (Gersten et al., 2009).

To arrange effective practice, the interventionist should first assess each student's fact proficiency and then present instructional activities in such a way that the individual can focus on two new facts in one instructional session. Flash cards can be used to assess the student's mastery of required facts. As the student answers each fact, the card is placed in one of two piles: (1) facts the student can answer in less than three seconds, and (2) facts the student cannot answer or takes more than three seconds to compute. When creating practice activities for this student, interventionists should include just two of the unknown facts and then add some of the known facts to fill out the activity and provide ongoing review. Once the student can consistently solve the two facts from the unknown pile in less than three seconds, the instructor can add two new facts to practice activities and continue in this manner until the student has mastered all facts for that operation. While this process may seem slow and tedious, students achieve automaticity far more quickly when they experience such focused practice opportunities.

The procedure described above for selecting unknown facts assumes that each individual fact counts as one item in short-term memory, so that students with a capacity of two items should work on just two facts at a time. However, when information is clustered meaningfully, multiple facts may be grouped together and still count as just one item in working memory. Consider the analogy of a small change purse that is only large enough to hold two coins at a time. If we put two pennies into the purse, the purse is totally filled with just two cents. But if we instead place two dimes in the purse, that same purse can hold twenty cents. When information is grouped into meaningful clusters, the brain can hold more content than if each fact is considered in isolation. We can apply this principle to help students master basic facts. For example, "one" is the identity element in multiplication, because multiplying a number times one yields a product that is the same as the original factor, as illustrated by the fact $7 \times 1 = 7$. Students who understand this concept can practice all the $\times 1$ facts simultaneously without overloading working memory, just as a dime can be placed in the coin purse without exceeding its capacity. Other strategies that help students compute fluently include counting by fives to find the answer to multiplication problems that contain a factor of 5, or using the inverse relationship between multiplication and division to determine the answer to an unfamiliar division problem if the related multiplication fact is known. Competent students use such strategies independently, but students receiving tiered support may need direct strategy instruction to develop efficient strategies (Moser, 1992).

The method of strategy instruction that is currently advocated by mathematics educators relies heavily on discussion. Students are given a problem and asked to devise a way to solve it, often by working together in small groups to explore different approaches. Then the groups are asked to share their strategies, and a discussion follows. The expectation is that students will benefit from their peers' explanations, use the opportunity to experiment with a variety of strategies, and eventually select one or more to use consistently. Such methods can be very effective with some students, but Woodward and Baxter (1997) found that students with mathematical disabilities showed significantly less growth in classrooms that used this type of discussion approach. We know that students who struggle with mathematics often have attention problems, vocabulary deficits, and language-processing problems, as well as deficits in short-term memory (Bryant et al., 2006; Hallahan et al., 2005), and each of these problems can interfere with an individual's ability to benefit from class discussion. Individuals with deficits in short-term memory learn best when information is introduced in small, carefully sequenced chunks and when they are given ample opportunity to practice and consolidate what they have learned before they are asked to process any additional information. Students receiving tiered interventions will benefit from direct instruction that uses clear, unambiguous examples and that follows the guidelines for explicit instruction that were described in Chapter 5.

Executing a strategy consumes short-term memory capacity (Baddeley, 1980; Case, 1985; Kahnemann, 1973), so interventionists should be judicious in the use of strategies with students who have deficits in short-term memory. When students first encounter a new strategy, using the strategy may consume most, if not all, of their cognitive capacity. Extensive practice may be necessary before students can execute a strategy fluently and automatically (Logan, 1985; Pressley & Afflerbach, 1995; Schneider, Dumais, & Shiffrin, 1984). Once students understand and can successfully execute a particular practice, they will then need carefully planned massed and distributed practice in order to use the strategy efficiently without taxing their working memory capacity.

Research has not yet established an optimal sequence for teaching basic facts (Hudson & Miller, 2006), but many experts recommend organizing instruction around specific strategies, such as the "x1" identity element strategy discussed above. Counting by fives, using reciprocals, and a variety of other methods that facilitate efficient retrieval of a particular group of facts can reduce cognitive load and facilitate computational fluency (Bley & Thornton, 2001; Cathcart, Pothier, Vance, & Bezuk, 2000; Kame'enui & Simmons, 1990). The Common Core Standards describe a variety of addition and subtraction strategies that students should master in first grade:

> CC.1.OA.6: Use strategies such as counting on; making ten (e.g., $8 + 6 = 8 + 2 + 4 = 10 + 4 = 14$); decomposing a number leading to a ten (e.g., $13 - 4 = 13 - 3 - 1 = 10 - 1 = 9$); using the relationship between addition and subtraction (e.g., knowing that $8 + 4 = 12$, one knows $12 - 8 = 4$); and creating equivalent but easier or known

sums (e.g., adding $6 + 7$ by creating the known equivalent $6 + 6 + 1 = 12 + 1 = 13$). (National Governors Association Center for Best Practices, Council of Chief State School Officers, 2010)

We recommend that interventionists chunk math facts by strategy, introduce one strategy at a time, and provide plenty of practice time before introducing additional strategies. Students first need to understand how a strategy works and then practice using the strategy to compute fluently. To develop automaticity, students will initially need massed practice with many short opportunities to practice a limited amount of material. The IES practice guide suggests limiting practice sessions to just two unfamiliar math facts or fact clusters at a time. Once students master this material, they need distributed practice with review opportunities gradually becoming less frequent.

Much has been written about the overuse of "drill and kill" techniques, and teachers sometimes hesitate to spend much time drilling facts. However, drill does have an important role in developing computational fluency. As Van de Walle explains,

> Drill—repetitive non-problem-based activity—is appropriate for children who have a strategy that they understand, like and know how to use but have not yet become facile with it. Drill with an in-place strategy focuses students' attention on that strategy and helps to make it more automatic. Drill plays a significant role in fact mastery, and the use of old-fashioned methods such as flash cards and fact games can be effective if used wisely. (Van de Walle, 2004, p. 158)

While timely drill is effective, premature focus on computational fluency can be counterproductive. If students do not have an efficient strategy for calculating the answer to basic facts, they may rely on inefficient strategies such as counting objects or counting on their fingers. In this situation, drill may produce nothing but faster finger counting, which will never become efficient enough to allow students to become proficient. Therefore, we recommend that teachers focus first on developing conceptual understanding of the operation and then spend time helping students learn to use a specific strategy, before introducing fact drills. Once students can use a strategy efficiently, they can engage in drill activities that use that strategy. While they are practicing the first strategy, they can also begin learning a second strategy. After students master both strategies, they need practice deciding which of the two strategies would be best to use with any given problem.

In the next sections we discuss a variety of strategies that can help students develop automaticity with basic facts. Following these strategy descriptions, we will discuss ways to differentiate instruction to meet individual student needs.

Strategies for Addition Facts

Counting On

When students first learn to add, they use concrete objects to represent the first addend, then represent the second addend, and then join the two sets to find the sum. As previously discussed, most students need about three experiences using concrete objects, then three opportunities to model problems with pictures and other visual representations, in order to develop conceptual understanding of the addition process. Once they understand what addition means, they can focus on learning to find answers quickly and effortlessly. Repeated practice is needed for students to progress from conceptual understanding to computational fluency.

Students who struggle with basic facts often continue to rely on counting every object in order to solve basic fact problems long after their peers have committed these facts to memory or developed more efficient strategies to help with fact retrieval (Siegler, 1988). For example, given the problem 6 + 7, a student who struggles with basic facts will continue to hold up six fingers or draw six tally marks, then add seven more, and then join the two groups and count each object one at a time, beginning with the number 1 and continuing until all thirteen objects have been counted. This process produces the correct answer, but it is an inefficient strategy. To become more efficient, students first need to learn to "count on" from a given number, so that when they join two sets they no longer need to recount everything but instead can begin counting on from the first number to obtain the total. Most students develop this strategy independently as early as age four (Siegler & Jenkins, 1989). However, second-grade students who struggle with mathematics may still not have mastered this skill (Tournaki, 2003). Research suggests that systematic and explicit instruction can help these students learn to use the strategy to facilitate fluent fact retrieval (Gersten et al., 2009).

Group counting can provide modeling and practice in using the counting-on strategy. Ask one student to begin counting aloud, beginning at 1. After that student counts "1, 2, 3, 4," tell her to stop and ask a second student to continue counting "5, 6, 7, 8," and so on. Another effective activity for practicing the counting-on strategy is to draw a large number line on the floor. Students can stand on a number and then count as they walk down the number line. They can also use the ten-frames that were introduced in Chapter 7 to practice counting on. Have students represent a number like 6 on the ten-frame, then add one more counter to change the number to 7, then to 8, and so forth. Initially students will need to recount all the counters beginning with the first one, but with practice they will be able to count on from the last number shown. To model numbers larger than 10, use one full ten-frame card to model the 10, then begin filling a second card to represent 11, 12, and so on. Sequencing activities can also help students learn to generate the next number without having to recount from 1. Students can sequence a set of ten-frame cards in order from 1 to 10 and then use the cards

Figure 8.2 +1 and +2 Facts

+	0	1	2	3	4	5	6	7	8	9
0										
1		2	3	4	5	6	7	8	9	10
2		3	4	5	6	7	8	9	10	11
3		4	5							
4		5	6							
5		6	7							
6		7	8							
7		8	9							
8		9	10							
9		10	11							

to practice counting forward out loud. To provide an added challenge, turn over one card in the sequence and have students identify which number was turned over.

Plus-One and Plus-Two Facts

Once students understand the process of counting on, they can use it to identify facts that are one more than a given number and then facts that are two more than a given number. There are thirty-two addition facts where one of the addends is one or two, so almost one third of the 100 addition facts can be calculated using this simple strategy. See Figure 8.2.

To introduce this strategy, begin with an activity similar to the oral counting introduced for practicing counting on. Call on one student to start counting aloud, beginning at 1 and continuing until the teacher says, "Stop." Then select another student, who says the next number in the sequence and then states the complete number fact. For example, the first student might count "1, 2, 3, 4." Then the teacher says "Stop" and points to another student. The second student says, "Five. Four plus 1 is 5." When practicing plus-two facts, the second student would say the next two numbers in the sequence and then state the complete number fact: "Five, 6. Four plus 2 is 6."

A number line drawn on the floor is also a useful tool to practice +1 and +2 facts. Let a student stand on a number; then tell him to add one more or add two more. The student steps on the answer and states the complete math sentence out loud. For example, to model 4 + 1 the student would stand on 4. When the teacher says, "Add one more," the student would step or jump to 5 and say, "Four plus 1 is 5."

Ten-frame cards can also be used to practice plus-one and plus-two facts. Have the students represent a one-digit number; then challenge them to calculate what the answer would be if they add one more to that number. Write the fact problem on the board so they connect the concrete experience with the ten-frames to the abstract number problem. For example, write 4 + 1 on the board, and let students represent the 4 on their ten-frame mat. Challenge them to predict what the answer will be when they add one more; then let them add the additional counter and count to confirm their prediction. Once students can use counters to accurately predict the results of adding one more to their ten-frame boards, try flashing a ten-frame card and asking them to state one more than the amount shown. The same activity can then be repeated at the abstract level by replacing the ten-frame cards with numeral cards. A calculator can also be used to practice +1 and +2 facts. Let students enter a fact problem such as 6 +1, try to predict the result, and then press the equals sign to check their prediction. Once students can quickly and accurately identify the sum when a number is increased by one, begin working on adding two more, using the same strategies. To solidify these facts in long-term memory, students will need additional practice activities. Flash cards and worksheets can be used for practice, but most students will be more motivated by games that allow them to practice their facts with classmates. In Appendix B we provide ideas for using games to develop computational fluency. The first two activities in that section describe board games and egg carton games to practice the "+1" and "+2" facts.

The Commutative Property of Addition

The commutative property of addition states that a + b = b + a. Thus, if 7 + 5 is known, then 5 + 7 is also known. Instead of memorizing 100 addition facts, students who understand this property can learn just fifty facts and automatically solve the other fifty. Students should first experience the commutative property at the concrete level by creating two sets of objects and comparing the results when they add the facts together, beginning with one addend, then the other addend. Repeated experiences using concrete objects and pictures will help them recognize that the answer will be the same no matter which order they use to solve the problem. Dominoes provide an excellent visual representation of the commutative property, because a domino can be flipped backward and forward without changing the total quantity. Younger students will enjoy practicing the commutative property with the "Fishy Facts" activity described in Appendix B. Having students explain the commutative property in words will provide additional reinforcement and help consolidate their understanding.

Facts with Zero

There are nineteen facts that have zero as one of the addends (see Figure 8.3). Zero is the identity element in addition, because if you add zero to any

Figure 8.3 Zero Facts

The Identity Property of Addition: a + 0 = a										
+	0	1	2	3	4	5	6	7	8	9
0	0	1	2	3	4	5	6	7	8	9
1	1									
2	2									
3	3									
4	4									
5	5									
6	6									
7	7									
8	8									
9	9									

number, the result is your original number (a + 0 = a). Students sometimes find the idea of adding zero confusing, and they will benefit if objects, drawings showing two parts with one part empty, and word problems are all used to illustrate this concept. Students who have been introduced to both addition and multiplication sometimes confuse the role zero plays in the two operations. Adding zero to a number has no effect on the original quantity, but multiplying by zero results in a product of zero. Again, providing concrete and visual representation can clarify the difference in the two operations. The games suggested to practice plus-one and plus-two facts can be easily adapted to practice zero facts.

Doubles

There are ten facts that are formed by doubling single-digit numbers, as shown in Figure 8.4. To help them remember these facts, students can create drawings of real-life examples of doubles, as shown in Figure 8.5 (see p. 162). Including the written number fact with the drawing will connect the visual and abstract representational forms and will further support computational fluency.

Some authors suggest using doubles pictures that show the entire fact in a single object. For example, insects have three legs on one side of the body and three legs on the other side, so one insect can be used to illustrate 3 + 3 = 6. We can also use the entire insect to illustrate the number six. If we

Figure 8.4 Doubles

+	0	1	2	3	4	5	6	7	8	9
0	0									
1		2								
2			4							
3				6						
4					8					
5						10				
6							12			
7								14		
8									16	
9										18

Figure 8.5 Double Drawings

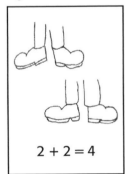

2 + 2 = 4

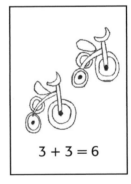

3 + 3 = 6

8 + 8 = 16

do that, then two insects show that 6 + 6 = 12. While either format works for addition facts, if we choose the second option, then our doubles drawings also apply later when we introduce multiplication facts. If students associate an insect with the number six, then three insects have eighteen legs, four insects have twenty-four legs, and so on. Using consistent pictures reduces the memory load and facilitates generalization, which can help students master the multiplication facts more quickly.

Calculators can also be used to practice doubles. If you first enter the "double maker" (2 × =), then a student can enter a one-digit number like 6, predict the answer of the doubles fact (6 + 6 = 12), and then press the equals sign to check the prediction. Because doubles are often awarded special significance in board and dice games, students who have experience with these games may find it fairly easy to memorize facts that involve doubles. In Appendix B we describe two games that students can play to practice their doubles facts—Egg Carton Doubles and Double Trouble.

Near-Doubles

The eighteen facts referred to as near-doubles include all those combinations where one addend is one more than the other addend, as shown in Figure 8.6. To calculate the sum of near-doubles, students double the smaller digit and then add one more. This strategy therefore requires students to already know their doubles facts and also to have mastered the plus-one strategy. It can be introduced by presenting a list of near-double facts and then engaging the students in a discussion about how they can use facts they already know to solve these new facts. Students can practice computing near-doubles by rolling a single die and stating the near-double fact that can be created using the number rolled. For example, if a student rolled a 3, he would say, "Three plus 4 is 7." The games described to practice doubles can be adapted to practice near-doubles by using this procedure. For example, to use the Double Trouble game described in Appendix B to practice near-doubles, students roll a pair of dice as explained in the directions; when they roll a double, they transform it into a near-double and write the near-double fact on their paper. The student who records the most near-doubles in five minutes wins the round.

Figure 8.6 Near-Doubles

+	0	1	2	3	4	5	6	7	8	9
0	0	1								
1	1	2	3							
2		3	4	5						
3			5	6	7					
4				7	8	9				
5					9	10	11			
6						11	12	13		
7							13	14	15	
8								15	16	17
9									17	18

Figure 8.7 Ten Sums

+	0	1	2	3	4	5	6	7	8	9
0										
1										10
2									10	
3								10		
4							10			
5						10				
6					10					
7				10						
8			10							
9		10								

Ten-Sums

When given a group of numbers to add, experienced mathematicians often try to find combinations that total ten. Although there are only nine combinations whose sums total ten (see Figure 8.7), they are so useful that it is worth spending time helping students master these facts.

Ten-frames provide a valuable visual representation to support acquisition of ten-sum facts, because when a number less than ten is represented on the frame, the empty spaces illustrate the number of items needed to make ten. Students can practice representing a number on the ten-frame and then deciding how many more counters they must add to reach ten. As students gain proficiency, you can flash a ten-frame card or a written numeral card and ask students to decide how many more would be needed to make ten. Number lines provide another valuable tool to help students master ten-sums. The MathLine described in Chapter 7 uses a red ring to highlight 10 and all multiples of 10, so if students represent the first addend on Math-Line, they can easily see how many more are needed to make ten. Developing a mental number line appears to be a critical component of numerical reasoning (Tarver & Jung, 1995). For additional practice, students can play the games described in Appendix B, Finding Ten-Sums, Ten-Sums Fish, Guess My Hand, and Toss 'n' Cross.

Near-Tens

The eighteen facts referred to as near-tens include all those facts whose sums are one more or one less than 10, as shown in Figure 8.8. Students can use

Figure 8.8 Near-Tens

+	0	1	2	3	4	5	6	7	8	9
0										9
1									9	10
2								9	10	11
3							9	10	11	
4						9	10	11		
5					9	10	11			
6				9	10	11				
7			9	10	11					
8		9	10	11						
9	9	10	11							

their knowledge of ten-sums to calculate the near-tens. For example, when presented with the fact 7 + 4, a student who knows that 7 + 3 = 10 can determine that, since 4 is one more than 3, the sum will be one more than 10. Similarly, since 2 is one less than 3, 7 + 2 must result in an answer one less than 10. Again, ten-frames and MathLine provide concrete and visual representation to support the students' acquisition of these facts.

Facts Solved by Making a Ten

If students can decompose two-digit numbers into tens and ones, they can use this knowledge to solve fact problems involving larger numbers like 8 or 9. There are 20 addition facts where one addend is 8 or 9. See Figure 8.9. To solve these problems, students begin with the 8 or 9 and count up to 10, then add on the remaining amount to obtain the total. For example, to add 9 + 6, count up one from 9 to 10. Instead of 9 + 6 we now have 10 + 5, and students who understand the base-ten number system will recognize that 10 + 5 is another way of saying 15. An example of this strategy is provided in Common Core Standard 1.OA.6, which states that students should be able to use decomposition strategies to solve a problem like the following: 8 + 6 = 8 + (2 + 4) = (8 + 2) + 4 = 10 + 4 = 14. Manipulating discs on ten-frames provides a physical model that can help students understand this concept. Students can also model the process on a number line or on MathLine, just as they did earlier when finding ten-sums. The Make-a-Ten War game described in Appendix B describes a game that uses this strategy to practice solving facts containing addends of 8 or 9.

Figure 8.9 Facts Solved by Making a Ten

−	0	1	2	3	4	5	6	7	8	9
0									8	9
1									8	10
2									10	11
3									11	12
4									12	13
5									13	14
6									14	15
7									15	16
8	8	9	10	11	12	13	14	15	16	17
9	9	10	11	12	13	14	15	16	17	18

The Leftovers

After students have mastered the addition fact strategies described above, there are four facts remaining. If students apply the commutative property to these facts, then they really only have to learn two more facts to have mastered all 100 basic addition facts. See Figure 8.10.

Selecting a Strategy

Extensive research has been conducted on the use of strategies, and researchers have concluded that students must first learn to execute the strategy and then practice identifying situations in which the strategy could be appropriately applied (Pressley, Borkowski, & O'Sullivan, 1984, 1985; Pressley, Harris, & Marks, 1982; Pressley, Levin, & Ghatala, 1988; Pressley, Ross, Levin, & Ghatala, 1984; Pressley & Woloshyn, 1995). Once students know both *how* to use the strategy and *when* to use the strategy, they still need continued cues and prompts reminding them to use the strategy before its use becomes habitual. Without this scaffolded support, individuals generally return to old, familiar habits, even if these old methods were less efficient. In the case of basic fact computation, students are likely to revert to using their fingers to determine sums of unfamiliar facts. Therefore, interventionists will need to provide systematic practice in strategy selection and application. Each of the activities described above focuses on a specific strategy, and all of the examples are selected to practice just that strategy. To increase the probability that students will select and use these strategies appropriately in the future,

8.10 The Leftovers

+	0	1	2	3	4	5	6	7	8	9
0										
1										
2										
3						8				
4										
5			8					12		
6										
7					12					
8										
9										

interventionists will need to provide lessons that require students to select a strategy. After students have learned two different strategies, provide them with a set of math facts and ask them to describe which strategy they think would be most appropriate to help them solve a particular fact. For example, after students have worked on both the +2 facts and doubles, give them both types of facts and ask them to select a strategy that would be a good choice for a given fact and explain their choices. To practice this decision-making skill, they can sort facts into piles of facts that would all be solved using the same strategy. They can also be given worksheets containing a variety of facts that would best be solved using two or more different strategies. Instead of asking students to solve the problems, have them identify the most appropriate strategy with each fact and then justify their choices.

However, even when students can select an appropriate strategy and execute it efficiently, they are still not likely to use it independently when the need arises. Students need prompts to use the strategy throughout the day when situations arise in which a particular strategy would be useful. They will need many prompts and reminders before they begin to generalize a strategy and use it autonomously when computing basic facts.

Strategies for Subtraction Facts

Subtraction is the inverse of addition. There are 100 addition facts formed by combining two one-digit numbers, and 100 related subtraction facts formed

Figure 8.11 100 Basic Subtraction Facts

−	0	1	2	3	4	5	6	7	8	9
0	0	1	2	3	4	5	6	7	8	9
1	1	2	3	4	5	6	7	8	9	10
2	2	3	4	5	6	7	8	9	10	11
3	3	4	5	6	7	8	9	10	11	12
4	4	5	6	7	8	9	10	11	12	13
5	5	6	7	8	9	10	11	12	13	14
6	6	7	8	9	10	11	12	13	14	15
7	7	8	9	10	11	12	13	14	15	16
8	8	9	10	11	12	13	14	15	16	17
9	9	10	11	12	13	14	15	16	17	18

by reversing the process, as shown in Figure 8.11. To model subtraction, we generally teach students to represent the total amount, cross off the amount to be taken away, and then count to determine how many are left. This provides an accurate representation of the subtraction process, but it is an inefficient way to calculate answers in problem-solving situations. Students who continue to rely on such counting strategies will struggle when faced with more advanced mathematics. Fluent computation requires that students memorize the subtraction facts or develop an efficient strategy for solving the problem.

Related Facts

Once students have mastered their addition facts, we can use the inverse relationship between addition and subtraction to help them solve subtraction fact problems fluently. For example, if students know that 4 + 3 = 7, then they can use this knowledge to determine that 7 − 3 = 4 and 7 − 4 = 3. Dominoes provide a great visual illustration of fact families and can be used to help students connect subtraction to known addition facts. Show students a domino and have them state the addition and subtraction facts represented on the domino, as illustrated in Figure 8.12.

For example, the domino shown in Figure 8.12 illustrates 6 + 3 = 9. After students identify the addition fact, cover the dots on one side of the domino and discuss the resulting subtraction fact. If we cover the six dots on the left side of the domino, we have illustrated the subtraction fact 9 − 6 = 3. Once students are comfortable with this process, try showing them just half a domino while keeping the dots on the other side hidden. Tell them

Figure 8.12 Representing Related Facts

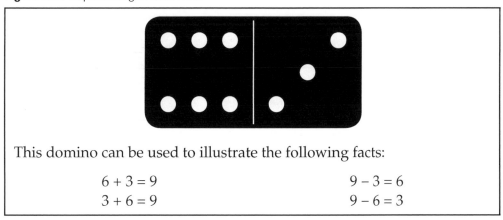

This domino can be used to illustrate the following facts:

6 + 3 = 9	9 − 3 = 6
3 + 6 = 9	9 − 6 = 3

the number of dots on the complete domino, and see if they can determine the number of dots that are hidden from view. For example, if the complete domino contains two dots on one side and six on the other, hide the two dots, show them six dots, and tell them there are eight dots in all. Challenge them to identify the missing addend and then to state the subtraction fact you have illustrated: 8 − 2 = 6. A worksheet can be created that uses the domino pattern to provide focused fact drill. Create an entire page of problems that all revolve around a single domino, and let students practice associating the two numbers on the domino with the four facts that can be formed using that domino. For example, if one side of the domino contains four dots and the other side contains nine dots, you can use the domino to create the combinations 4 + 5 = 9, 5 + 4 = 9, 9 − 5 = 4, and 9 − 4 = 5. Create about twenty questions that use these four numbers, with the unknown quantity in different positions, such as 4 + 5 = ?, 4 + ? = 9, 9 − 5 = ?, 9 − ? = 4, and so on. This process is illustrated in Figure 8.13.

Another way to help students associate subtraction with the related addition fact is with small flash cards. Create a set of small addition flash cards for each student. Write a subtraction fact problem on the board, and ask students to hold up the two addition facts that can help them solve the subtraction problem. For example, if you write the problem 8 − 3 on the board, students can hold up the flash cards containing 3 + 5 and 5 + 3. This activity is most effective if students only practice a limited number of facts at one time. Additional games to practice related subtraction facts are described in Appendix B.

Counting Down: −1 and −2 Facts

Another way to determine subtraction remainders is to count down. As we have already discussed, counting up is an inefficient addition strategy; counting down is equally inefficient. The exception is the facts formed by subtracting one or two. The same strategies used to teach students to count up when adding one or two are equally effective when teaching students to

Figure 8.13 Developing Fact Fluency

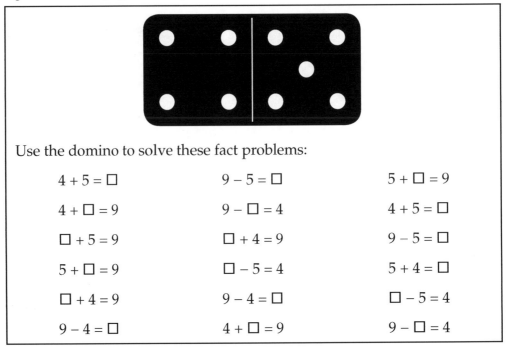

Use the domino to solve these fact problems:

4 + 5 = ☐	9 − 5 = ☐	5 + ☐ = 9
4 + ☐ = 9	9 − ☐ = 4	4 + 5 = ☐
☐ + 5 = 9	☐ + 4 = 9	9 − 5 = ☐
5 + ☐ = 9	☐ − 5 = 4	5 + 4 = ☐
☐ + 4 = 9	9 − 4 = ☐	☐ − 5 = 4
9 − 4 = ☐	4 + ☐ = 9	9 − ☐ = 4

count down when subtracting one or two. There are thirty-two subtraction facts that can be solved by counting down one or two, so almost one-third of the 100 subtraction facts can be mastered using this strategy. In order to use the counting-down strategy, students need to be able to count backward from ten to solve first-grade facts and from eighteen to solve second-grade facts. The same strategies used to teach counting on can be used to practice counting down. Let one student begin counting backward; then have that student stop and ask a different child to continue. Once students can count backward easily, model how to use this process to solve facts that involve subtracting one. For example, to model 8 − 1, have the student begin at 8, count back one number to 7, then state the entire fact: 8 − 1 = 7. The same process can be used to practice −2 facts. Let students use their bodies to model this process by walking backward on a large number line taped to the floor. The games described in Appendix B to practice +1 and +2 facts can be adapted to practice the counting-down strategy.

Subtracting Zero

There are nineteen facts with zero as one of the addends (see Figure 8.3) and ten related subtraction facts that involve subtracting zero from a single digit number. Just as adding zero to a number does not change the total, when we subtract zero from a number the result is the original number (a − 0 = a). Concrete and visual examples will help students develop this concept. The games used to practice −1 and −2 facts can be easily adapted to practice subtracting zero.

Subtracting the Same Number

When a number is subtracted from itself, the result is zero—for example, $8 - 8 = 0$. A few experiences modeling these facts with concrete or pictorial representation are usually sufficient for students to learn this rule.

Decomposition Strategies

Decomposition strategies involve decomposing a number to create a simpler or familiar fact and then using that fact to solve the harder fact. For example, to find $14 - 5$, students can decompose 5 into $4 + 1$. They subtract the 4 from 14 to get to 10, then subtract the remaining 1 to obtain the answer of 9. To subtract $15 - 9$, students might first subtract 5 to get to 10 and then be able to solve the simpler fact that remains: $10 - 4 = 6$. Or students could count up from 9 to get to 10 and then realize that they need to count up 5 more to reach 15, so in all they count up 1 and 5 more, which means they count up 6 in all: $15 - 9 = 6$. Students who are competent in math frequently employ decomposition strategies when adding and subtracting, but students with a history of mathematical difficulty may struggle with this approach. All of the subtraction facts can be solved using related addition facts, so students who find decomposition strategies frustrating can obtain computational fluency if they focus on mastering addition facts and then using this knowledge to solve the related subtraction facts.

Strategies for Multiplication Facts

Multiplication involves repeated addition, so helping students connect multiplication to their existing knowledge of addition will facilitate their acquisition and mastery of the 100 multiplication facts. Before working for computational fluency, students first need to develop conceptual understanding of the multiplication process. In Chapter 7 we discussed ways to use counters, number lines, arrays, and area models to create concrete and visual representations of multiplication problems. These models were illustrated in Figure 7.22. When students label a representation with both the addition fact and the matching multiplication fact, it helps them connect the two operations.

The commutative property applies to multiplication as well as addition, and the physical and pictorial representations that students use for multiplication facts can help them understand this fundamental principle. Have students create arrays to represent a fact like 3×5, then rotate the array to show 5×3. They can also draw 3 sets of 5 and 5 sets of 3, and then count to prove that the products are the same.

Once students understand what multiplication means and can consistently model multiplication problems, they can begin to work on developing computational fluency. Strategies for solving multiplication facts focus on connecting multiplication to students' existing knowledge of addition and of skip counting. The first three strategies we discuss can help students

Figure 8.14 ×2 Facts

×	0	1	2	3	4	5	6	7	8	9
0			0							
1			2							
2	0	2	4	6	8	10	12	14	16	18
3			6							
4			8							
5			10							
6			12							
7			14							
8			16							
9			18							

develop these connections and can be used to solve more than half of the 100 multiplication facts.

×2

Multiplying by two is often the easiest table for students to understand, so it is often the first table introduced. There are twenty multiplication facts that have 2 as a factor, as shown in Figure 8.14. These are equivalent to the ten doubles addition facts students should already have mastered, so the major focus of doubles instruction in multiplication is to help students connect the multiplication facts to their existing knowledge of addition. The same illustrations that students created to illustrate the addition doubles shown in Figure 8.5 can also show the multiplication doubles. Calculators were discussed as a strategy for practicing addition doubles; the same strategy can be applied to multiplication problems that have 2 as a factor. Press 2 × = to generate multiplication doubles. The games Egg Carton Doubles and Double Trouble described for addition in Appendix B can also be adapted to help students master the twenty multiplication doubles.

Fives

Twenty multiplication facts have 5 as a factor, as shown in Figure 8.15. Students who can count by fives can use their knowledge to rapidly calculate products of the ×5 facts. The Tally Up! game described in Appendix B can help activate students' prior knowledge of skip-counting by fives. When students are proficient at skip-counting, we can relate multiplying by fives

Figure 8.15 ×5 Facts

×	0	1	2	3	4	5	6	7	8	9
0						0				
1						5				
2						10				
3						15				
4						20				
5	0	5	10	15	20	25	30	35	40	45
6						30				
7						35				
8						40				
9						45				

to skip-counting. One easy strategy is to give students a ×5 fact problem and have them hold up the number of fingers indicated by the factor that is not a five, then count the fingers by fives. For example, to calculate 4 × 5 or 5 × 4, students hold up four fingers and then count those extended fingers by fives: 5, 10, 15, 20.

We can also develop real-life connections for the fives table by using the multiplication facts to find the value of a group of nickels. The Counting Nickels game described in Appendix B can be used to practice this skill.

Counting by fives is also used to tell time, and developing this connection is another way to help students see the real-life applications of the ×5 table. Draw a large clock face with a minute hand and discuss how we count by fives when reading the minute hand. For example, when the minute hand points to 3, it is fifteen minutes past the hour. Relate this idea to the ×5 multiplication facts. Show students a flash card containing a ×5 fact, point to the number on the clock face that matches the second factor on the fact card, and state the complete multiplication fact. For example, show the fact 4 × 5, point to the 4 on the clock, and say 4 × 5 = 20. It is 20 minutes past the hour. The Star Points game described in Appendix B provides another way to practice the ×5 facts.

Zeros and Ones

There are thirty-six facts that contain 0 or 1 as a factor, as shown in Figure 8.16. The rules for solving these facts are best developed through concrete and visual representations. One is the identity element in multiplication, so any number multiplied by one results in a product that is the same as the

Figure 8.16 ×0 and ×1 Facts

×	0	1	2	3	4	5	6	7	8	9
0	0	0	0	0	0	0	0	0	0	0
1	0	1	2	3	4	5	6	7	8	9
2	0	2								
3	0	3								
4	0	4								
5	0	5								
6	0	6								
7	0	7								
8	0	8								
9	0	9								

original number—for example, $8 \times 1 = 8$. After students represent the facts in the ×1 table, ask them to identify the pattern and generate the rule for solving these facts. Use a similar process to help them understand the effects of multiplying by zero. If we ask them to illustrate the ×0 table, they will quickly conclude that any number multiplied by zero is zero. Using concrete and visual representation to generate the rules creates deeper understanding than simply telling them the rule, thus helping students apply the rules meaningfully in problem-solving situations.

Although the basic concept of multiplying by zero or one seems relatively easy, students often struggle with these facts because they confuse the results of multiplying by zero and one with the effects of adding zero or one. Adding a zero leaves the original number unchanged, while multiplying by zero results in a product of zero. Adding one increases the original number by one, but multiplying by a factor of one leaves the original number unchanged. Because students may confuse these two processes, we recommend practicing doubles and ×5 facts first, then focusing on the ×0 and ×1 multiplication facts.

Nines

Nineteen facts contain at least one factor of 9, as shown in Figure 8.17. If students have not memorized the ×9 facts, there are several patterns they can use to help them determine the product. The result of multiplying a number by a factor of 9 is always one set less than multiplying the same number by a factor of 10. Students who know the ×10 table or can skip-count by 10s and

Figure 8.17 ×9 Facts

×	0	1	2	3	4	5	6	7	8	9
0										0
1										9
2										18
3										27
4										36
5										45
6										54
7										63
8										72
9	0	9	18	27	36	45	54	63	72	81

then subtract can use this strategy to solve ×9 facts. The strategy is shown in Figure 8.18.

To find the product of 9 × 6 or 6 × 9, think 6 sets of 10, and then remove the tenth block from each set of 10. Students think, "Six times 10 equals 60, minus 6 leaves 54."

The same results can be obtained using the fingers of both hands to represent the product. Hold up all ten fingers, as shown in Figure 8.18. Count from left to right, and turn down the finger that represents the factor in the problem that is not nine. For example, to multiply 6 × 9 or 9 × 6, hold down the sixth finger, which is illustrated by the turned-down thumb on the second hand. The fingers to the left of the turned-down finger represent the tens in the product, and the fingers to the right of the turned-down finger represent the ones. In this example, there are five fingers on the left side and four fingers on the right, so 6 × 9 = 54. To multiply 9 × 9, we would turn down the ninth finger, which is the ring finger on the right hand. The eight fingers to the left of that ring finger represent the eight tens in the answer, and the one finger to the right of the turned-down ring finger represents the one in the answer, so the student can see that 9 × 9 = 81.

Other Strategies

When students have mastered the tables discussed above, they will be able to solve seventy-five of the 100 multiplication facts. Of the remaining twenty-five facts, ten can be solved using the commutative property, leaving just fifteen facts for students to learn. These are highlighted in Figure 8.19.

Figure 8.18 Representing ×9 Facts

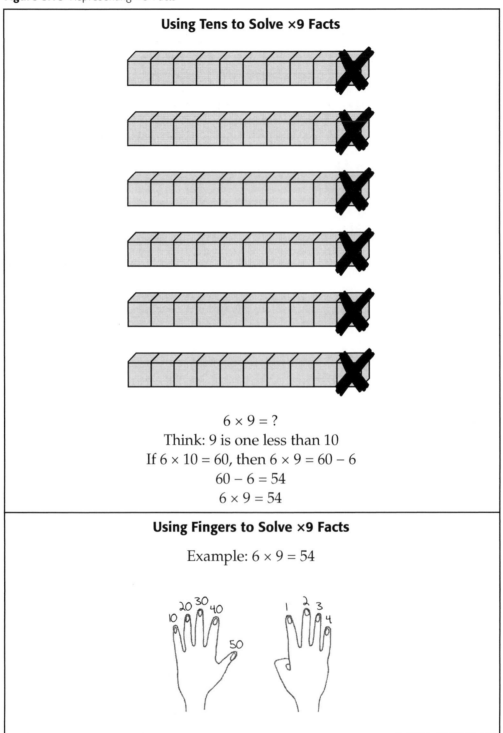

Figure 8.19 The Leftovers

×	0	1	2	3	4	5	6	7	8	9
0										
1										
2										
3				9	12		18	21	24	
4				12	16		24	28	32	
5										
6				18	24		36	42	48	
7				21	28		42	49	56	
8				24	32		48	56	64	
9										

The strategies often recommended for solving these facts are relatively complex. Some students may learn them easily, while others may find them too difficult.

Facts in the ×4 table can be solved by first finding the related ×2 fact and then doubling the product. For example, 4×6 is the same as $(2 \times 6) + (2 \times 6)$, or $2(2 \times 6)$. See Figure 8.20.

Using this strategy requires students to be able to double large numbers like $12 + 12$ or $16 + 16$. Some students may find the mental doubling more challenging than simply memorizing the ×4 table.

Figure 8.20 Double Doubles

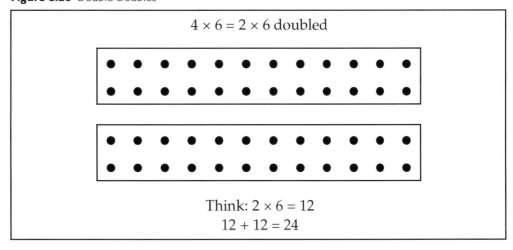

$4 \times 6 = 2 \times 6$ doubled

Think: $2 \times 6 = 12$
$12 + 12 = 24$

Facts in the ×3 table can be solved by relating them to familiar ×2 facts and then adding one more set. For example, to solve 3 × 4, think 2 × 4 = 8, and then add one more set of 4, to make a total of 12. To solve 3 × 7, think 2 × 7 = 14, and then add one more set of 7 to make a total of 21.

If students are able to use familiar facts to determine unknown facts, then practicing these strategies may be a worthwhile use of intervention time. If students find these strategies too challenging, however, interventionists may choose to focus instead on the mnemonic strategies discussed below in order to master the remaining multiplication facts.

Strategies for Division Facts

There are ninety division facts students need to master. Because division is the inverse of multiplication, these facts are best learned by linking them to their related multiplication facts (Fuchs et al., 2005; Fuchs, Fuchs, Hamlett et al., 2006; Fuchs, Seethaler et al., 2008). For example, if students know that 3 × 4 = 12 or 4 × 3 = 12, they can use this knowledge to determine that 12 ÷ 4 = 3 and 12 ÷ 3 = 4. Mastering the multiplication facts and then establishing connections between these multiplication facts and their inverse division facts are key to mastering the ninety division facts. The same activities described to help students associate subtraction facts with their related addition facts can be used to link division facts to previously mastered multiplication facts. Figure 8.21 shows an example of the type of worksheet that can help students associate the numbers in related fact families. A game to practice division facts is included in Appendix B.

Figure 8.21 Developing Fact Fluency: Providing Massed Practice with the 4 Facts in One Fact Family

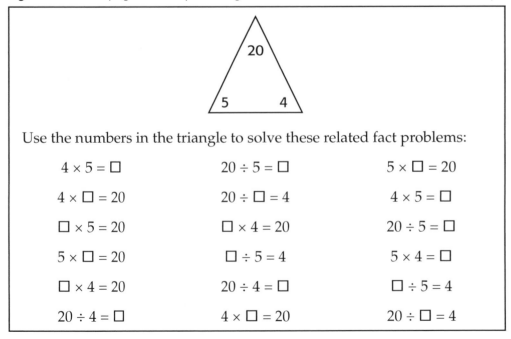

Use the numbers in the triangle to solve these related fact problems:

4 × 5 = □	20 ÷ 5 = □	5 × □ = 20
4 × □ = 20	20 ÷ □ = 4	4 × 5 = □
□ × 5 = 20	□ × 4 = 20	20 ÷ 5 = □
5 × □ = 20	□ ÷ 5 = 4	5 × 4 = □
□ × 4 = 20	20 ÷ 4 = □	□ ÷ 5 = 4
20 ÷ 4 = □	4 × □ = 20	20 ÷ □ = 4

Figure 8.22 Commonly Used Pegwords

1	bun, sun
2	shoe, zoo
3	tree
4	door, floor
5	hive
6	sticks, bricks
7	heaven
8	skate, gate
9	vine, line
10	hen, pen

Mnemonics

Mnemonic devices use verbal links or visual images to support recall. Many adults learned the acronym HOMES to remember the names of the five Great Lakes (Huron, Ontario, Michigan, Erie, Superior). The benefits of using mnemonics to aid recall are well documented for students with memory difficulties, intellectual disabilities, learning disabilities, behavioral disabilities, and emotional disturbance, as well as students who are gifted and those who are achieving normally (Greene, 1999; Mastropieri & Scruggs, 1991; Mastropieri & Scruggs, 2005; Wolgemuth, Cobb, & Alwell, 2008).

Pegwords are a type of mnemonic device that use a list of rhyming words to help individuals remember specific numbers. Figure 8.22 shows a list of commonly used pegwords. Once students learn the pegwords, they can use them to create visual images or verbal links to help them remember any math fact. For example, to remember that 2 × 4 = 8, a student might create an image of two shoes running across the floor toward a gate. To remember that 6 × 6 = 36, students can chant, "Sticks, sticks, dirty sticks." In Appendix C we list a variety of books, websites, and commercially available materials that use mnemonics, songs, and raps to support the memorization of basic facts.

As is true with any of the strategies we have described, if students are to use mnemonics independently to help them recall basic facts during activities that require computational fluency, they must first learn the mnemonic and then engage in massed practice activities in order to move the information out of working memory into long-term memory. They will then need distributed practice to retain the information and learn to recall it appropriately when needed for fluent computation.

Using Technology to Practice Basic Facts

A multitude of computer programs and apps advertise that they will help students master basic facts. Efficient drill activities provide targeted practice in just a couple of unfamiliar facts or a particular strategy, coupled with periodic review of any previously mastered facts. Programs that provide customized drill matched to individual student needs can indeed facilitate fluent fact retrieval. Some programs allow teachers to individualize the activity to include only those facts a particular student needs to practice, and other programs assess student mastery and generate an individualized list of facts to practice. Such programs can be very effective. Unfortunately, many computerized programs offer random practice of too many facts, such as those that practice all the 100 addition facts or multiplication facts. While students may enjoy spending time on the computer, providing such brief exposure to a large number of facts is unlikely to build automaticity. Intervention time is valuable, and instructors must choose wisely to provide the type of focused practice that will help students develop computational fluency.

Differentiating Practice

Fact practice should be individualized to allow each student to focus on the specific facts he or she needs to learn. The IES practice guide suggests that students should focus on just two unfamiliar facts at a time, coupled with ongoing review of previously mastered facts (Gersten et al., 2009). Interventions are typically provided in small-group settings, and it is rare that all students in the group should be focusing on the exact same set of facts or fact clusters. To achieve optimal learning outcomes, interventionists need to differentiate practice activities for small groups with like needs or to match individual student needs. A variety of formats can be used to provide this differentiated practice with basic facts.

1. **CRA Continuum:** As we discussed in the previous chapter, students need to understand what an operation means before they begin to work on developing computational fluency with abstract numbers. Within a group of students, it is likely that some will already understand the underlying concepts and be ready to focus on developing automaticity, while others in the group may still need to practice modeling problems with objects or drawings. Allowing students to use concrete or visual representation as needed is one way to differentiate practice activities.

2. **Worksheets**: Students generally view completing worksheets as a rather dull activity, so worksheets should be used sparingly.

However, occasional worksheet practice can be beneficial, and it is easy to provide individualized worksheets that focus on a particular fact or fact cluster. The worksheets illustrated in Figures 8.13 and 8.21 are a good example. Everyone in the group could be completing a fact worksheet, but the sheets can be individualized to allow each student to practice just the one or two unfamiliar facts or fact clusters he needs to master. Accelerated Math (www.renlearn.com) provides a computer software program that creates math assignments tailored to each student's current level. Teachers can select an instructional objective and the program will generate a "worksheet" that contains multiple problems practicing the same skill.

3. **Computer Programs:** If the group has access to multiple computers, then each student can work on a computer program that is specifically selected to focus on the facts that she needs to master. As mentioned above, effective drill provides targeted practice in a limited number of facts, coupled with periodic review of previously mastered facts. Programs that allow the instructor to select the exact facts each student will practice provide an easy and efficient way to differentiate fact practice.

4. **Peer Tutoring:** Research studies have demonstrated that peer tutoring can produce strong gains in mathematical proficiency (see the Best Evidence Encyclopedia report at www.bestevidence.org). The benefits of using peer tutoring were discussed in Chapter 4, and Figure 4.1 describes several evidence-based peer tutoring programs. Any of these programs can be used to differentiate instruction.

   Another peer tutoring activity that can be used to differentiate basic fact practice is called the Flashcard Game (www.kaganonline .com). Each student must have an individualized set of flash cards containing the facts she needs to master, as well as a pile of mastered facts to review periodically. From these cards, the student should select two unfamiliar facts and three review facts. Next, students pair up and exchange cards. One student is the tutor and quizzes his partner on the partner's five cards. In Round One, the tutor first shows the tutee the front of the card containing the problem, then the back of the card that shows the answer. The front of the card is shown again, and the tutee states the answer. If the answer is correct, the tutor returns the card to the tutee. If the answer is incorrect, the tutor helps the tutee identify the fact and then places the card at the back of the pile so it can be reviewed again. Once the first student has correctly identified all five cards, the partners trade roles and the process is repeated. In Round Two, few clues are given, and in Round Three, students should be able to identify the facts without cues. Once a student masters a fact, the card can be moved to the pile of review facts and replaced with a card from the pile of facts the student still needs to master. The

Flashcard Game could be played for ten minutes each day to provide the recommended practice in basic facts. The game allows everyone in the group to be involved in the same activity, but practice is differentiated so that each person can practice an individualized set of facts.

5. **Board Games:** Almost any board game can be used to practice math facts by simply providing a stack of fact flash cards and requiring students to correctly solve a fact before advancing their game piece. Commercial board games designed for practicing math facts generally provide a stack of flash cards. The cards are placed in the middle of the board, and every student draws from that same pile of cards. However, if the facts do not match each student's individual needs, then little learning may occur. Instead, allow each student to use her own set of flash cards, selected as described in the Flashcard Game above. The individualized flash cards allow each student to experience differentiated practice on the specific facts she needs to master.

6. **Card Games:** Students enjoy playing games, and their increased engagement and motivation can facilitate learning. Card games are easy to differentiate. All the students in the class can learn to play a basic card game like the Make-a-Pair or Concentration games described in Appendix B. When it is time to practice math facts, students working on the same sets of facts can be grouped together and given a deck of cards that contains only the facts those students need to practice. All students in the class can be playing the same card game, but if their cards are differentiated, then they are receiving the type of targeted practice that has been shown to maximize learning outcomes.

7. **Stations:** Learning stations can be adapted to provide differentiated practice in basic math facts (Forbringer & Fahsl, 2007, 2009). They are especially effective in the regular classroom where teachers need to differentiate practice for large groups of students. When using differentiated stations, students are grouped homogeneously so that all the students in the group need to work on a similar set of facts. Before a group of students enters the station, the activity is modified to focus on just the fats the students in that group need to learn or review.

For example, a class might contain a group of students who are working on adding doubles, and another group who are multiplying by fives. One of the stations could contain the egg carton game described in Appendix B. In this game, a numeral from 0 to 9 is written inside each cup of an empty egg carton. Students take turns rolling or dropping a small ball into the egg carton, and the number written in the cup where their ball lands is used in a fact calculation. Students compete to see who will be the first to accumulate 100 points. In the group practicing doubles, students would double the number where their ball lands and use that as their score for the round. Those working on the five tables could multiply the number by five, while a third group of students who are working on counting-on could add one to the number in the cup. Each group would play the same egg carton game, but the activity would be differentiated to provide targeted practice in the facts those students need to master.

A second station in the same classroom might contain a card game like Make-a-Pair or Concentration, described in Appendix B. Before each group enters the station, the teacher would switch the deck of cards to provide just the facts that group of students needs to practice. Each group would play the same card game, but the teacher would differentiate the activity by providing a deck of cards that matches the needs of the students in the group.

When using differentiated stations, it is advisable to adjust the time frame so the teacher is able to switch fact cards before each group's arrival at a station. Instead of having students rotate through all the stations in a single period, they can rotate over the course of several days. For example, if there are five stations, then students could complete a different station each day, and in a week everyone will go through every station. This allows the teacher time after school to switch fact cards at each station, so when the students arrive the station is prepared with cards appropriate for the students scheduled to use the station that day. The activity itself will look the same, so students may not even realize that the facts they practice are differentiated.

Summary

Computational fluency is an essential component of mathematical proficiency. Students are expected to have mastered the addition and subtraction facts by the end of second grade, and the multiplication and division facts by the end of fourth grade. Individuals who meet these benchmarks can focus their attention on problem solving and higher-level computational procedures, while those who must still focus on the process of computing basic facts will have less cognitive capacity available for complex mathematical procedures. Because fact fluency is such an important skill, the IES practice guide recommends that ten minutes of each intervention session focus on developing fluency with basic facts (Gersten et al., 2009).

In Chapter 6 we provided an overview of the CRA continuum, and in Chapter 7 we discussed using the CRA continuum and explicit instruction to develop conceptual understanding of whole numbers. Once students understand whole-number concepts, they can begin to focus on developing automaticity with basic facts, which was the focus of this chapter. In the next chapter we will discuss strategies to help students understand rational numbers.

Chapter 9

Representing Rational Numbers

In the early grades, interventions provided for students in Tier 2 and Tier 3 should emphasize counting, number value, place value, and operations with whole numbers, as discussed in Chapters 7 and 8. Once students have mastered this content, the focus should shift to rational numbers, including understanding the meaning of fractions, decimals, ratios, and percents, and operations using rational numbers (Gersten et al., 2009). These topics represent foundational proficiencies and are prerequisites for further mathematical progress.

While many of the methods for introducing rational numbers during interventions are similar to those used in the core curriculum, interventions differ in two important ways. First, instruction during interventions should be explicit and systematic (Gersten et al., 2009). Second, interventionists need to carefully follow the CRA continuum and explicitly link the representation systems (Gersten et al., 2009). In this chapter we will discuss ways to incorporate both of these instructional strategies when introducing rational numbers.

Developing Fraction Concepts

Fractions present one of the greatest challenges students encounter. NAEP test results reveal that American students have consistently struggled with basic fraction concepts (NMAP, 2008; U.S. Department of Education, 2009, 2011; Wearne & Kouba, 2001). Since understanding fraction concepts is a prerequisite to meaningful computation of fractions, as well as fundamental for understanding decimals, percents, and ratio and proportion, it is not surprising that students continue to struggle when they encounter these later topics. Even students who have not experienced previous mathematical difficulty can be challenged by fractions. For students with a history of mathematical difficulty, the problem is magnified.

To understand fractions, students must master a few big ideas. First, fractional parts are formed when a whole or unit is divided into equal parts. In other words, to understand a fraction, students first need to identify the unit and then make sure it is divided into equal parts. The second big

Figure 9.1 Modeling Fractions

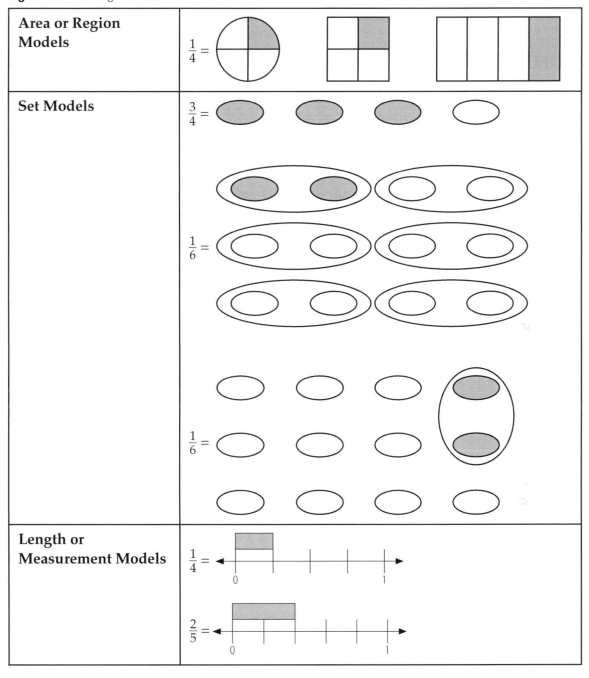

idea that students need to understand is how fractions are labeled. In other words, they need to know that the denominator tells how many equal parts are in the unit and the numerator tells how many of those parts we have. Models play an important role in helping students understand these big ideas. Figure 9.1 provides examples of three different types of models used to illustrate basic fraction concepts: (1) area models, (2) set models, and (3) measurement models.

Area models involve dividing a whole object into equal parts. They are generally the easiest fraction models for students to understand, because in a whole object the unit and the object are synonymous. A variety of materials are available to help students learn to create area models of fractions, but the most commonly used manipulative is the fraction circle. When cut like a pizza pie, fraction circles provide an excellent, concrete way to help students understand the relative value of fractional parts of wholes. Unfortunately, too often fraction circles are the only type of fractional representation that students encounter. NCTM (2000) recommends that all students experience multiple representations of mathematical concepts and have the opportunity to translate among representations, because connecting one form of representation to another enhances understanding. When modeling fractional parts of wholes, using shapes such as squares, rectangles, and triangles can help students develop a more solid understanding of the concept (see Figure 9.1). Manipulatives like pattern blocks, Cuisenaire rods, and geoboards can also be used to model fractions. Fraction towers are especially useful, because the pieces snap together like the pop cubes used for counting whole numbers and so are less likely to be jostled out of place than some other manipulatives. See Figure 9.2 for an illustration of these manipulatives.

Once students are comfortable using area models to represent fractional parts of whole numbers, they need experiences with other types of models. Set models present a greater challenge, because when students see a set of objects, they tend to find it harder to identify what constitutes the unit. Sets vary in size; they may contain two items or two thousand. For example, a set might be a dozen eggs, all the students in the classroom, or a box of crayons. Whatever its size, the entire collection of items in the set forms the unit, which is counted as one. When we divide a set into parts, each of the fractional parts is a subset of the unit. This is illustrated in the first example of set models shown in Figure 9.1. The example depicts a set of four counters, three of which are shaded. In this example, the four counters form the unit. Each individual counter represents one subset or fractional part, so 3 out of 4 counters, or ¾ of the counters, are shaded. In the second and third examples of set models, the unit consists of 12 counters. The unit is divided into 6 groups or subsets, each of which contains 2 counters. One subset contains shaded counters, so it represents ⅙ of the unit. Because the number of objects forming the unit and its subsets varies from one set model to another, students sometimes find set models confusing.

The third type of model is the measurement model, commonly seen in rulers and number lines. In a measurement model, the unit is the distance from 0 to 1, and the space between subdivisions represents the fractional parts. Locating fractions on a number line challenges many learners, and individuals who struggle with mathematics will need explicit instruction if they are to succeed with this method of representation. The effort is worth it, however, because a number line can be used to represent any fraction, decimal, or percent. When students use fraction circles or fraction bars to

Figure 9.2 Concrete Representations of Fractions

Modeling ½ with a geoboard

Modeling 1 whole and ½
with pattern blocks

Modeling 1 whole, ½, ¾, and ⅛
with Cuisenaire rods

Modeling 1 whole, ½, and ¾
with fraction towers

represent fractional parts of a whole, they draw a different model for each different denominator. A number line provides a consistent model that students can use to represent any quantity, so once students develop a mental number line they can easily compare the values of any rational numbers.

Because students generally find it more difficult to master set and measurement models, it is helpful to wait to introduce these concepts until after the student has demonstrated mastery of area models. Transitioning too quickly from area models to set and measurement models can lead to confusion. For a thorough discussion of the use of models to develop fraction concepts, see Van de Walle's text *Elementary and Middle School Mathematics: Teaching Developmentally* (2004).

Using the CRA Sequence with Advanced Fraction Skills

While most programs use some form of concrete or visual representation to introduce the concept of fractions, few programs follow the CRA continuum when introducing more complex skills such as converting mixed numbers to improper fractions, or adding, subtracting, multiplying, and dividing fractions. In a 2008 study, Hodges, Cady, and Collins examined three middle-school textbook series to determine how well they incorporated representations into their lessons on fractions. In the texts they examined, the use of concrete representation ranged from a mere 0.25 percent up to a high of only 5.12 percent. Visual representations of fractions appeared between 7.28 percent and 27.31 percent of the time, while the vast majority of lessons relied only on abstract words and symbols. If these findings are typical, then it is not surprising that American students are struggling with fractions. The lack of concrete and visual representation in upper-level textbooks suggests that many students will have only abstract experiences with fractions.

When skills are introduced using only abstract symbols or words, students often memorize rote procedures without fully understanding what they are doing. For example, the process of converting mixed numbers to improper fractions is often taught abstractly. Students are told to multiply some numbers and add others, but concrete and visual representations of the process are seldom provided. In the fourth National Assessment of Educational Progress (NAEP), seventh graders were asked to convert a mixed number to an improper fraction. Although about 80 percent of them were able to make the conversion successfully, fewer than half recognized that 5¼ was the same as 5 + ¼ (Kouba et al., 1988). This type of anomaly occurs when students are taught to perform rote procedures without understanding the underlying concepts. Until representation is routinely incorporated into fraction instruction, American students will continue to struggle.

Because meaningful information is more easily remembered (Wolfe, 2001), students who use concrete and visual representations to develop an understanding of the underlying concepts are also more likely to remember and be able to apply their knowledge in the future. Figure 9.3 shows how

Figure 9.3 Mixed Numbers and Improper Fractions

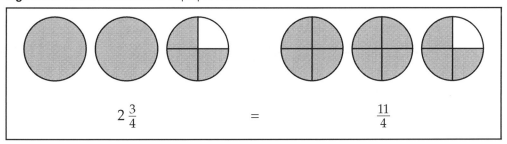

$$2\frac{3}{4} \qquad = \qquad \frac{11}{4}$$

a model can help students understand the relationship between improper fractions and mixed numbers.

When the models are presented along with the abstract explanation, the process of converting between the different representations becomes meaningful, and students are therefore more likely to learn and retain the information. In this example, the mixed number 2¾ is shown using two whole circles, plus another circle that is divided into fourths and has three of the fourths shaded. Building on students' previous understanding of equal shares, we can partition the two whole circles into fourths, so that all the circles are divided into equal-size pieces. Counting the parts, students discover that when they cut two wholes into four parts they end up with eight parts. This is the 2 × 4 = 8 mentioned in the abstract explanation, now given meaning through the visual representation. The model also makes it clear that there are three additional parts in the partially shaded circle. If we count all the shaded parts, we find that 8 + 3 = 11. Therefore we have a total of 11 parts. We did not change the size of the individual parts. They are still fourths, so the denominator stays the same, and the solution is: 2¾ = 1¼. When the abstract explanations are meaningfully associated with a concrete or visual representation, the steps are more easily understood and retained. Even if students forget the abstract set of steps presented in the verbal explanation, if they understand the underlying concepts, they can figure out the solution by creating a quick sketch.

Equivalent Fractions

Fraction equivalence is another big idea in understanding fractions. Students need a variety of concrete experiences in order to understand that the same fractional portion of a whole can be expressed using different symbolic representations. For example, the same portion of a whole can be labeled as ½, ²⁄₄, ³⁄₆, and so on. Students who understand the concept of equivalence will be better prepared to understand decimals and percents such as .5 or 50 percent.

To help students recognize that the same fractional portion can be created using different fraction pieces, we can ask them to begin with a fraction piece that represents a familiar fraction such as ½ or ⅓, and use fraction

Figure 9.4 Equivalent Fraction Strips

1 whole

$\frac{1}{2}$	$\frac{1}{2}$

$\frac{1}{3}$	$\frac{1}{3}$	$\frac{1}{3}$

$\frac{1}{4}$	$\frac{1}{4}$	$\frac{1}{4}$	$\frac{1}{4}$

$\frac{1}{5}$	$\frac{1}{5}$	$\frac{1}{5}$	$\frac{1}{5}$	$\frac{1}{5}$

$\frac{1}{6}$	$\frac{1}{6}$	$\frac{1}{6}$	$\frac{1}{6}$	$\frac{1}{6}$	$\frac{1}{6}$

$\frac{1}{8}$	$\frac{1}{8}$	$\frac{1}{8}$	$\frac{1}{8}$	$\frac{1}{8}$	$\frac{1}{8}$	$\frac{1}{8}$	$\frac{1}{8}$

$\frac{1}{10}$	$\frac{1}{10}$	$\frac{1}{10}$	$\frac{1}{10}$	$\frac{1}{10}$	$\frac{1}{10}$	$\frac{1}{10}$	$\frac{1}{10}$	$\frac{1}{10}$	$\frac{1}{10}$

manipulatives to find as many single-fraction names for the area as possible. For example, they could use fraction circles to illustrate ½ and then try laying other single-fraction denominators on top of the ½ model to determine which can be used to cover ½ exactly. This provides a concrete model that helps students understand that ½ is the same amount as ¼ or ⅛. Length models can also be used to develop the concept of equivalence. For example, strips of paper can be folded to represent different fractions. An unfolded strip would represent one whole, and other strips of the same length can be folded in half, thirds, fourths, and so on. When the strips are laid out below each other, fractions that are equivalent are readily apparent. See Figure 9.4.

Fraction bars, towers, or pop cubes provide a different experience with length models. The cubes are especially well suited to modeling equivalent fractions because the plastic cubes snap together to form sturdy towers. Once they are snapped together, the pieces of adjacent towers cannot slide around as fraction circles or strips of paper sometimes do, and the stability makes it easier for students to identify fractions that are truly equivalent. These same factors make this manipulative effective when students are comparing fractions. See Figure 9.5.

In addition, fraction towers can be laid out side by side, so it is possible to compare several sizes at once to see which combinations are equivalent. In contrast, fraction circles must be laid on top of each other, which obscures

Figure 9.5 Using Fraction Towers to Compare Fractions

Comparing 1 whole, ½, and ¾

the bottom pieces and so makes it more difficult to compare multiple sizes simultaneously.

One of the most effective models to help students find equivalent fractions is an area model of a simple square, with vertical and horizontal lines drawn to create fractional pieces.

Figure 9.6 shows a square shaded to represent ½. Drawing horizontal lines on the square separates the region into equal slices, providing a quick way to model equivalent fractions. The second, third, and fourth squares in the figure show what happens when the region is cut into four, eight, or sixteen equal parts. Students can easily sketch squares on paper, so they can use this representation independently, even when they do not have access to manipulatives.

Fraction overlays are a three-dimensional version of the squares described above. The overlays are cut from overhead transparency sheets, with lines drawn on each square in permanent marker to create halves, thirds, and so on. By shading parts of the square with a dry-erase marker, students can represent specific fractions. Just as we modeled with the squares in Figure 9.6, students can turn an unshaded overlay on its side so that the lines run horizontally, and then place it on top of the shaded overlay to create an equivalent fraction. See Figure 9.7.

Figure 9.6 Fraction Squares

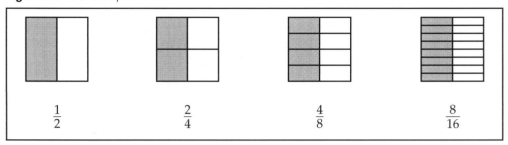

$$\frac{1}{2} \qquad\qquad \frac{2}{4} \qquad\qquad \frac{4}{8} \qquad\qquad \frac{8}{16}$$

After students have had multiple experiences using concrete and visual representation to model equivalent fractions, they will eventually need to learn the equivalence algorithm so that they will be able to perform operations with fractions fluently. The algorithm for finding equivalent fractions is this: multiply or divide both the numerator and denominator by the same non-zero number. This symbolic procedure for finding equivalent fractions is based on the identity property of multiplication, which says that multiplying a number by one does not change the number. Therefore, we can multiply any number by a fraction equivalent to 1, such as ²⁄₂, ³⁄₃, or ¼. Consider these examples:

$$\left(\frac{2}{2}\right)\frac{1}{3} = \frac{2}{6} \qquad \left(\frac{3}{3}\right)\frac{3}{4} = \frac{9}{12}$$

Sketched squares or fraction overlays are an excellent way to illustrate the algorithm, because when we turn a clear overlay horizontally and lay it on top of a shaded overlay, we are actually multiplying the fraction by an equivalent of 1. Figure 9.7 shows how a clear overlay representing ½ is placed over the square shaded to represent ⅔, creating ⁴⁄₆. In other words, (²⁄₂)⅔ = ⁴⁄₆. Because the algorithm involves multiplication, it should not be taught until students begin multiplying fractions. Early experiences with equivalence should focus on concrete and visual models.

Many textbooks, especially at the middle-school level, rely on a strictly symbolic approach to teach equivalent fractions. Students are taught the algorithm without fully understanding its significance, and as a result may forget it, confuse it, or execute the procedure by rote without being able to apply it meaningfully in problem-solving situations. Students need many experiences manipulating equivalent fractions before they are introduced to the algorithm. Explicitly linking the algorithm to students' experiences with the overlays will allow them to understand the meaning that underlies the procedure. They will therefore be more likely to remember the algorithm and to successfully apply it in the future. If the available program does not make sufficient use of concrete and visual models, then interventionists will need to add this component to their lessons.

Figure 9.7 Fraction Overlays

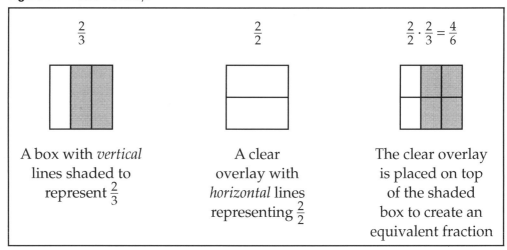

A box with *vertical* lines shaded to represent $\frac{2}{3}$

A clear overlay with *horizontal* lines representing $\frac{2}{2}$

The clear overlay is placed on top of the shaded box to create an equivalent fraction

Figure 9.8 Adding and Subtracting Fractions

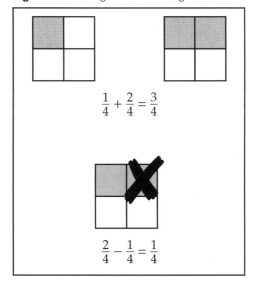

Adding and Subtracting Fractions

Concrete and visual representations are equally useful when introducing addition and subtraction of fractions. When students first learn these operations, the most frequent error they make is to add or subtract the denominator along with the numerator. Given the fractions ¼ + ²⁄₄, they may mistakenly calculate the sum as ⅜. This error reveals a lack of conceptual understanding. If students first use manipulatives to solve this problem, as shown in Figure 9.8, the error is far less likely because they can see that the size of the pieces has not changed.

Figure 9.9 Adding Mixed Numbers with Like Denominators

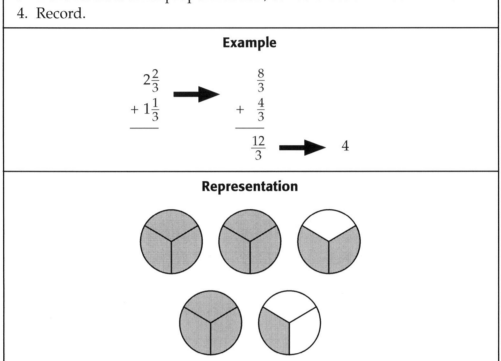

Skill Steps

1. Change the mixed numbers to improper fractions.
2. Add.
3. If the result is an improper fraction, convert it to a mixed number.
4. Record.

Example

Representation

Once students are comfortable adding and subtracting fractions with like denominators, they can tackle addition and subtraction of mixed numbers with like denominators. Although there are several possible methods for adding mixed numbers, perhaps the simplest is to first convert all the mixed numbers to improper fractions, then add, expressing the answer as a mixed number. See Figure 9.9 for an example and list of steps to follow when teaching this process.

The procedure for subtracting mixed numbers is similar to that described for addition. First, convert the mixed numbers to improper fractions, then subtract, expressing the answer as a mixed number. Again, teachers should incorporate concrete and visual representation and provide students with an explicit list of steps to follow. Figure 9.10 shows subtraction of mixed numbers with like denominators.

If students understand how to find equivalent fractions, how to add and subtract fractions with like denominators, and how to multiply fractions before they encounter addition and subtraction with unlike denominators, then performing operations with unlike denominators should not present a conceptual challenge. However, students who are still struggling with these

Figure 9.10 Subtracting Mixed Numbers with Like Denominators

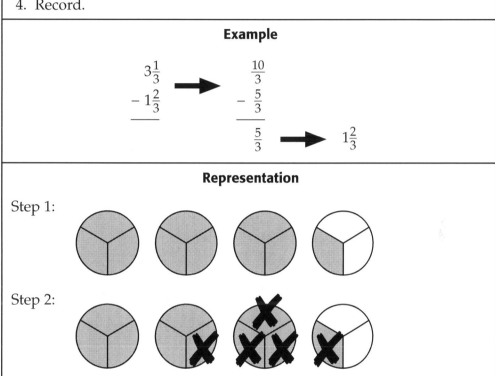

---

prerequisite skills will become overwhelmed when compelled to use them all in a single problem. Additionally, students requiring supplemental support are likely to stumble because of the lengthy number of steps required to solve problems involving unlike denominators. To support students in this process, interventionists should provide a list of skill steps and encourage students to check off each step as they complete it. A list of suggested skill steps for adding and subtracting fractions and mixed numbers with unlike denominators is provided in Figure 9.11.

Step one of this procedure is to rewrite the problem using a common denominator. The simplest, most straightforward way to identify a common denominator is to multiply the denominators provided; the resulting product represents a common denominator. For example, to find a common denominator for $\frac{2}{3} + \frac{1}{4}$, we multiply 3×4 to obtain the common denominator of 12. This process is identical to the process described previously for crisscrossing fraction overlays to find equivalent fractions. For some students, it may be best to continue to rely on this procedure without bothering to introduce the idea of lowest common denominator. Multiplying denominators produces

Figure 9.11 Adding and Subtracting with Unlike Denominators

Skill Steps: Adding & Subtracting Fractions
1. Rewrite with common denominators.
2. Add or subtract.
3. Rewrite the answer in lowest terms, if needed.

Skill Steps: Adding & Subtracting Mixed Numbers
1. Rewrite with common denominators.
2. Change mixed numbers to improper fractions.
3. Add or subtract.
4. Rewrite the answer in lowest terms, if needed.

Example #1: Adding Fractions

$$\begin{array}{r} \frac{2}{3} \\ +\ \frac{1}{2} \\ \hline \end{array} \rightarrow \begin{array}{r} \frac{4}{6} \\ +\ \frac{3}{6} \\ \hline \end{array} \rightarrow \begin{array}{r} \frac{4}{6} \\ +\ \frac{3}{6} \\ \hline \frac{7}{6} \end{array} \rightarrow \begin{array}{r} \frac{4}{6} \\ +\ \frac{3}{6} \\ \hline 1\frac{1}{6} \end{array}$$

Example #2: Subtracting Fractions

$$\begin{array}{r} \frac{4}{5} \\ -\ \frac{1}{3} \\ \hline \end{array} \rightarrow \begin{array}{r} \frac{12}{15} \\ -\ \frac{5}{15} \\ \hline \end{array} \rightarrow \begin{array}{r} \frac{12}{15} \\ -\ \frac{5}{15} \\ \hline \frac{7}{15} \end{array}$$

Example #3: Adding Mixed Numbers

$$\begin{array}{r} 1\frac{2}{3} \\ +\ 2\frac{1}{2} \\ \hline \end{array} \rightarrow \begin{array}{r} 1\frac{4}{6} \\ +\ 2\frac{3}{6} \\ \hline \end{array} \rightarrow \begin{array}{r} \frac{10}{6} \\ +\ \frac{15}{6} \\ \hline \end{array} \rightarrow \begin{array}{r} \frac{10}{6} \\ +\ \frac{15}{6} \\ \hline \frac{25}{6} \end{array} \rightarrow 4\frac{1}{6}$$

Example #4: Subtracting Mixed Numbers

$$\begin{array}{r} 4\frac{1}{3} \\ -\ 1\frac{1}{2} \\ \hline \end{array} \rightarrow \begin{array}{r} 2\frac{2}{6} \\ -\ 1\frac{3}{6} \\ \hline \end{array} \rightarrow \begin{array}{r} \frac{26}{6} \\ -\ \frac{9}{6} \\ \hline \end{array} \rightarrow \begin{array}{r} \frac{26}{6} \\ -\ \frac{9}{6} \\ \hline \frac{17}{6} \end{array} \rightarrow 2\frac{5}{6}$$

Figure 9.12 The Shortcut Method for Finding Lowest Common Denominators (LCD)

> 1. Look at the denominators. Can the larger numeral be divided evenly by the smaller denominator?
> 2. If YES, then the larger numeral is the LCD.
> 3. If NO, double the larger numeral and try again.
> 4. Continue to triple, quadruple, and so on until you find the LCD.

a correct answer, and instructional time may be more effectively spent on other topics.

However, if the denominators being multiplied contain multidigit numbers, the resulting common denominator can be very large and unwieldy. For this reason, the interventionist may decide to introduce least common denominators. We have found that a shortcut method is effective when teaching students to find the least common multiple that will produce a common denominator. Steps for the short-cut method are listed in Figure 9.12.

Using the shortcut method to find a common denominator for the fractions $\frac{4}{6}$ and $\frac{5}{12}$, we would first examine the two denominators. The numeral 12 represents a larger quantity than the numeral 6, so we will attempt to divide 12 by 6. Note that we are focusing on the size of the numeral in the denominator, not the size of the fraction. Sixths are larger fraction pieces than twelfths, but we are looking at the numerals 6 and 12, and the numeral 12 represents a larger quantity than the numeral 6. Step 2 of the procedure asks whether the larger numeral can be divided evenly by the smaller denominator. In this case, the answer is yes: $12 \div 6 = 2$. Since twelve can be evenly divided by 6, we know that 12 is the lowest common denominator. If the answer is no, then we would proceed to step 3. For example, to find the lowest common denominator for the fractions $\frac{1}{6}$ and $\frac{1}{9}$, we would identify 9 as the larger numeral. Since 9 is not evenly divided by 6, we would proceed to step 3 and try doubling 9. The result of 18 can be evenly divided by 6, so it is the lowest common denominator. The fractions $\frac{1}{3}$ and $\frac{1}{4}$ illustrate a problem that requires tripling to find the lowest common denominator. Four is not evenly divisible by 3, and if we double the 4, the quantity of 8 is not evenly divisible by 3 either. However, if we triple 4 to obtain 12, we have found a number that can be evenly divided by 3, and so we have identified the lowest common denominator. Students generally find the shortcut process fairly simple, and it is easily modeled using fraction overlays. If we first model the fraction whose denominator contains the larger numeral and then crisscross a clear overlay depicting $\frac{2}{2}$ on top of the model, we have illustrated the doubling process. If we crisscross $\frac{3}{3}$ on top of the fraction, we have modeled tripling the number. The shortcut method may enable students to quickly identify lowest common denominators when working with large numbers.

Adding and subtracting fractions challenges students because of the large number of complex steps involved. Students with executive processing

Figure 9.13 Modeling Multiplication

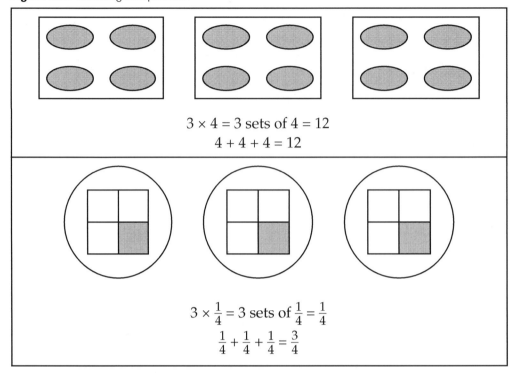

$3 \times 4 = 3$ sets of $4 = 12$

$4 + 4 + 4 = 12$

$3 \times \frac{1}{4} = 3$ sets of $\frac{1}{4} = \frac{1}{4}$

$\frac{1}{4} + \frac{1}{4} + \frac{1}{4} = \frac{3}{4}$

problems or short-term memory deficits may become confused. As with all topics we have discussed, when providing interventions it is important to first model the process with concrete and visual representation and to provide a clear list of steps for students to follow. This scaffolded support can be gradually faded as students gain confidence and proficiency.

Multiplying Fractions

Multiplication of fractions builds on students' previous knowledge of multiplying whole numbers. According to the Common Core Standards, in fourth grade students learn to multiply a fraction by a whole number and relate this process to multiplication of whole numbers. In other words, they understand that, if 3 × 4 indicates 3 sets of 4, then 3 × ¼ indicates 3 sets of ¼. Figure 9.13 shows the similarity between modeling multiplication of whole numbers and multiplication of fractions.

Multiplication is repeated addition, and the models in Figure 9.13 clearly reflect this connection. In fifth grade, students extend their understanding to multiplying a fraction or whole number by a fraction. Because multiplying by a fraction is less intuitive, students may struggle when they reach this point. If the factors are multiples of each other, the problem can be represented using the same type of models that students have used in the past. An example of using fraction circles to multiply by a fraction is illustrated in Figure 9.14.

Figure 9.14 Multiplying by a Fraction

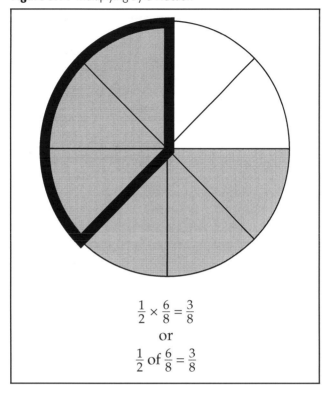

$$\frac{1}{2} \times \frac{6}{8} = \frac{3}{8}$$
or
$$\frac{1}{2} \text{ of } \frac{6}{8} = \frac{3}{8}$$

The model works well when one factor is a multiple of the other fraction. However, when the factors are not multiples of each other, fraction circles are not effective. For example, the fraction circles would not work well to illustrate a problem like ¼ × ⅔. In this case, a pan of brownies provides a simple but meaningful concrete experience to model the process. Let's say I bake a pan of brownies for a group of six students. To my dismay I discover that, before I can get the brownies to school, my family has eaten ⅓ of them, leaving just ⅔ of the pan for my students. When I reach school, a former student stops by to say hello, sees the brownies, and asks for ¼ of the brownies I have left. If I say yes, how much of the original pan of brownies would that student eat? In other words, what is ¼ of ⅔? I show the pan of brownies, which is ⅔ full. I have cut a vertical line down the middle of the brownies in the pan, so students can clearly see that we have ⅔ of the brownies and that ⅓ are missing. See Figure 9.15.

To link the concrete representation to its symbolic form, I will write the equation on the board. When we multiply fractions, the multiplication symbol is read as "of," so I will write the equation both ways:

$$\frac{1}{4} \text{ of } \frac{2}{3} = \square \qquad \text{or} \qquad \frac{1}{4} \times \frac{2}{3} = \square$$

This is a good place to elicit students' ideas about how to proceed. With their agreement, I can use horizontal cuts across the pan to divide the remaining

Figure 9.15 Modeling Multiplication

brownies into 4 slices. We need ¼ of the brownies in the pan, which means we need one of the 4 slices. There are 2 brownie pieces in that slice. They represent 2 out of 12 brownies in the original pan of brownies, so ¼ of ⅔ = ²⁄₁₂. Students who can calculate equivalent fractions may recognize that ²⁄₁₂ is the same as ⅙, but expressing the fraction in lowest terms is not necessary at this point and should not be allowed to distract students from the essential focus on multiplication.

The fraction squares and overlays we used to help students understand equivalent fractions provide a perfect two-dimensional representation of the brownie pan multiplication problem. To model ¼ of ⅔, we first show the amount we have, which is stated in the *second* fraction in the equation (in this example, ⅔). See Figure 9.16.

If we are drawing squares to create our models, we show the denominator using *vertical* lines to separate the region into sections (in this example, we need 3 sections), and then shade the number of pieces indicated by the numerator (in our problem, 2). Then we consider the first fraction in the equation, which tells us how much of the model we will use. Our problem says to take ¼ of that region, so we draw *horizontal* lines to divide the region into 4 equal slices, and then shade one of the 4 slices. The product is the region where the shaded slices overlap, which contains 2 squares. Those 2 brownie squares represent ²⁄₁₂ of the original pan of brownies.

If we use fraction overlays to model this problem, the process is similar. First we represent the second fraction by arranging our square so that the lines run vertically. Then we use another overlay to represent the first fraction, ¼. We crisscross the first fraction (¼) on top of the second fraction (⅔) so that the lines on the top overlay run horizontally. On the overlays, the product is the region where the two shaded overlays overlap.

Using fraction squares or overlays to model multiplication is similar to the method described earlier for modeling equivalent fractions with overlays. When we created equivalent fractions, we were actually multiplying the given quantity by a fraction equivalent to one, such as ²⁄₂ or ¼. Normally when we are using the whole unit, we would color in the entire square. However, that would make it difficult to see the original fraction when we crisscross the overlays on top of each other, so when we find equivalent fractions we just use lines and omit shading on the square that represents the

Figure 9.16 Modeling Multiplication with Fractions Squares and Overlays

Problem: $\frac{1}{4} \times \frac{2}{3}$

Drawing Fraction Squares		
Step 1	**Step 2**	**Step 3**
Show how much we have (the *second* fraction). Draw a square. Draw *vertical* lines to show the total number of parts stated in the denominator, then shade the number of parts stated in the numerator.	Show how much we want (the *first* fraction). On the same square, draw *horizontal* lines to show the amount stated in the denominator, then shade the number of parts stated in the numerator.	The product is the area where the two models overlap.
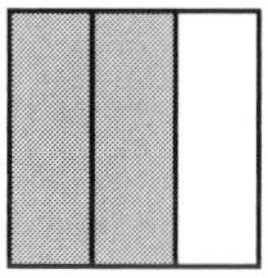 $\frac{2}{3}$	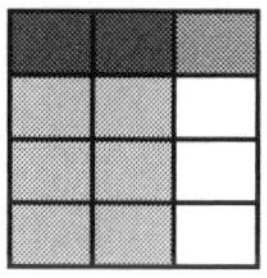 $\frac{1}{4}$	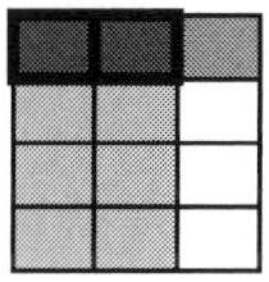 $\frac{2}{12}$

Fraction Overlays		
Step 1	**Step 2**	**Step 3**
On one overlay, use *vertical* lines to show how much we have (stated in the *second* fraction).	On a different overlay, use *horizontal* lines to show how much we want (stated in the *first* fraction).	Crisscross the two overlays. The product is the area where the two models overlap.
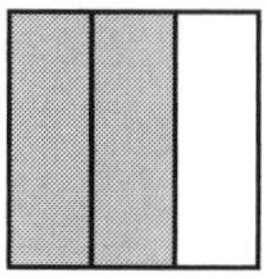 $\frac{2}{3}$	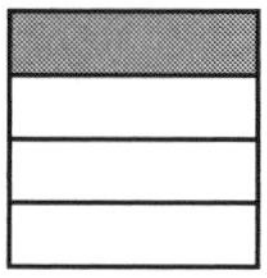 $\frac{1}{4}$	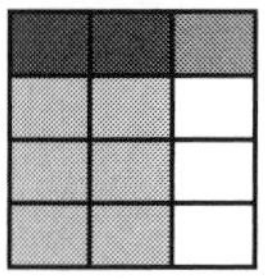 $\frac{2}{12}$

whole. It may be helpful to demonstrate the process with a shaded-in template or drawing so students can connect the process for finding equivalent fractions to the multiplication algorithm, and then have a discussion about why it is preferable to omit the shading when modeling equivalent fractions.

When students first begin to multiply a number by a fraction, they may be puzzled by the answer. In their previous experiences multiplying whole numbers, the product is usually bigger than the factors. (The exception is when we multiply by a factor of zero or one.) When we multiply by a proper fraction, the product is always smaller than the original amount. Using concrete and visual representation helps students understand why this happens, and this understanding is essential in order for them to estimate products and judge whether an answer is reasonable.

Dividing Fractions

Division of fractions is one of the most challenging topics for students and their instructors, described by Liping Ma as "a topic at the summit of arithmetic" (Ma, 1999). In a much-discussed study, Ma asked teachers in the United States and China to represent and solve the following problem: $1\frac{3}{4} \div \frac{1}{2}$. In her samples, only 39 percent of American teachers could solve the problem, and only 4 percent of them could represent it. In contrast, 100 percent of Chinese teachers were able to correctly solve the problem, and 90 percent could also represent it. If American teachers struggle themselves with these operations, it is not surprising that their students will have difficulty as well.

When we use the CRA sequence to introduce multiplication and division of fractions, we can prevent much of this confusion, especially if we also provide a meaningful context for our problems. To solve Ma's problem, we will first put it in a familiar context. Let us say that we have $1\frac{3}{4}$ hours of free time available to watch TV. How many $\frac{1}{2}$-hour shows can we watch in $1\frac{3}{4}$ hours? Figure 9.17 shows a graphic illustration of this problem.

In $1\frac{3}{4}$ hours, we can watch 3 complete $\frac{1}{2}$-hour shows and $\frac{1}{2}$ of another show. Note that, although we have $\frac{1}{4}$ hour left over, that does not mean we can watch $\frac{1}{4}$ of the last show. When we described how much free time we had, the hour was divided into quarter-hour segments. But when we are calculating the number of shows we can watch, a complete show lasts $\frac{1}{2}$ hour, and so our unit changes to $\frac{1}{2}$ hour. After we watch 3 complete shows, there will be $\frac{1}{4}$ hour remaining, which is exactly half of a $\frac{1}{2}$-hour show. Our answer therefore is that we can watch $3\frac{1}{2}$ half-hour TV shows. The changing whole (unit) presents an enormous challenge for students (Izsak et al., 2008), who will need multiple experiences dividing fractions in order to master the process.

There are two approaches to teaching division of fractions. The method most commonly used in U.S. schools has been to teach students the inversion algorithm. For example, to solve the problem $\frac{1}{4} \div \frac{2}{3}$, we invert the second fraction, then multiply to obtain our answer: $\frac{1}{4} \div \frac{2}{3} = \frac{1}{4} \times \frac{3}{2} = \frac{3}{8}$. In practice,

Figure 9.17 Liping Ma's Problem

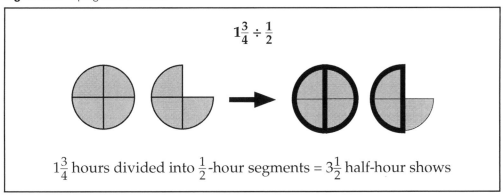

$1\frac{3}{4} \div \frac{1}{2}$

$1\frac{3}{4}$ hours divided into $\frac{1}{2}$-hour segments = $3\frac{1}{2}$ half-hour shows

this has sometimes meant telling students, "Don't ask why. Just invert and multiply!" The algorithm works, but explaining why is abstract and difficult.

The alternative to teaching the invert-and-multiply algorithm is to teach students a division algorithm based on finding common denominators. This algorithm is not commonly used, but it has the advantage of being much easier to model and explain. To teach this algorithm, it is helpful to build on students' existing knowledge of division with whole numbers. For example, students might first be asked to solve the following problem that involves division of whole numbers:

> I want to make cookies. I have 8 cups of flour. My recipe calls for 3 cups of flour for each batch of cookies. How many batches of cookies can I make?

This is a measurement division problem. We have 8 cups of flour, and we need to divide them into groups of 3. The question is, "How many groups of 3 can we make from 8 cups?" The equation is written as follows: $8 \div 3 = ?$

Figure 9.18 shows 8 cups divided into groups of 3. We can make 2 groups of 3 cups, with 2 cups left over. These 2 cups provide ⅔ of the amount needed for the next batch of cookies. Therefore, from 8 cups of flour we can make exactly 2⅔ batches of cookies. The completed equation is $8 \div 3 = 2⅔$. Once students can successfully solve this problem, they can apply their knowledge to the next problem, which is similar except that it involves dividing by a fraction rather than a whole number:

> I want to make cookies. I have 2 cups of sugar. My recipe calls for ¾ cup of sugar for each batch of cookies. How many batches of cookies can I make?

Like the previous example, this is a measurement division problem. We have 2 cups of sugar, and we need to divide them into groups of ¾. The question

Figure 9.18 Review: Modeling Division of Whole Numbers

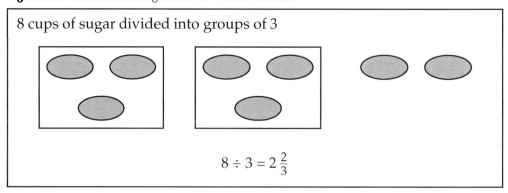

8 cups of sugar divided into groups of 3

$$8 \div 3 = 2\frac{2}{3}$$

is, "How many groups of ¾ can we make out of 2 cups?" We write the equation as follows: 2 ÷ ¾ = ?

When modeling the common denominator algorithm to divide fractions, the following skill steps are useful:

1. Write the equation.
2. Represent the dividend and divisor.
3. Show the models with common denominators.
4. Rewrite the equation using common denominators.
5. Solve.

Using these steps to solve the cookie problem above, we would first represent the dividend (2 cups of sugar) and the divisor (¾ cup of sugar needed for each batch of cookies). See Figure 9.19.

Next, we show both numbers using common denominators. In this example, one of the cups is divided into fourths, so we need to divide all the cups into fourths. When we do that, the two whole cups of sugar become ⁸⁄₄. The illustration of the ¾ cup that is needed for each batch of cookies does not change. The equation, rewritten using common denominators, becomes

$$\frac{8}{4} \div \frac{3}{4} =$$

Both fractions refer to fourths of cups. The question under consideration is *how many batches we can make*. We can find the answer by simply dividing the numerators: 8 ÷ 3 = 2⅔. If we have 2 cups of flour, we can make 2⅔ batches of cookies. Note that this is the same equation used in our previous example when we divided whole numbers. By connecting the division of fractions to students' previous understanding of whole numbers, we build more meaningful understanding. Although the division algorithm based on finding common denominators is seldom taught, it is a much easier algorithm to model and explain meaningfully. Van de Walle suggests it in his text, and

Figure 9.19 Modeling Division of Fractions

Problem: 3 cups of sugar divided into groups of $\frac{3}{4}$

1. Write the equation.

$$2 \div \frac{3}{4} =$$

2. Represent the dividend and divisor.

2 cups of sugar $\frac{3}{4}$ cup per batch of cookies

3. Show the models with common denominators.

2 cups of sugar $\frac{3}{4}$ cup per batch of cookies

4. Rewrite the equation using common denominators.

$$2 \div \frac{3}{4} = \frac{8}{4} \div \frac{3}{4}$$

5. Solve.

$$2 \div \frac{3}{4} = \frac{8}{4} \div \frac{3}{4}$$

We are solving for the number of batches, so

$$8 \div 3 = \frac{8}{3} = 2\frac{2}{3} \text{ batches of cookies}$$

we believe it can lead to greater understanding for those students who have struggled with more traditional approaches.

Just as students may have been confused by the answers they obtained when multiplying fractions, the results of dividing fractions may also surprise them. When we divide whole numbers, the quotient is smaller than the original amount (the dividend). For example, when we divide 8 cups of flour into 3 groups, the quotient is 2⅔, which is less than the 8 cups we

Figure 9.20 Resources for Teaching Fractions

Books
Van de Walle, J. A. (2004). *Elementary and Middle school Mathematics: Teaching Developmentally* (5th ed.). Boston: Pearson.   Witzel, B. S., & Riccomini, P. J. (2009). *Computation of Fractions: Math Interventions for Elementary and Middle Grades Students.* Upper Saddle River, NJ: Pearson.

YouTube Videos
Subtracting Fractions: • www.youtube.com/watch?feature=endscreen&v=fH9abI7jlog& NR=1   **Multiplying Fractions:**   • www.youtube.com/watch?feature=endscreen&v=NBFS3KW_aIY& NR=1   • www.youtube.com/watch?v=wGQw5-sAgi0   • www.youtube.com/watch?v=8p-XwgBfFmI   • www.youtube.com/watch?feature=endscreen&v=_X2nqjj_Q5E& NR=1   **More YouTube Videos**   • www.youtube.com/watch?feature=endscreen&v=fH9abI7jlog& NR=1   • Math-U-See fraction overlays, www.youtube.com/watch?v= MtEFZ8RfoFM

Sources for Fraction Overlays
Math Fun, http://mathedufun-store.stores.yahoo.net/index.html   Math-U-See, www.exodusbooks.com/details.aspx?id=10546

had initially. When we divide fractions, the opposite is true. In the fraction example, the solution is $2 \div \frac{3}{4} = 2\frac{2}{3}$. The quotient of $2\frac{2}{3}$ is a larger number than the two cups we had at the beginning of the problem. The use of concrete and pictorial models allows students to see that, when we divide the unit into fractional pieces, we create smaller groups. It takes more tiny groups to equal the whole, so our quotient will be larger than our original number. Providing time for students to explain and justify their solutions will help solidify this concept.

Although NCTM's standards advocate using representation to develop students' understanding in all areas of mathematics, examination of popular textbooks suggests that instruction in advanced fraction concepts relies

Figure 9.21 Modeling Decimals with DigiBlocks

Modeling the number 15.2

primarily on abstract words and symbols. Interventionists will therefore need to add concrete and visual representation to many of the commercially available materials used to teach higher-level fractions. Figure 9.20 provides a list of resources to help with this process.

Decimals

Most students have some previous experience with decimals because our monetary system uses decimal values. Some students may also have experience with baseball statistics, which use decimals to report batting averages and other player information. Since decimals use the base-ten number system to express fractional quantities, we can facilitate students' ability to understand decimals by connecting decimal instruction to their previous experiences with fractions and place value. The same manipulatives that we used to introduce fractions can also be used to represent decimal values. DigiBlocks, which were described in Chapter 7, include blocks specifically designed to represents tenths. These miniature blocks are one-tenth the size of the DigiBlocks unit block, so they provide a concrete model of the relative size of a tenth compared to a whole unit. In Figure 9.21 a student is modeling the number 15.2 with DigiBlocks.

Figure 9.22 Connecting Fractions and Decimals

$$\frac{1}{2} = 0.5$$

Students can also use the fraction bars that were described in Chapter 7 to create models of decimal tenths. In addition to the standard sets of fraction bars, versions are available that are labeled on one side as a fraction and on the other side show the decimal equivalent, so students have a concrete model that illustrates how the same amount can be represented as either a fraction or a decimal. See Figure 9.22. In addition, measurement models such as meter sticks and number lines can be used to help students understand decimal values.

Base-ten blocks are another excellent tool that can provide concrete representation of decimal values and also help students connect decimal notation to their previous experiences with place value. When we use base-ten blocks to represent whole numbers, a unit cube represents 1.0, a rod is worth 10, a flat is 100, and the big cubes represent 1000. We can use the same cubes to represent decimal numbers by changing which cube we designate as having a value of 1.0, as shown in Figure 9.23. To understand decimals, students must first recognize that a decimal point is a symbol used to show the location of the ones place, so they can therefore use the decimal point to identify the place value of all the digits in a number. Base-ten blocks allow students to create concrete models of decimal numbers, which makes the abstract concept of place value more comprehensible.

Graph paper enables students to create two-dimensional representations that are similar to the three-dimensional representations they created with base-ten blocks. If they mark off a 10 × 10 section of paper, the shape is similar to the 10 × 10 flat. If this square is labeled as the unit, or 1.0, then a column

Figure 9.23 Representing Decimals with Base-Ten Blocks

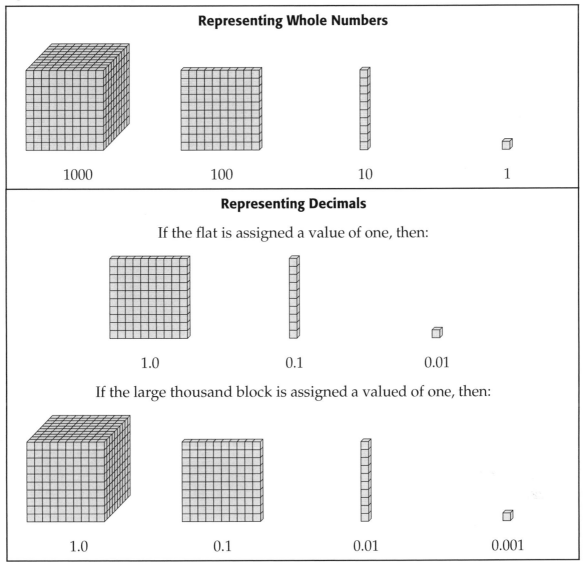

of 10 squares would represent 0.1 and each individual square would have a value of 0.01. See Figure 9.24.

Students can use graph paper drawings to demonstrate their understanding of decimal values and to make comparisons between decimals. For example, students working with abstract numbers sometimes focus on the face value of the digits in a decimal and forget to consider the digit's place value. This can lead them to mistakenly conclude that a number like 0.4 is less than 0.18 because 4 is less than 18. When students use concrete or visual models to represent the quantities, relative values are more easily perceived. Figure 9.25 provides an example of this comparison.

A similar model can be used to help students understand decimal equivalence. When we add zeroes to the right of a decimal, its value is unchanged.

Figure 9.24 Representing Decimals on Graph Paper

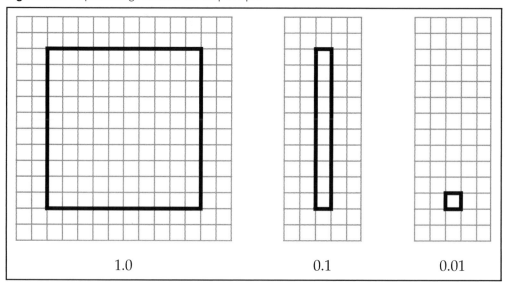

Figure 9.25 Comparing Decimals

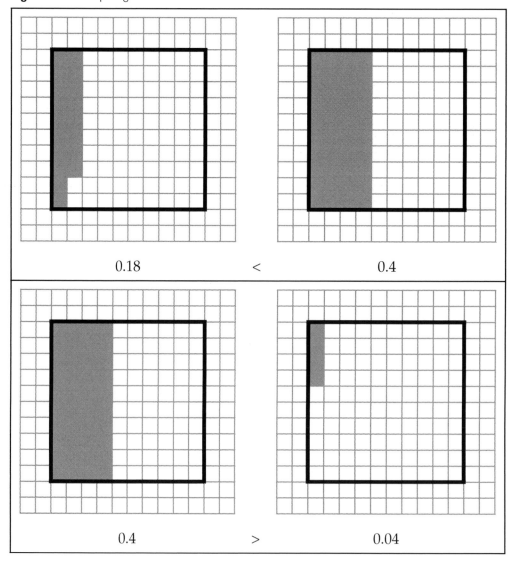

Figure 9.26 Modeling Decimal Equivalence

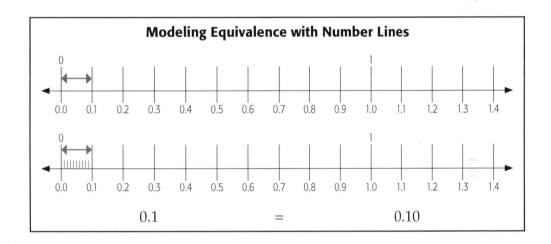

For example, 0.1 is equivalent to 0.10 and 0.100. Using graph paper, students can illustrate each of these decimal numbers and see that they cover the same area. See Figure 9.26.

The concept of decimal equivalence can also be modeled with number lines, and this is also shown in Figure 9.26.

When students progress to performing operations with decimals, these graph paper models continue to be useful. One of the most frequent errors students make with decimal computation is to ignore place value. For example, when asked to add quantities like 2 and .8, they may forget to line up the decimal points and so report the sum as 10 instead of 2.8. Modeling the problem with blocks or graph paper can clear up the confusion. See Figure 9.27.

Similarly, when students subtract decimals they may ignore place value, with the result that they may set up a problem like 4 − 1.25 as follows:

Figure 9.27 Adding Decimals

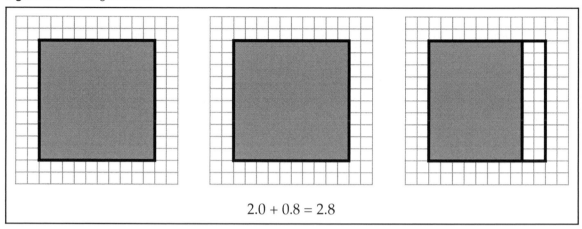

$$2.0 + 0.8 = 2.8$$

Figure 9.28 Modeling Multiplication with Overlays

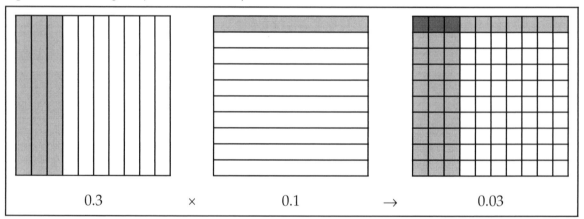

0.3   ×   0.1   →   0.03

$$\begin{array}{r} 1.25 \\ -4 \\ \hline \end{array}$$

Again, concrete or visual representations will clarify the problem and help students avoid such errors in the future.

To represent multiplication of decimals, students can use the same models they used when representing multiplication with fractions. For example, to multiply 0.1 × 0.3, we can use the same fraction overlays used to multiply fractions. We model 0.3 and 0.1, as shown in Figure 9.28. When we crisscross the overlays, the region where the two overlap is the product, 0.03. Asking students to think about and explain why this answer is expressed in hundredths can help them solidify decimal concepts.

When we multiply a quantity by a fraction, the resulting product is smaller than the original factor. The same is true when we multiply by a decimal. For example, if we eat ½ of 4 cookies, we have just 2 cookies left. If we express the factor ½ as a decimal, we will obtain the same result: .5 × 4 = 2.

Figure 9.29 Modeling Dividing by a Decimal

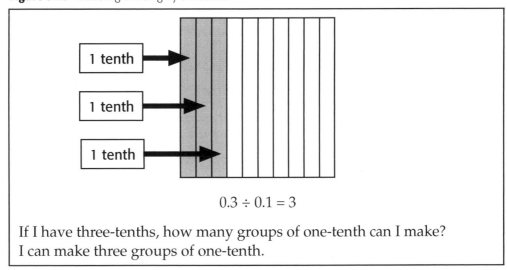

$$0.3 \div 0.1 = 3$$

If I have three-tenths, how many groups of one-tenth can I make?
I can make three groups of one-tenth.

In contrast, when we multiply by whole numbers greater than one, the product is always larger than our original amount. Physical and pictorial models like those provided in Figure 9.28 can help students understand these principles; such understanding is essential in order for students to learn to estimate answers and judge whether an answer makes sense.

Division by fractions and decimals also produces results that differ from the results obtained when performing operations with whole numbers. When we divide by a fraction or decimal, the resulting quotient is greater than the original amount, because we have divided the original quantity into multiple smaller pieces. Students may initially find these results puzzling because they are used to dividing by whole numbers, where the resulting quotient is smaller than the original amount. Creating a model helps students understand the effects of dividing by a decimal, as illustrated in Figure 9.29.

Decimals are typically introduced in upper elementary grades. Too often, operations with decimals are introduced as rote procedures. Although students may learn to execute the computations accurately, they will have trouble applying their knowledge in problem-solving situations if they do not understand the underlying principles. Because upper elementary math materials currently rely on abstract representation for most lessons, interventionists will frequently need to add concrete and visual representation activities in order to support students who are receiving supplementary support.

Percent

Percentages are commonly encountered in everyday situations. Meteorologists report the chance of storms as a percentage: "There is a 40 percent chance of rain today." Sales tax and income tax are calculated based on a

Figure 9.30 Fraction–Decimal–Percent Equivalents

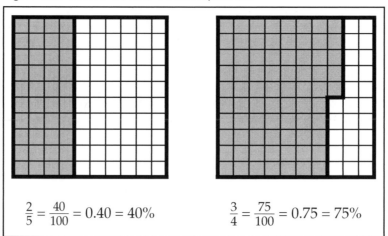

$$\frac{2}{5} = \frac{40}{100} = 0.40 = 40\%$$ $$\frac{3}{4} = \frac{75}{100} = 0.75 = 75\%$$

percentage of cost or income. The term "percent" derives from the Latin meaning "per hundred," and percent provides another way to represent fractional or decimal hundredths. We can therefore use the same models we introduced for fractions and decimals to represent percent. Activities that explicitly link fraction–decimal–percent equivalents can help students construct an understanding of percent. For example, we can shade a portion of a 100-square section of graph paper and express the quantity as a fraction, a decimal, and a percent, as shown in Figure 9.30.

Our representations should include quantities greater than 1 as well as models of quantities less than 1. These larger numbers, such as 150% or 200%, are most easily understood when modeled in relation to an illustration of 100%. See Figure 9.31.

Using a variety of types of representations to model a single concept deepens students' conceptual understanding. Therefore, we should not limit our representations of percent to using 100-square grids, but also include models that use pattern blocks, geoboards, meter sticks, number lines, and other concrete and visual images, just as we did when introducing fractions and decimals.

Summary

Rational numbers involve some of the most challenging content students encounter, yet most current instructional materials provide limited opportunities for students to experience concrete or visual representations of these difficult concepts. Representation allows students to organize information, describe mathematical relationships, and communicate mathematical ideas to others. The process of representing their ideas helps students construct meaning, as well as organize and clarify their thinking. Research indicates that understanding follows a developmental sequence, beginning at the

Figure 9.31 Using Comparison Illustrations to Model Percent

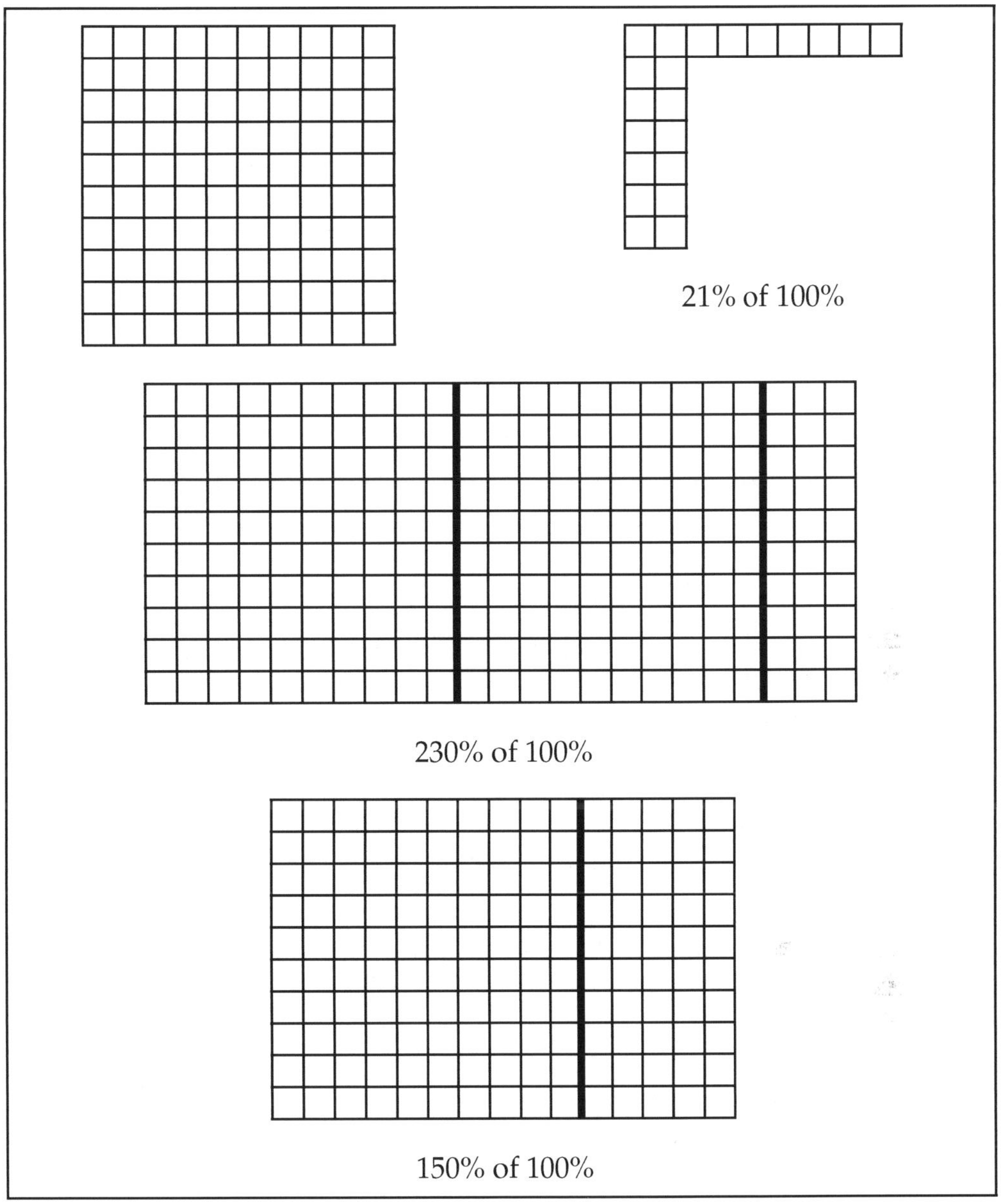

21% of 100%

230% of 100%

150% of 100%

concrete level when students physically manipulate concrete objects, then progressing to visual representation such as drawings, tallies, and graphs, and finally moving to abstract words and symbols. Linking various representations of the same mathematical concept or procedure deepens students' mathematical understanding. Providing explicit strategies and rigorously following the CRA sequence will allow all students to become proficient with rational numbers.

Chapter 10

Problem Solving

The ultimate goal of mathematics instruction is for students to use mathematical concepts and procedures to solve real problems. Mathematicians define problem solving as "engaging in a task for which the solution method is not known in advance" (NCTM, 2000, p. 52) or "finding a way out of a difficulty, a way around an obstacle, attaining an aim which is not immediately attainable" (Polya, 1965). Both the NCTM's Principles and Standards for Mathematics (2000) and the Common Core Standards emphasize problem solving at every grade level. However, international assessments show that American students struggle when asked to solve problems, and the task is especially difficult for students who have the greatest difficulty with mathematics (Geary, 2003; Hanich et al., 2001). The metacognitive competencies required for problem solving are precisely those skills that students with mathematical disabilities find difficult: (1) processing the language of the problem and understanding what is being asked, (2) identifying and organizing relevant information, (3) selecting a problem-solving strategy, (4) remembering and executing the strategy steps in the proper sequence, (5) performing necessary computations and accurately recording solutions, and finally (6) checking to make sure the computation was executed successfully and that the answer makes sense. For students who have difficulty with executive functioning, this is a daunting task.

Math programs designed for use as a core curriculum use a variety of different approaches to problem solving. Many use a variation of Polya's (1945) four-step process: (1) understand the problem; (2) devise a plan; (3) carry out the plan; (4) look back and reflect. These are critical steps for successful problem solving, but they do not provide enough guidance for many students. Students with language-processing problems, reading problems, or for whom English is a second language may not understand the problem. Students with deficits in executive functioning will have difficulty devising a plan or executing a plan and often struggle when asked to reflect on what they have done. They need more detailed support at each phase of this four-step process than is provided in most core programs. For example, to help students understand the problem and devise a plan, core materials often encourage the learner to paraphrase the story, visualize it, or represent it using two- or three-dimensional figures. These are excellent strategies, but struggling learners may need explicit instruction before they can use these strategies effectively. If they try to use pictures and diagrams, research shows that the representations they create are often of poor quality or focus on superficial features that do not reflect the problem's underlying semantic or problem structure (Montague & Applegate, 1993a, 1993b, Montague & Jitendra, 2006; Montague et al., 1991; van Garderen & Montague, 2003). In the regular classroom, students are taught to select from a menu of problem-solving strategies, including representing the problem by drawing a picture, acting it out, using a model, or making a table or chart (Van de Walle, 2004). All of these are useful strategies, but individuals with deficits in metacognitive functioning will be easily overwhelmed by the choices. Instead of evaluating the problem and selecting the most appropriate strategy, they often resort to a simple "guess and check" approach. They may look for superficial clues such as key words or assume that every problem presented can be solved using whatever operation has just been taught (Carpenter et al., 1999).

Although some students encounter extreme difficulties with problem solving, research studies suggest a promising approach to help these learners become proficient problem solvers. Multiple high-quality studies demonstrate that students struggling in mathematics can make significant progress if they are taught to recognize the common underlying structures found in word problems (Darch, Carnine, & Gersten, 1984; Fuchs et al., 2003a; Fuchs et al., 2003b; Fuchs, Fuchs, Prentice et al., 2004; Fuchs, Fuchs, Craddock et al., 2008; Fuchs, Seethaler et al., 2008; Jitendra et al., 1998; Xin, Jitendra, and Deatline-Buchman, 2005). Although advanced problems may combine multiple problem types, all can be broken down into a few basic underlying problem structures. The IES practice guide recommends:

> Interventions should include instruction on solving word problems that is based on common underlying structures. . . . When students are taught the underlying structure of a word problem, they not only have greater success in problem solving but can also gain insight into the deeper mathematical ideas in word problems. (Gersten et al., 2009, p. 26)

Problem Structures for Addition and Subtraction

A schema is "a general description of a group of problems that share a common underlying structure requiring similar solutions" (Xin & Jitendra, 2006). Teaching students to recognize schema is a conceptual approach to problem solving that helps students organize information and so reduces cognitive load and facilitates effective problem solving. U.S. mathematics textbooks typically contain three types of addition and subtraction word problems: *change*, *group*, and *compare* (Marshall, 1990; Marshall, Pribe, & Smith, 1987; Van de Walle, 2004). Teaching students to recognize the salient features of each type of problem helps them understand the problem and also facilitates problem solution.

Change problems describe a scenario in which the quantity of an item changes over time. For example, the problem might involve the number of children in the classroom. At the beginning of the story there are a given number of children in the room. Then more children arrive or some children leave, so the number of children at the end of the story is different from the number in the room at the beginning. In change problems, the story is always about the same type of item, but the quantity of that item changes over time because some items are added or subtracted. Here is a typical change problem:

> Melissa had 5 cookies. She ate 2 of them. How many cookies does she have now?

The whole story is about Melissa's cookies, but the quantity of cookies changes over time. Here is another example:

> Aaron collects baseball cards. He was given 5 new cards for his birthday. Now he has 123 cards. How many cards did Aaron have before his birthday?

This whole story is about Aaron's baseball cards, but the number of cards changes over time. Change problems can involve addition or subtraction and the information can be presented in any order, but the problems always describe a situation in which the quantity of the *same* item changes over time.

Group or *part/whole* problems involve parts that are combined to make a whole. Unlike change problems, group problems present a snapshot of the quantity of items or sets of items at a particular moment in time. A group problem might ask about the total number of students in the classroom, some of whom are boys and some of whom are girls. Together the two parts (boys and girls) form the whole (children in the classroom). Here is an example of a group or part/whole problem:

> Allison had 6 red M&M's and 5 yellow M&M's. How many M&M's did she have in all?

The whole, or superordinate set, is the total number of M&M's. The parts, or subordinate sets, are the red and yellow M&M's. There is no change over time; the problem asks about the quantity of parts and the whole at one particular moment. Here is another example of a group problem:

Figure 10.1 Examples of Part-Whole Relationships in Group Problems

Whole	Parts
students	boys, girls
pets	cats, dogs, birds
vegetables	corn, peas, broccoli
fruit	apples, bananas
M&M's	red M&M's, blue M&M's
rooms in a house	kitchen, bedroom, bathroom
toys	dolls, trucks, puzzles, balls

For Mother's Day, Shameka picked a bouquet of tulips, hyacinths, and daffodils for her mother. She picked 12 flowers. If 5 of the flowers were daffodils and 3 were hyacinths, how many were tulips?

This is a group problem because it describes parts (tulips, hyacinths, and daffodils) that combine to make a whole (flowers). The story describes the quantity of flowers at a given moment, not change over time. The critical concept for students to understand is that the whole is equal to the sum of its parts. Group problems always contain a whole that is separated into two or more parts. Examples of part-whole relationships are listed in Figure 10.1.

Compare problems compare two or more different items or sets of items using a common unit. The problem may ask students to identify which of the sets is greater or lesser, taller or shorter, faster or slower, bigger or smaller, or any other comparison question. For example, students might be given the ages of two children and asked who is older, or the weight of two objects and asked which is heavier, or the cost of three items and asked which costs the most. Unlike change problems that address the quantity of the same items over time, compare problems always involve comparing two or more *different* items or sets of items. For example:

Maria read 4 books. Her friend Jessica read 5 books. How many more books did Jessica read than Maria?

In this example the two items being compared are the quantity of books read by Maria and the quantity of books read by Jessica. Time is irrelevant. The focus of the story is the comparison between different sets using a common unit (the number of books read). Another example of a *compare* problem is the following:

Figure 10.2 Examples of Comparison Situations for Compare Problems

Which is more? Which is less?
Which is taller? Which is shorter?
Which is older? Which is younger?
Which is higher? Which is lower?
Which is bigger? Which is smaller?
Which is fatter? Which is thinner?
Which is longer? Which is shorter?
Which is faster? Which is slower?

James can lift a 100-pound weight. If his brother Marcus can lift 25 more pounds than James, how much weight can Marcus lift?

Two items are being compared: the amount of weight James can lift compared to the amount of weight Marcus can lift. Compare problems always involve a comparison between two or more different items or sets using a common unit of measure. Examples of comparison situations are listed in Figure 10.2.

Additional examples of the three types of addition and subtraction problems (change, group, and compare) are provided in Figure 10.3. During initial instruction, one type of problem is introduced at a time. Students practice recognizing examples and nonexamples of the problem type and then learn solution strategies for that type of problem before another problem structure is introduced.

Representing and Solving Addition and Subtraction Problems

In schema-based instruction, students use graphic organizers to record the facts of the problem and demonstrate the relationships among those facts. Since graphic organizers fall in the middle of the CRA continuum, at the representational level, they are not introduced when students first begin to work with story problems. Students' first experiences in problem solving should be at the concrete level, following the CRA continuum described in Chapter 6. Concrete experiences are essential for developing conceptual understanding. Once students are proficient with concrete representation, they can progress to representing problems using two-dimensional illustrations such as charts, drawings, diagrams, and graphic organizers like the ones used in schema-based instruction. Research shows that students benefit when given experiences with two-dimensional representation before tackling problems involving only words and numbers. Arranging the information on a graphic organizer is helpful because the student no longer needs to hold the facts and their relationships in working memory. This reduces the

Figure 10.3 Examples of Addition and Subtraction Word Problems

Change Problems:
- Thomas has 8 tropical fish in his tank. He bought 7 more. How many fish does he have now?
- Patrick had 4 CDs. His mother gave him 2 more CDs for his birthday. How many CDs does he have now?
- John has 6 CDs. Two of them were birthday presents from his mother. How many CDs did John have before his birthday?
- Amy had $5.00. She bought an ice cream cone for $2.29. How much money does she have left?
- I had 6 M&M's. I ate 3 of them. How many do I have left?
- I had some M&M's. I ate 3 of them. Now I have 2 left. How many did I start with?

Group Problems:
- Keri has 1 dog and 2 cats. How many pets does she have in all?
- There are 5 M&M's on the table. 3 of them are white. How many are not white?
- I have some beads on my bracelet. 3 of them are red. 4 of them are blue. How many beads do I have in all?
- Mother made 36 cupcakes. She put vanilla frosting on some of them, and chocolate frosting on the rest. There are 24 cupcakes with chocolate frosting. How many cupcakes have vanilla frosting?
- Sally and Marissa are selling Girl Scout cookies. Sally sold 23 boxes of cookies. Marissa sold 35 boxes of cookies. How many boxes of cookies did the two girls sell?
- Chris collects baseball cards. He has 100 cards in his collection. If 25 of his cards are of rookies, how many are not rookie cards?

Compare Problems:
- I have 6 M&M's. My friend only has 2. How many more M&M's do I have than my friend?
- My friend has 7 M&M's. I have 2 less than she has. How many M&M's do I have?
- Beth is 4 feet tall. She is 1 foot shorter than Whitney. How tall is Whitney?
- Kyle weighs 125 pounds. Andrea weighs 100 pounds. How much less does Andrea weigh?
- Michael is 14 years old. His sister Amanda is 8 years old. How much older is Michael than his sister Amanda?
- Michael is 14 years old. He is 6 years older than his sister Amanda. How old is Amanda?

cognitive load and allows the student to focus on analyzing and solving the problem (Polya, 1957). In addition, since graphic organizers involve nonlinguistic representation, students with language-processing problems or for whom English is a second language benefit because the amount of verbal explanation can be minimized.

Using graphic organizers is an evidence-based practice to support students who struggle academically. However, in most core programs students are exposed to a variety of two-dimensional representations, and students are often encouraged to create their own representation in order to ensure that their drawing is personally meaningful. As mentioned previously, students who struggle mathematically experience great difficulty when they attempt to design their own graphic representations, and research studies have found that the representations they create are often of poor quality or focus on superficial features that do not reflect the problem's underlying structure. In schema-based instruction, students are taught to use a specific type of diagram for each problem type. The schematic diagrams help students organize the information from any addition or subtraction problem into a recognizable pattern that facilitates problem solution. Instead of approaching each addition or subtraction problem as a new and unique challenge, students who have learned to recognize the underlying structural patterns need only learn to solve three types of addition and subtraction problems. This vastly simplifies the cognitive task.

Teaching students to recognize a problem's underlying structure is a conceptual teaching approach that enables students to successfully execute Polya's first step, "Understand the problem." It also provides guidance for the second step, "Devise a plan." Once students understand the pattern and can identify the problem type, they can use that information to develop a solution strategy. Each type of problem has specific solution strategies. For example, in a group problem, the whole is equal to the sum of its parts. Therefore, if the parts are given, the student can add them together to find the whole. If the whole and one part are given but another part is missing, subtracting the portion provided from the known whole will reveal the missing quantity. Research studies document that, when students are taught to identify problems types and effective solution strategies for each type of problem, achievement increases significantly (for example, see Fuchs, Fuchs, Craddock et al., 2008; Fuchs, Seethaler et al., 2008; Xin, Jitendra, and Deatline-Buchman, 2005).

Materials for teaching the three types of addition and subtraction problems use a variety of schematic diagrams. The two most prevalent versions are the model-drawing approach used in Singapore Math and the schematic diagrams used in schema-based instruction (SBI) programs. We will describe both types of diagrams, beginning with the model drawing used in Singapore Math. Singapore has scored at or near the top in every Trends in International Math and Science Study (TIMSS) comparison study since 1995. The use of model drawing for problem solving has received international attention. The graphic models help students transform the mathematical relationships provided in abstract words and numbers into schematic representations that visually demonstrate both the facts of the problem and the relationships among those facts. English is not the native language for students in Singapore, but it is the language used in the classroom. Model drawings help students develop conceptual understanding without the need for lengthy verbal explanations. Therefore, model drawing is an excellent approach to use with English Language Learners or with students who have language-processing problems.

Group Problems

Students' first experiences with model drawing should use very simple illustrations. In the Singapore model-drawing method, when students first transition from concrete representation to the use of more abstract drawings, they are taught to use a discrete method of modeling, which means they draw one small square to represent each object in a problem. At first, students model complete statements that provide all the facts and have no missing information. For example, the following statement might be presented:

Christopher has 5 toys. He has 3 cars and 2 trucks.

Students would draw three squares to represent the cars and two squares to represent the trucks. In early experiences with model drawing they would draw pictures of cars in three of the boxes and trucks in the other two boxes. As they gain proficiency, they would progress to labeling each square with a word ("cars" or "trucks") or an abbreviation (C or T). See Example #1 in Figure 10.4. However, once the student masters the concept of cardinality, he can progress from a discrete method where each object is represented by a single block to a continuous model where unit bars represent multiple objects. For the example above, a student using a continuous model would draw a unit bar to represent the total number of toys and label the bar "5 toys." Then he would divide the bar into two sections with a vertical line, and label one section "3 cars" or "3 C" and the other "2 trucks" or "2 T." Example #2 in Figure 10.4 shows a continuous model. This same type of model can be used to represent problems with multiple addends. For example, if Christopher had 3 cars, 2 trucks, and a ball, the unit bar would still represent the total number of toys (6), but it would be divided into 3 sections labeled "3 cars," "2 trucks," and "1 ball." This is illustrated in Example #3 in Figure 10.4.

Students need multiple experiences organizing complete information into the models before tackling problems with missing information. Once they understand the relationship between the parts and the whole in the diagram, the problem can be changed to "Christopher has 3 cars and 2 trucks. How many toys does he have?" Students can then use a question mark to represent the missing information in their drawing, as illustrated by Example #1 in Figure 10.5 (see p. 225).

Figure 10.4 Discrete and Continuous Model Drawings

Example #1: Discrete Model	Christopher has 5 toys. He has 3 cars and 2 trucks. | C | C | C | T | T |
Example #2: Continuous Model	Christopher has 5 toys. He has 3 cars and 2 trucks. | 3C | 2T |
Example #3: Continuous Model with Multiple Addends	Christopher has 6 toys. He has 3 cars, 2 trucks, and 1 ball. | 3C | 2T | 1B |

Schematic diagrams facilitate problem solution. The model visually demonstrates that the whole is equal to the sum of its parts. If the parts are given and the whole is missing, then the student adds the parts to obtain the whole. In the example above, Christopher has 3 cars and 2 trucks. A question mark represents the whole quantity. Through demonstration and discussion the child learns that, if the whole is missing, it can be found by adding the parts $(3 + 2 = 5)$. This rule will apply to every schematic drawing where the whole is unknown. See Example #2 in Figure 10.5 for another problem of this type.

If the whole is known but a part is missing, then the problem requires subtraction:

Christopher has 3 cars. He also has some trucks. He has 5 toys in all. How many trucks does he have?

See Example #3 in Figure 10.5. Through demonstrations and discussion the child learns that a missing part can be determined by subtracting the known part from the whole $(5 - 3 = 2)$. Whenever the whole is known and one piece is missing, it is a subtraction problem. These two rules enable a student to solve any group problem:

1. To find the whole when the parts are given, add.
2. To find a part when the whole is given, subtract.

Examples #4 and #5 illustrate additional group problems. If students create a unique drawing for each new problem they encounter, it is harder to see the pattern. Using a similar schematic drawing to represent every group problem helps students make connections between the problem type and the solution strategy.

Figure 10.5 Model Drawing for Group Problems

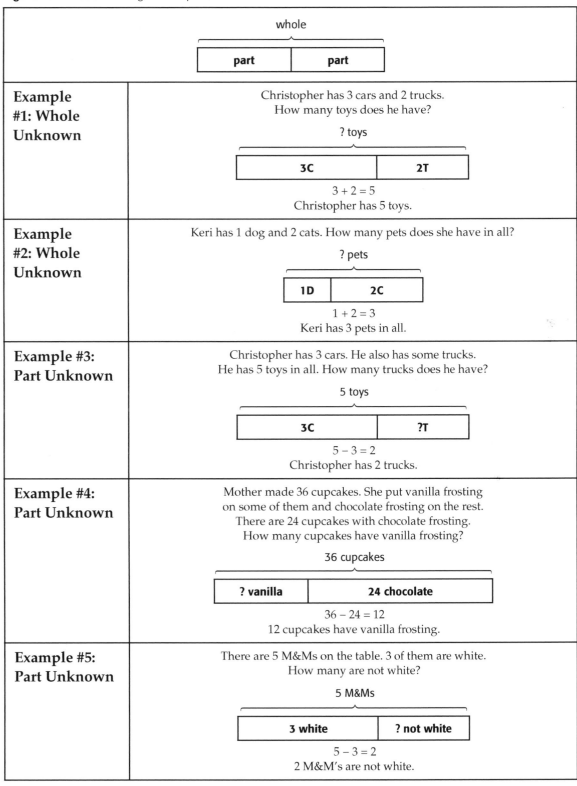

Change Problems

Singapore Math uses the same model to represent both group and change problems. Examples of the model drawings for group problems were provided in Figure 10.5. The same type of graphic organizer is used to represent a change problem. However, in a change problem, instead of labeling the whole, the student must determine which component represents the biggest quantity or total, and use this figure to label the whole unit bar. See Figure 10.6.

Sometimes the biggest quantity occurs at the beginning of the problem, as in Example #1:

Sarah had $59. She spent $45 on a pair of shoes. How much did she have left?

Sarah had the most money at the beginning of this problem, so $59 is the total quantity used for the whole unit bar. Sometimes the biggest quantity occurs at the end of the problem, as in this example illustrated in Example #2:

Samantha had 37 seashells. Her best friend gave her 8 more. How many seashells does she have now?

The total in this problem is the quantity of seashells at the end of the story, so that would be the amount represented by the whole unit bar. Students must read and understand the problem in order to determine which part of the story represents the biggest quantity. Figure 10.6 shows how these and other change problems would be represented using model drawing. The rules for solving change problems are the same rules students learned for solving group problems. If the whole or biggest number is missing, then add. If the whole or biggest number is provided, then subtract to find a missing part.

Compare Problems

Compare problems have a unique schematic representation, because they compare two or more *different* items or sets of items using a common unit of measure. For example:

Maria read 4 books. Her friend Jessica read 5 books. How many more books did Jessica read than Maria?

In Singapore model drawing, each item or set of items in a compare problem is illustrated using a separate unit bar. A bigger bar is used to represent the bigger quantity (in this example, the number of books Jessica read) and a smaller bar is drawn below it to represent the smaller quantity (in the example, the number of books Maria read). The difference between the length of the smaller bar and the length of the bigger bar represents

Figure 10.6 Model Drawing for Change Problems

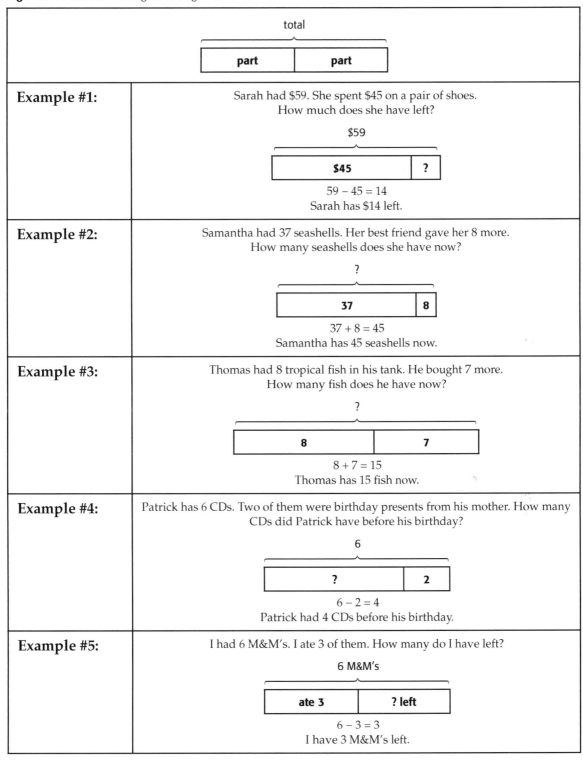

Figure 10.7 Model Drawing for Compare Problems

	Larger quantity	
	Smaller quantity	← **Difference** →
Example #1	Maria read 4 books. Her friend Jessica read 5 books. How many more books did Jessica read than Maria?	
	Jessica's books	5
	Maria's books	4 ◄?►
	5 – 4 = 1 Jessica read 1 more book than Maria.	
Example #2	Beth is 4 feet tall. She is 1 foot shorter than Whitney. How tall is Whitney?	
	Whitney's height	?
	Beth's height	4' ◄1'►
	4 + 1 = 5 Whitney is 5 feet tall.	
Example #3	Kyle weighs 125 pounds. Andrew weighs 100 pounds. How much less does Andrew weigh?	
	Kyle's weight	125 lbs
	Andrew's weight	100 lbs ◄?►
	125 – 100 + 25 Andrew weighs 25 pounds less than Kyle.	
Example #4	Michael is 14 years old. His sister Amanda is 8 years old. How much older is Michael than his sister Amanda?	
	Michael's age	14
	Amanda's age	8 ◄ ? ►
	14 – 8 = 6 Michael is 6 years older than his sister Amanda.	
Example #5	Michael is 14 years old. He is 6 years older than his sister Amanda. How old is Amanda?	
	Michael's age	14
	Amanda's age	? ◄ 6 ►
	14 – 6 = 8 Amanda is 8 years old.	

the difference between the two quantities (in this example represented by a question mark). Figure 10.7 shows model drawings for this and several other compare problems.

Compare problems are solved using a strategy similar to that used to solve group and change problems, except that instead of using the "whole" or "total" quantity, you use the "bigger" quantity. If the bigger quantity is given, you subtract. If the bigger quantity is not given, you add. Solution statements are included for each problem in Figure 10.7.

Asha Jitendra has conducted extensive research on using schema-based instruction (SBI) to solve mathematical word problems. The conceptual process in SBI is similar to the model-drawing approach we have described, but the graphic organizers look different. SBI introduces one schematic diagram for group problems, a different one for change problems, and a third graphic organizer for compare problems. Just as with model drawing, in SBI students first learn to identify the type of problem type (group, change, compare); then they learn to organize the information on the appropriate graphic organizer. They identify which portion of the drawing represents the total, whole, or biggest number and note whether or not that quantity is given. The rules for solving the problem are the same as in the previous discussion of model drawing. If the total is given, you subtract. If the total is not given, you add. Students are taught an explicit strategy to follow when solving these problems. Figure 10.8 shows Jitendra's explicit strategy for problem solving, which includes a mnemonic to help students remember the strategy.

Extending Addition and Subtraction

For each of the three types of addition and subtraction problems, we have described how to solve one-step problems requiring a single calculation. After students have mastered one-step problems, they can progress to solving two-step problems that require two separate calculations. For example, consider the following problem:

> Alex had $10. He bought a movie ticket for $7 and a soda for $2.50. How much money does he have left?

To solve this problem, the student must first determine the total amount of money Alex spent ($7 + $2.50 = $9.50), then subtract that amount from the money Alex had originally in order to determine how much he has left ($10 − $9.50 = $.50). The solution requires two separate model drawings, one to show how much money Alex spent, and a second model to show the amount of money left after he made his purchases. Two-step problems can involve any combination of problem types. They are systematically introduced after students have mastered one-step problems using the component model drawings.

Word problems that involve the addition and subtraction of decimals contain the same schematic structures as word problems that involve the addition and subtraction of whole numbers. Decimal word problems follow

Figure 10.8 FOPS: An Explicit Strategy for Problem-Solving

Step 1. **F**ind the problem type.
- Did I read and retell the story?
- Did I ask if it is a change problem? (Did I look for the beginning, change, and ending? Do they all describe the same thing?)

Step 2. **O**rganize the information in the problem using the diagram (change, group, or compare).
- Did I underline the label that describes the beginning, change, and ending and write the label in the diagram?
- Did I underline important information, circle numbers, and write numbers in the diagram?

Step 3. **P**lan to solve the problem.
- Do I add or subtract? (If the total or whole is given, subtract. If the total or whole is not given, add.)
- Did I write the math sentence?

Step 4. **S**olve the problem.
- Did I solve the math sentence?
- Did I write the complete answer?
- Did I check if the answer makes sense?

Source: Jitendra, A. K. (2007). *Solving math word problems: Teaching students with learning disabilities using schema-based instruction.* Austin, TX: Pro-Ed.

the same change, group, and compare patterns and are solved using the same solution strategies as other addition and subtraction problems. If students have mastered solving word problems with whole numbers, they can apply the same patterns to solve decimal word problems.

The graphic organizers used in model drawing or SBI are also useful when introducing algebra. By substituting a letter for the question mark used in the above examples, students can use the same graphic organizers to model algebraic expressions. For example, consider this problem:

Juanita brought 5 pencils to school. She loaned some of her pencils to friends and now she only has 2 pencils left. Write an algebraic equation to describe this problem.

This is a change problem that can be represented using the standard model drawing used for change problems, as illustrated in Figure 10.9. If students already know that they must subtract to find the missing part when the total is given, then they can easily create the algebraic equation $5 - 2 = x$ to solve this problem.

Figure 10.9 Representing Algebra

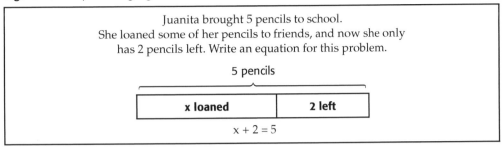

Juanita brought 5 pencils to school.
She loaned some of her pencils to friends, and now she only
has 2 pencils left. Write an equation for this problem.

5 pencils

x loaned	2 left

$x + 2 = 5$

The CRA continuum applies to algebra as it does to all other mathematical concepts. Students' initial experiences with algebra should be at the concrete level, acting out equations with their bodies or objects. When the graphic organizers are introduced, they should be explicitly paired with concrete experiences to help students make the connection between the concrete and graphic representations. Pairing numbers and words with these representations creates a smooth transition to algebra.

Problem Structures for Multiplication and Division

Equal Groups

Multiplication is repeated addition, and the model drawings clearly illustrate this relationship. In an addition group problem, the whole is equal to the sum of its parts; in multiplication, the whole is also equal to the sum of its parts. However, the parts in an addition problem represent addends of varying values (each of the numbers that will be added together). In a multiplication problem, the parts represent equal sets. Here is an example of an introductory multiplication problem:

A bicycle has 2 wheels. How many wheels are there on 4 bicycles?

To illustrate this problem, the student would draw a unit bar to represent the whole (i.e., the number of wheels on 4 bicycles). The unit bar would contain four boxes to represent the number of groups or sets (4 bicycles), with the number 2 written in each box to represent the 2 members of each set (the wheels on each bicycle). See the first example in Figure 10.10.

The drawing clearly shows that $2 + 2 + 2 + 2 = 4 \times 2 = 8$ wheels in all. The model drawing also demonstrates the relationship between multiplication and division, because the whole (8 wheels) is clearly divided into 4 sets of 2. The fact that division is repeated subtraction is also evident in the drawing.

The process for solving multiplication and division problems is similar to that for solving addition and subtraction problems. If the whole (total) is not given, multiply. If the whole (total) is given, divide. In the above example, the total number of wheels is not given, so the student would multiply to find the solution ($4 \times 2 = 8$).

Figure 10.10 Model Drawings for Multiplication & Division

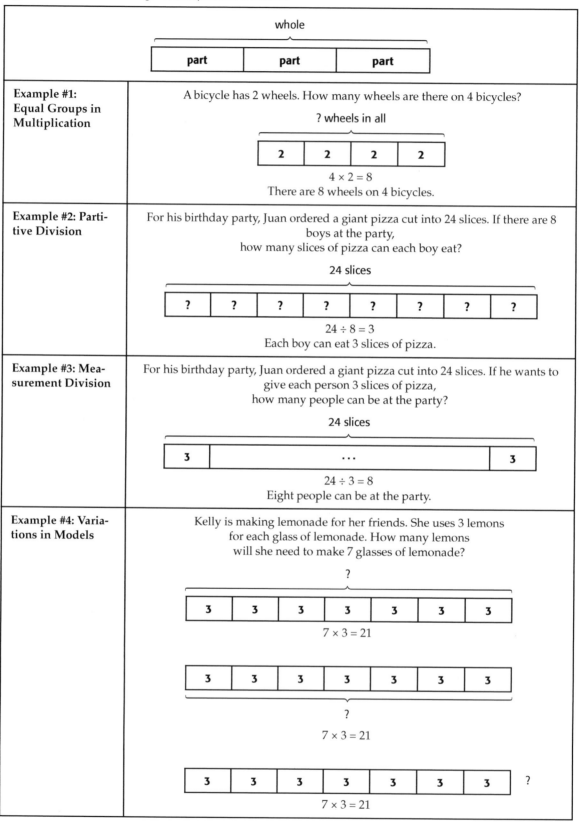

Here is an introductory division problem:

> For his birthday party, Juan ordered a giant pizza cut into 24 slices. If there are 8 boys at the party, how many slices of pizza can each boy eat?

To model this problem, the student would draw a unit bar to represent the 24 slices available, divided into 8 boxes to represent each of the 8 boys at the party. The number of slices each boy can eat is unknown, so a question mark would be placed in each box. The rule states, "If the whole (total) is given, divide." Since the total number of slices is given (24), the student would divide to find the number of items in each of the 8 sets. See the second example in Figure 10.10.

The pizza problem above is an example of partitive division. Both the total (24 slices of pizza) and the number of sets (8 boys) are provided, and the student must find the number of items in each set (number of slices each boy can eat). In measurement division problems, the opposite is true; the total and the number of items in each set are provided and the student must find the number of sets. For example, the partitive division example described above could be changed into the following measurement division problem:

> For his birthday party, Juan ordered a giant pizza cut into 24 slices. If he wants to give each person 3 slices of pizza, how many people can be at the party?

To model a measurement division problem, the student would first draw the unit bar to represent the total (24 slices of pizza). Since the number of sets (people at the party) is unknown, the student cannot simply use a box to represent each of the boys at the party as in the previous example. Instead, after drawing the unit bar the student would draw the first box at the left end of the unit bar and write 3 inside it to represent the 3 slices of pizza each person could eat. Then he would draw the last box at the end of the unit bar and write 3 inside it as well. Inserting three dots between the boxes indicates that the pattern continues between the first and final values. This is illustrated in the third problem in Figure 10.10. The problem can be read, "3 times some number equals 24" or "24 divided by some number equals 3." It is solved the same way as the partitive division problem. Since the total number of slices is given (24), the student would divide by the number of items in each set (3) to find the number of sets (8).

Variations exist among the different authors who describe the process of model drawing. Some books show problems modeled as described above, with the total value labeled with a bracket over the unit bar. Others use a similar model, but the bracket and total value are placed below the unit bar. Still others place the total value to the right of the unit bar. See Example #4 in Figure 10.10 for illustrations of these variations in model drawing. Each variation effectively models word problems, and each one would help students understand the underlying pattern. Since students who struggle mathematically often become confused when they encounter slight variations in presentation, we suggest selecting one model format and using it consistently in the core curriculum and in tiered interventions.

Multiplicative Comparison Problems

Multiplicative comparison problems are similar to the compare problems in addition and subtraction because they compare two people or things using a common unit such as weight or age. However, instead of the comparison words used in addition and subtraction such as "more than" or "less than," multiplicative comparison problems use words such as "3 times as many" to describe the relationship between the two sets. Here is an example of a multiplicative comparison problem:

> Mark ate 3 cookies. His brother David ate 4 times as many cookies as Mark. How many cookies did David eat?

To illustrate this problem, students must first identify the two units being compared. In this example, the units being compared are the number of cookies Mark ate and the number of cookies David ate. Students would draw a unit bar to represent the smaller unit (in this example, the number of cookies eaten by Mark) and label it (3), then draw a unit bar to represent the larger unit (the number of cookies eaten by David). Since David ate 4 times as many cookies as Mark, David's cookies will be represented by a larger unit bar containing four boxes, each labeled 3. See Example #1 in Figure 10.11. The model drawing clearly shows that David ate 4×3 cookies, or 12 cookies.

In model drawing the same schematic diagrams can be used to represent ratios. Consider the following problem illustrated in Example #2:

> For every $3 Scott earns, he saves $2. How much will he save if he earns $150?

This problem can be illustrated with two unit bars to represent the 2 items being compared (the amount of money Scott earns and amount he saves). Since he saves $2 for every $3 he earns, the amount saved contains 2 boxes and the amount earned contains 3 boxes. The problem states that the amount earned totals $150. Students have already learned that when the whole is given, they can divide by the number of sets to find the value of each individual set. When we divide 150 by 3 the answer is 50, so each box in the drawing is worth $50. The amount saved is shown as two boxes, so Scott saved $100.

In model drawing, multiplicative comparison problems are represented using similar graphics to those used for the compare problems students encountered in addition and subtraction. Using the graphic organizers helps students connect multiplication and division to the familiar pattern for solving addition and subtraction problems. When this connection is explicit and

Figure 10.11 Multiplicative Comparison Problems

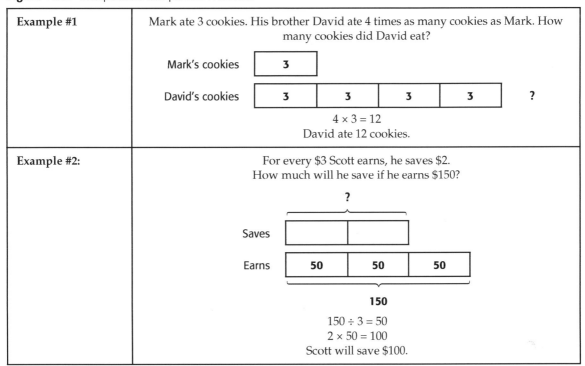

students can recognize the pattern, the cognitive load is reduced and students who have struggled in mathematics can experience increased success.

SBI uses different graphic organizers to represent the various types of multiplication problems contained in most math programs. Students are taught to represent *multiplicative compare* problems involving relationships with whole numbers and fractions using one type of schematic drawing. They are taught to use a different graphic organizer for *vary* problems involving ratios and proportions. These schematic models are more abstract than those used in model drawing, so they may be more difficult for students to master. However, the graphics are similar to the equations taught in most core programs and this may be a benefit. To solve multiplicative compare and vary problems, SBI teaches students to use cross multiplication. For students who have not yet mastered equivalent fractions, using cross multiplication would be a rote process rather than a meaningful solution strategy. Before introducing cross multiplication, instructors will need to make sure students are familiar with equivalent fractions, can represent them using fraction templates or other manipulatives described in Chapter 5, and can execute cross multiplication as a meaningful process.

Extending Multiplication and Division

The same schematic representations used for multiplication and division of whole numbers can be used to represent word problems involving decimal numbers. They are equally effective for representing algebra word problems. See Figure 10.12 for examples of these model drawings. For students with

Figure 10.12 Extending Multiplication & Division

Example #1: Multiplication with Decimals	Joshua is building a birdhouse. The plans say he needs 4 sections of wood that are each .4 meters long. How long a piece of wood should he buy? ? total length .4 .4 .4 .4 $4 \times .4 = 1.6$ Joshua needs to buy a piece of wood that is 1.6 meters long.
Example #2: Division with Decimals	A piece of rope was cut into 4 equal pieces. If the original rope was 11.2 meters long, how long is each piece? 11.2 meters ? ? ? ? $11.2 \div 4 = 2.8$ Each piece is 1.6 meters long.
Example #3: Multiplicative Comparison with Decimals	Chris jogged 1.3 k on Monday. He went 3 times as far on Tuesday. How far did Chris jog on Tuesday? 1.3k ? $3 \times 1.3 = 3.9$ Chris jogged 3.9 k on Tuesday.
Example #4: Algebra	Kevin's class has invited parents to watch the students present a skit they wrote. The teacher asks Kevin to set up 24 chairs for the parents in the back of the room. If he arranges the chairs in 3 rows, how many chairs should he put in each row? Write an equation for this problem. 24 ? ? ? $x = \dfrac{24}{3}$

deficits in working memory or metacognition, helping them make these connections can significantly increase achievement outcomes.

Scaffolding Support

Students who are at risk for failure in mathematics need scaffolded support. Academic scaffolding is similar to the scaffolding erected around buildings that are under construction; both are designed to support fragile structures and provide access to areas that would otherwise be inaccessible. The following is a list of evidence-based practices that can provide scaffolded support for students receiving tiered interventions:

♦ Follow the CRA continuum. Students' initial experiences with problem solving should be at the concrete level, using their bodies and concrete objects to act out story problems. Schematic diagrams can be introduced after students have developed conceptual understanding at the concrete level. Students who struggle with mathematics learn more easily when the connection between the concrete and more abstract representations is explicitly demonstrated.

♦ Teach students to recognize the underlying schematic structures in word problems, as described above. Most basal programs introduce a mixture of problem types without providing clear guidance to help students recognize the semantic structure of the problem. Research studies show the benefits of teaching one type of story problem at a time. When faced with story problems, students who have experienced difficulty in mathematics tend to jump to computation before they fully understand the problem. If they first encounter complete stories with no information missing, they can focus attention on the semantic structures rather than on racing to find a solution. Problems with missing information can be introduced after students learn to recognize the underlying semantic patterns. When instructors first introduce a problem type, all examples should illustrate that structure. Diverse story elements can be gradually introduced so that students learn to discriminate among types of problems.

♦ Explicitly teach students how to use schematic diagrams. These graphic organizers provide nonlinguistic representation of the facts in a problem and the relationships among those facts. Students need to be taught how to organize the information into these diagrams. Begin by demonstrating the relationship between students' concrete experiences and the graphic organizers. Students who struggle with problem solving may grab numbers from a problem in the exact order they appear in the story. Providing clear, consistent modeling followed by guided practice can ensure that students create models that reflect an accurate understanding of the story.

♦ Provide an explicit strategy. Problem solving is a complex task that requires multiple steps to be accurately executed in a particular sequence. Students with deficits in metacognitive reasoning tend to have difficulty remembering and executing steps in sequence, so they benefit when taught an explicit strategy that provides step-by-step guidance. Because these students often fail to notice whether their calculations are accurate or their answer makes sense, they need to be taught to evaluate their work; this should be included as one of the steps in the strategy. A checklist of strategy steps provides a useful visual prompt that can be systematically faded once students can successfully execute the strategy steps.

♦ Carefully sequence problems from simple to complex. The current trend in mathematics instruction is to present students with complex problems that have multiple entry points. Some students find this complexity so overwhelming that they are unable to focus on the salient features of the problem, discern patterns among problems, or generalize solution strategies from one example to the next. Students who find problem solving an uncomfortable challenge benefit when problems are carefully sequenced. They need to experience success with routine problems first, with nonroutine formats introduced after they have demonstrated proficiency with the simpler problems. Examples of the kinds of changes that should be systematically introduced include changing the order in which information is presented, adding unfamiliar vocabulary or complex sentence structure, introducing irrelevant information, presenting information with charts, graphs, diagrams, or other visual representations, and providing problems that require multistep solutions. These changes should be systematically and explicitly introduced, discussed, and practiced so students realize that superficial changes do not change the underlying story structure. Figure 10.13 shows a set of sample skill steps for teaching group problems in addition and subtraction.

♦ Follow the explicit instruction model. For each new concept or skill step, provide teacher-mediated instruction followed by guided practice followed by independent practice. Students who struggle with mathematics learn best when each step is explicitly taught. Once students demonstrate proficiency with one skill, they are ready to tackle the next skill in the sequence. While some students are able to progress rapidly from simple to more complex problems, others may need multiple experiences with each skill step before they are ready to move on to the next step in the sequence.

♦ Systematically fade support. Students who receive math interventions need scaffolded support to gain proficiency, but the goal of tiered support is for them to function successfully in the regular classroom. They need to learn to handle complex instruction with information introduced in bigger chunks. When instructors gradually fade support while continuing to monitor performance, students are able to transition more easily back into the regular instruction.

Selecting Appropriate Problem-Solving Materials

Research strongly supports providing instruction in problem solving that is based on underlying structures. However, most textbooks currently in use in the United States do not organize word problems by problem type, nor do they provide the type of systematic instruction in problem solving that has been found effective in research studies. Most teachers have not been trained in this method. Therefore, interventionists will need additional support,

Figure 10.13 Scaffolding Instruction: Sample Skill Steps for Group Problems

- Act out group problems.
- Use concrete objects to model group problems.
- Identify group problems (part + part = whole) presented with no information missing.
- Organize group problems on a graphic organizer.
- Solve group problems for missing whole (part + part = ?).
- Solve group problems for missing part (part + ? = whole) or (? + part = whole).
- Identify and ignore irrelevant information.
- Solve problems with multiple addends (e.g., part +part + part = whole).
- Solve group problems containing money.
- Solve group problems when information is presented in nonstandard formats, such as tables, charts, maps, graphs, drawings, and advertisements.
- Solve multistep problems.
- Solve problems containing complex vocabulary.
- Solve problems containing information presented in an unusual order.
- Solve problems with large numbers.

including both training and instructional materials, if they are to effectively implement this recommendation. While the number of available programs is small, materials do exist that teach students to recognize problem types and to use schematic drawings to help them organize information. Figure 10.14 provides links to a variety of instructional materials.

Summary

Teaching students to identify underlying structures in story problems is an evidence-based practice that has been shown to result in significant improvement in problem-solving ability among students who have traditionally struggled in mathematics. Schema-based instruction provides students with a few simple categories and solution strategies that vastly reduce the cognitive load typically associated with problem solving. Because the evidence supporting this approach to problem solving is so strong, the What Works Clearinghouse recommends it for all students receiving tiered interventions: "Teach students about the structures of various problem types, how to categorize problems based on structures, and how to determine appropriate solutions for each problem type" (Gersten et al., 2009, p. 27). Teaching students to recognize underlying structures is an evidence-based strategy that can enable all students to become proficient problem solvers.

Figure 10.14 Sources for Problem-Solving Materials

Go Solve: Using Graphic Organizers to Understand and Solve Word Problems
www.tomsnyder.com

Go Solve is a set of three software programs that use the graphic organizers taught in schema-based instruction to solve addition, subtraction, multiplication, and division word problems. The program contains clear explanations and appealing graphics, but it moves very quickly from one skill to another. Students who have struggled with word problems would need additional instruction and many more examples, but could benefit from this program as a supplemental material.

Pirate Math: Let's Find x
For ordering information, contact flora.murray@vanderbilt.edu

Pirate Math is a complete tutoring program for students experiencing difficulty with addition and subtraction word problems. It contains forty-eight scripted lessons for teaching students to identify and solve the three types of addition and subtraction problems, along with blackline masters for creating flash cards and other supplemental materials. The variable x is used to represent the unknown, so it creates a smooth transition to solving algebra word problems. The program does not teach students to use any form of graphic organizer or drawing to assist them when solving these problems.

Singapore Math
www.singaporemath.com

Singapore Math provides a complete core math curriculum for grades K–6. It includes teacher resources that focus on model drawing to solve word problems.

- *The Singapore Model Method for Learning Mathematics*
  This monograph provides an overview of the Singapore model method, explains its history, and discusses how it is used for teaching problem-solving in elementary and middle-school math.
- *Bar Modeling: A Problem-Solving Tool*
  This book is designed to teach educators how to use bar modeling as a problem-solving tool. It does not provide lessons for students, but does include extensive examples to help teachers develop their own expertise.

Figure 10.14 *(cont)* Sources for Problem-Solving Materials

- *Step-by-Step Model Drawing: Solving Problems the Singapore Way*
  This book is designed to teach teachers how to use model drawing for problem-solving. It includes an overview of the process and scripted lessons for solving problems involving addition, subtraction, multiplication, and division of whole numbers, fractions, decimals, ratio, rate, and introductory algebra. The book provides one model lesson and one or two additional examples for each type of problem.
- *Model Drawing for Challenging Word Problems: Finding Solutions the Singapore Way*
  This book provides scripted lessons for teaching students to solve problems involving whole numbers, fractions, decimals, rate/distance, ratio, percent, two unknowns, and algebra.

Singapore Math Practice

www.carsondellosa.com

This series of workbooks provides activities for a variety of Singapore Math strategies, including using model drawing to solve story problems. Two workbooks are available at each grade level from first though eighth grade. An answer key provides sample model drawings for each word problem.

Solving Math Word Problems: Teaching Students with Learning Disabilities Using Schema-Based Instruction

www.proedinc.com

Asha Jitendra's book includes an overview of schema-based instruction (SBI) and its research foundation, and scripted lessons for using SBI to solve the three types of addition and subtraction word problems as well as multiplicative compare and vary word problems. The book contains five lessons for each skill covered, plus additional review lessons. Jitendra provides the scripted lessons as models, but encourages instructors to use their own words when presenting the lessons. A CD of blackline masters is included.

Word Problems for Model Drawing Practice

www.crystalspringsbooks.com

This series of six workbooks provides practice problems for students in levels 1 to 6 of Singapore Math. Each book contains one word problem for each day of the school year. An answer key can be purchased separately.

Chapter 11

Conclusion: Using RtI to Improve Achievement in Mathematics

Almost two-thirds of American students are not achieving expectations for mathematics. Results of the 2011 National Assessment of Educational Progress (NAEP), often called the "nation's report card," show that fewer than four in every ten fourth- and eighth-grade students are proficient in mathematics (U.S. Dept. of Education, 2011). Clearly, change is needed if our students are to be mathematically competent and our nation is to remain globally competitive.

Response to Intervention is a comprehensive school improvement model designed to help all learners achieve academic proficiency. A growing body of research documents the effectiveness of using this model to increase achievement outcomes in mathematics (Fuchs, Fuchs, & Hollenbeck, 2007; Fuchs, Seethaler et al., 2008; VanDerHeyden & Burns, 2005; VanDerHeyden, Witt, & Gilbertson, 2007). The core elements of RtI include (1) providing high-quality instruction for all students to prevent mathematics difficulties, (2) using data to guide instructional decision making and evaluate instructional effectiveness, and (3) providing support for students who are at risk for academic failure by providing multiple levels of increasingly intense, targeted interventions. In this final chapter we will provide a brief review of how the RtI framework can improve mathematics achievement for all learners and provide suggestions for locating the evidence-based instructional materials and strategies necessary to successfully implement RtI.

Locating Materials to Provide High-Quality Instruction

The core curriculum is the instructional program provided in the general education classroom. In the most recent tests of national achievement, only 34 percent of U.S. eighth-grade students and 39 percent of fourth-grade students scored at or above the proficient level in mathematics (U.S. Dept. of Education, 2010). One reason our current approach is not achieving the desired outcomes may involve inadequacies in the textbooks and other instructional materials we are using. An investigation by the National

Mathematics Advisory Panel found that available instructional tools and textbooks often do a poor job of adhering to important instructional principles for teaching and learning mathematics (NMAP, 2008).

The RtI model calls for using evidence-based instruction with all students. To help educators locate effective practices and materials, the U.S. Department of Education and several other organizations review pertinent research studies and publish their findings. Figure 11.1 contains a list of Internet resources provided by these organizations. They are an excellent starting point for districts searching for textbooks and other materials.

While most publishers advertise that their products are supported by research and will lead to significant academic growth, existing research does not support most of these claims. For example, the U.S. Department of Education's What Works Clearinghouse (WWC) lists thirty-seven general education programs and two special education programs that have been reviewed as of this writing. Of these, only three were found to cause significant improvements in student achievement, based on a review of all available research studies. The limited number of available programs designated as evidence-based poses a serious challenge for schools that are attempting to adopt high-quality mathematics programs.

One reason so few programs have been identified as effective is that there is a serious lack of high-quality research in mathematics. While many studies of commercial programs are conducted, very few use the rigorous methodology necessary to convincingly demonstrate that the program leads to improved achievement outcomes for students. This does not mean that these programs are ineffective. It does mean that districts must often purchase instructional programs without the benefit of adequate data to inform their decisions. As materials are developed that align with the new Common Core Standards, it may become even more difficult to find data to inform textbook selection. Lag time is inevitable between program development and the accumulation of sufficient scientific research to effectively evaluate new materials.

Although high-quality research evaluating complete math programs is currently sparse, a large body of research has identified instructional design features that can produce significant improvements in achievement. In Chapter 3 we provided a list of the National Math Advisory Panel's recommendations describing evidence-based instructional design features that should be present in any program selected for core instruction. We have used these recommendations to create a list of questions to use when selecting instructional programs for use as a core curriculum (see Figure 11.2).

The features included in this checklist do not include all the factors a district might want to consider when selecting core materials, such as how the materials portray diversity, the availability of support materials for teachers, program costs, and so on. Our list focuses on instructional factors that have been shown to improve achievement outcomes through multiple,

Figure 11.1 Internet Resources for Locating Evidence-Based Materials

Best Evidence Encyclopedia

Center for Data-Driven Reform in Education (Johns Hopkins University)

www.bestevidence.org/

> The Best Evidence Encyclopedia (BEE) reviews educational programs and provides an overview of the program, evidence of effectiveness ratings, and contact information for obtaining the materials. The site includes programs for use in the core curriculum and programs that are useful for interventions.

Center on Instruction

RMC Research Corporation

www.centeroninstruction.org/

> The Center on Instruction is funded by the U.S. Department of Education. It develops and identifies free resources to help educators provide high-quality education. The site does not evaluate specific math programs, but does provide articles, modules, practice guides, and archived WebEx resources on progress monitoring and math interventions.

Do What Works

U.S. Department of Education

http://dww.ed.gov/

> The mission of this government website is to "translate research-based practices into practical tools to improve classroom instruction." The website provides clear, step-by-step guidance on how to use RtI to support learners who struggle with mathematics.

Instruction Tools Chart

National Center on Response to Intervention

www.rti4success.org/tools_charts/instruction.php

> The National Center on Response to Intervention is funded by the U.S. Department of Education's Office of Special Education Programs and works in conjunction with researchers from Vanderbilt University and the University of Kansas. The center's stated mission

rigorous scientific studies in regular education settings. Because the instruction provided in the core curriculum should be responsive to the needs of *all* students, materials selected for core instruction should also include instructional procedures that are critical to support students who are at risk. Districts that have a high percentage of students failing to meet benchmark expectations should place special emphasis on these additional characteristics when selecting materials for the core curriculum.

Figure 11.1 *(cont)* Internet Resources for Locating Evidence-Based Materials

is to "provide technical assistance to states and districts and build the capacity of states to assist districts in implementing proven models for RtI." The interactive tools chart provides a detailed description of programs to use in math and reading interventions, lists the study or studies used to evaluate each program, the quality of the study, the effect size, and costs and training required to implement the program.

Promising Practices Network
RAND Corporation
www.promisingpractices.net/programs.asp

The Promising Practices Network provides descriptions of programs that have been evaluated and proven to improve outcomes for children. All programs featured on the site have evidence of positive effects in rigorous scientific studies. This site provides information on social and emotional issues as well as educational programs for students in the core curriculum and those with special needs. To locate programs related to math outcomes, follow the link for "Cognitive Development/School Performance."

What Works Clearinghouse
U.S. Department of Education, Institute of Education Sciences
http://ies.ed.gov/ncee/wwc/

The What Works Clearinghouse website states that its mission is "to be a central and trusted source of scientific evidence for what works in education." The clearinghouse reviews and synthesizes the research with the goal of providing educators with "the information they need to make evidence-based decisions." The site contains a variety of resources in addition to program reviews, including the practice guide, *Assisting Students Struggling with Mathematics: Response to Intervention (RtI) for Elementary and Middle Schools* (Gersten et al., 2009), which is the basis of this book. To locate evidence-based materials, go to "Publications and Reviews," click on "Find What Works!" and follow the directions provided.

Using Data to Inform Instructional Decisions

A cornerstone of RtI is the use of data to evaluate instructional effectiveness and to guide instructional decisions. When schools follow an RtI model, all students are screened two or three times per year. Screening provides districts with a wealth of data to evaluate the effectiveness of their core curriculum. A program is generally considered effective if at least 80 percent of

Figure 11.2 Evaluating Core Curriculum Materials

Evidence-Based Practice	Questions to Ask
1. Emphasize critical concepts and benchmark skills. Less is more.	• How well does the content align with state standards? • Are benchmark skills emphasized at each grade level?
2. Teach critical foundations to mastery.	• Are students required to demonstrate proficiency in critical foundations before teachers introduce more advanced material? • Are benchmark skills taught to mastery?
3. Teachers use formative assessments to inform instruction.	• Do frequent formative assessments allow teachers to evaluate individual students' understanding? • Are suggestions provided that help teachers revise instruction based on the results of formative assessment?
4. Students should develop immediate recall of arithmetic facts.	• Are students given opportunities to develop fact fluency through frequent focused practice with a *limited* number of arithmetic facts? • Does the material explicitly teach strategies for fact retrieval?
5. Balance conceptual understanding, fluency, and problem-solving.	• Does the material devote equal amounts of instructional time to developing conceptual understanding, computational fluency, and problem-solving, or is one area emphasized to the exclusion of others?

6. Use a combination of teacher-centered and student-centered approaches—that is, include both inquiry-style and explicit instruction.	• Does the material include inquiry-based lessons? Characteristics of inquiry lessons:
	  ▪ Students work collaboratively to explore problems and develop solutions.
	  ▪ Students share their solutions and use a variety of reasoning and proof techniques to prove or disprove their ideas.

students consistently perform at benchmark on screening measures. Note that even when learners experience high-quality instruction, up to 20 percent of students may need additional support in order to be successful.

If a district finds that 80 percent or more of the students consistently perform well on screening measures, then it may be reasonable to assume that the curriculum is effective. If less than 80 percent of the students are meeting instructional benchmarks, then the district should evaluate the core program to ensure that the program being used is evidence-based, that it is

Figure 11.2 *(cont)* Evaluating Core Curriculum Materials

	• Does the material include explicit instruction? Characteristics of explicit instruction:
	  ▪ Students actively review prerequisite skills and concepts before encountering new information.
	  ▪ Teachers provide clear models, use an array of examples, and use a think-aloud technique to model their reasoning.
	  ▪ Teachers provide guided practice and check student understanding before assigning independent practice.

7. Incorporate the progressive use of concrete manipulatives, representational models, and abstract symbols at every grade level.	• Are concrete manipulatives used at every grade level to introduce new concepts? • Is visual representation used at every grade level to develop conceptual understanding? • Are students given opportunities to connect concrete and visual representations with the abstract symbols in order to make the abstract symbols and procedures meaningful?
8. Allow mathematically gifted students to accelerate their learning.	• Are assessments included that provide data to help teachers recognize when students are ready to accelerate their learning? • Are suggestions and resources provided to support students who are ready to progress through the material at an accelerated pace?
9. Include design features that support students who struggle with mathematics.	• Does the program include sufficient design features that have been identified as necessary for students at risk of academic failure?

being implemented with fidelity (i.e., delivered for a sufficient time and in the manner intended), and that adequate resources are available to support effective instruction. The core curriculum should match the characteristics of the learners being served. The same program may work well in one district and be less effective in another due to differences in learner characteristics. If a high percentage of students are not meeting benchmark expectations, a district might consider selecting core materials that place greater emphasis on the evidence-based instructional practices recommended for use with students at risk for academic failure.

Analyzing detailed assessment results, rather than just considering overall scores, can also yield valuable insights. It may be that students score well on most subtests, but a high percentage of students in multiple classrooms perform poorly in one particular area. Based on analysis of the data, a district might decide to devote more time to that topic or provide teachers with additional training to enable them to teach that particular content more effectively. The district might also choose to supplement the curriculum in that area. Comparing assessment results across years can also yield valuable insights, because the results obtained using a particular program can vary over time depending on the specific group of students being served. Since students' background knowledge and mastery of skills can vary from year to year, it is possible that the core math curriculum will adequately meet students' academic needs in some years, while in other years, supplementary instruction or materials should be added in order to help students achieve benchmark expectations. By using data to evaluate instructional effectiveness, districts can fine-tune their curriculum to meet student needs.

Providing Evidence-Based Interventions

Even when learners experience high-quality instruction, it is possible that up to 20 percent of students will need additional support in order to meet benchmark expectations. Careful screening enables educators to detect problems early and provide timely interventions. RtI uses a tiered service delivery model to efficiently distribute instructional resources in order to provide early intervention to the greatest possible number of students. Individuals who are not making adequate progress in the core curriculum receive supplemental support through multiple tiers that provide increasingly intense interventions. These interventions should be targeted to match student needs and should employ evidence-based intervention strategies. Students can move in either direction between tiers or, if appropriate, go directly to the most intensive intervention level. Student progress is monitored carefully throughout these interventions, and the data are used to adjust instruction to increase learning outcomes.

Tier 1 represents the general classroom where the core instructional curriculum is delivered. In Tier 1, instruction should be differentiated to provide additional support for learners identified through the universal screening as not having mastered the core curriculum objectives. If differentiating instruction is not sufficient to meet these students' needs, they can receive Tier 2 support. In Tier 2, interventions are provided to small groups of three to five students who share common instructional needs. Students receive about 120 minutes per week of mathematics intervention in addition to the math instruction provided in the regular classroom. Interventions should focus on the essential content needed by the students in the group, as identified through universal screening, ongoing progress monitoring, and diagnostic assessments, and should employ evidence-based instructional strategies. Students who continue to struggle can receive more intense interventions targeted to match their individual needs through Tier 3 support.

Most states follow a three-tier model. However, states vary in the number of tiers they use and the point at which they begin the special education referral process.

Most of this book has been devoted to describing evidence-based interventions that support students who have demonstrated difficulty in mathematics. The interventions we have described are based on the WWC practice guide, *Assisting Students Struggling with Mathematics: Response to Intervention (RtI) for Elementary and Middle Schools* (Gersten et al., 2009), which summarizes existing research and lists recommendations for providing evidence-based interventions. These recommendations describe features that should be included in all RtI programs. As more districts have begun to use an RtI model, publishers have advertised a variety of materials that they claim will provide effective interventions for students struggling with the core curriculum. Some of these materials do employ the evidence-based instructional strategies we have discussed, but many do not. Figure 11.1 provides links to Internet sites designed to help educators locate evidence-based materials. In addition to evaluating materials for use in the core curriculum, these sites include materials and instructional procedures designed for use in intensive interventions. Educators seeking evidence-based intervention materials are urged to consult these websites.

Because students differ in the supplemental support they require, intervention materials are not "one size fits all." The WWC practice guide recommends that interventions for students in grades K–5 focus intensely on in-depth treatment of whole numbers, while interventions for students in grades 4–8 focus on rational numbers and advanced whole number topics (Gersten et al., 2009). However, as the authors point out, older students who have not mastered whole numbers may need to spend additional time on prerequisite skills involving whole numbers before they are prepared to tackle rational numbers. Just because students are the same age does not mean they need the same intervention support. Some publishers advertise RtI materials for specific grade levels, such as "RtI for fifth grade" or "RtI for your third-grade intervention students." These generic materials ignore the importance of data-based decision making. Students receiving tiered support should be grouped so that they share similar instructional needs, and then materials can be selected to address those particular needs. This requires that districts first locate instructional materials founded on evidence-based practices and then use those materials selectively by matching materials to students' identified needs. Districts may need to purchase a variety of programs and materials to support the range of needs present in the students they serve.

Although the websites listed in Figure 11.1 include many excellent intervention materials, additional materials are needed to address the full range of content required in intervention settings. A large number of existing materials have not yet been studied rigorously enough to allow them to be labeled "evidence-based." To help districts locate additional materials for

Figure 11.3 Evaluating Intervention Materials Evidence-Based Practice Questions to Ask

1. Focus interventions on in-depth treatment of whole numbers and rational numbers.	• For students in grades K–5, does the material focus almost exclusively on whole numbers? • For students in grades 4-8, does the material focus on advanced topics with whole number arithmetic and in-depth coverage of rational numbers? • Can older students who are still struggling with whole numbers receive the in-depth focus they need?
2. Use explicit instruction.	• Do lessons have clear, specific objectives? • Does each student actively review any prerequisite skills and concepts before the lesson introduces new concepts? • Are concepts introduced in small steps? • Are students given step-by-step models of how to perform operations? • Are sample think-alouds provided? • Are there sufficient examples for modeling? • Do students demonstrate understanding in guided practice before independent practice is assigned? • Is practice scaffolded, with the interventionist gradually transferring responsibility to students? • Do students have opportunities to verbalize their problem-solving strategies? • Does the material include suggestions for corrective feedback that teachers can use to clarify student responses and reteach as necessary? • Is sufficient cumulative review provided?
3. Include instruction on solving word problems that is based on common underlying structures.	• Are students taught to recognize underlying structures in word problems? (For example, are students taught to categorize addition and subtraction problems as "group," "change," or "compare"?) • Are students taught a strategy to solve each type of problem?

use in interventions, we used the WWC recommendations to develop a list of questions that can guide material selection (see Figure 11.3).

This list of questions can help districts locate intervention materials that employ evidence-based practices. In previous chapters we have described each of these features in detail and explained the rationale for why they are important. Providing high-quality interventions can improve achievement outcomes for students who are struggling to attain mathematical proficiency.

Figure 11.3 *(cont)* Evaluating Intervention Materials Evidence-Based Practice Questions to Ask

	• Are students systematically taught to transfer known solution methods from familiar to unfamiliar problems?
4. Use concrete, visual, and abstract representations and explicitly link representations to develop understanding.	• Are concrete manipulatives used to introduce new concepts? • Are manipulatives systematically faded? • Are students taught to use visual representations such as number lines, arrays, and strip diagrams? • Are there enough examples of visual representations? • Do materials explicitly link concrete and visual representations with the standard symbolic representations?
5. Devote about ten minutes in each intervention session to developing immediate recall of arithmetic facts.	• Are students given daily opportunities to develop fact fluency through focused practice with a *limited* number of facts? • Can interventionists easily select specific facts or fact clusters to use in focused practice activities?
6. Use frequent progress monitoring.	• Are grade-appropriate general outcome measures included that allow interventionists to monitor the progress of at-risk students at least monthly? • Do assessments show whether students are learning from the intervention? • Are suggestions provided for revising instruction based on the results of progress monitoring?
7. Include motivational strategies in Tier 2 and Tier 3 interventions.	• Does the material include ideas for recognizing and rewarding task-oriented behavior, in addition to academic accomplishment? • Does the material help students chart their progress and set goals for improvement?

Summary

Academic performance assessments reveal that the majority of American students are not achieving benchmark expectations for mathematics (U.S. Dept. of Education, 2011). Response to Intervention is a comprehensive school improvement model designed to help all learners achieve academic proficiency. The core elements of RtI include (1) providing high-quality instruction to prevent mathematics difficulties, (2) using data to guide instructional decision making and evaluate instructional effectiveness, and (3) providing support for students who are at risk of academic failure through multiple levels of increasingly intense, targeted interventions. In this chapter we reviewed the components of high-quality instruction and described how to locate high-quality materials for use with all learners in the core curriculum, as well as materials to support learners who need additional interventions. We discussed using data both to evaluate instructional effectiveness and to identify students at risk of academic failure, and we reviewed how RtI's tiered service delivery model can efficiently distribute instructional resources to provide early intervention for the greatest possible number of students. Using RtI effectively has the potential to allow all American students to become proficient in mathematics.

Appendix A: Sample Lesson Plans

Sample Lesson Plan: The Penny
Lesson Objective: *Given a real penny or a picture of the front or back of a penny, identify the coin as a penny and state its value as 1 cent.*
Prerequisites & Background Knowledge: • Count up to 5 objects and tell the number of objects • Ability to read and write numeral 1
Materials & Equipment: • Large display coins • Bag of mixed coins for each pair of students • Whiteboard and erasable marker for each student • Worksheet
Lesson Plan Outline

Introduction: Engage & activate background knowledge	• Discuss:
	  ▪ Have you ever bought something at the store?
	  ▪ What did you buy?
	  ▪ Do you know how much it cost?
	  ▪ What do you need to have in order to buy things at the store? (money)
	• "Today we're going to learn about money so you will be able to use money to buy things at the store. What are some things you might like to buy at the store?"
	• "First let's practice your counting skills."
	  ▪ Choral count.
	  ▪ Hold up 1 to 5 objects. Have students hold up corresponding number of fingers. Repeat several times.
	  ▪ Have students write the numeral 1 at their desk. Monitor their work.

Lesson Presentation: Instructional input & modeling	• Show a penny and ask what they know about it. If students cannot name it, tell them "This is a penny." Show back and front; discuss attributes. • "This penny is worth 1 cent. How much is it worth?"

	• "Here's how we write 1¢. I write a 1, then a c, and then draw a line through the ¢ like this. • On your whiteboard, everyone write 1¢." Monitor accuracy and reteach if necessary.
Guided Practice: Check for understanding	• Show other coins for discrimination. Ask: "Is this a penny? How do you know? What's different? Is this one worth one cent?" • Signaled responses: Hold up various coins. Students respond by writing 1¢ if it is a penny and holding up a blank whiteboard if it is not a penny. Continue until students are fluent. • Give each pair of students a bag of coins. Have them find the pennies in their bag. Trade with another pair and repeat. Continue until fluent.
Independent Practice	Worksheet: Color or circle the pennies on the worksheet. Write 1¢ next to each penny.
Closure	• "Today we learned about this coin. Whisper to your neighbor what it is called." • "Everyone, what coin is this?" • "Whisper to your neighbor how much this penny is worth." • "Everyone together, how much is a penny worth?" • "Tomorrow we'll practice using pennies to buy things."

Sample Lesson Plan: Skip Counting

Lesson Objective: *Skip count by 2s from 2 to 20.*

Prerequisites & Background Knowledge:
- Count to 20 by ones
- Count up to 20 objects and tell the number of objects
- Write numbers to 20

Materials & Equipment:
- Number line and objects for demonstration counting
- White board and erasable marker for each student
- Baggie containing even number of objects for each pair of students
- Post-It notes

Lesson Plan Outline	

Introduction: Engage & activate background knowledge	• Review counting by ones:
	  ▪ Have students choral count to 20.
	  ▪ Students write numerals 1–20 on individual white boards. (Repeat until students are fluent.)
	  ▪ Display 1–20 objects; students write corresponding numeral on their white boards. (Repeat until students are fluent.)
	• Introduce the book *Two Ways to Count to Ten* by Ruby Dee.
	  ▪ Preview: Examine cover and title and ask students what they think the book will be about.
	  ▪ Point to animals shown on cover and elicit students' previous knowledge of these animals.
	• Read aloud, pausing to discuss student reactions.
	• Ask students:
	  ▪ "How did the antelope win?"
	  ▪ "Did you notice anything unusual about the way the antelope counted?"
	• "Today we're going to learn to count like the antelope. It's called *skip counting.*"
	• Language: Elicit other meanings of the word "skip" and compare to the use of the word in math.

Lesson Presentation: Instructional input & modeling	• Have 10 students come to front of room and count off by ones. • Model counting them by 2s (whisper odd numbers; say even numbers loudly). • Repeat. Have students join in counting by 2s.

	<ul><li>Repeat, but this time direct students to only say the even numbers and "think" the odd numbers in their heads.</li><li>Discuss: "Did we just count the way the antelope counted?"</li><li>Skip count objects:<ul><li>Lay out 10 objects. Model counting objects by 2s (whisper odd numbers; say even numbers loudly).</li><li>Repeat. Have students join in.</li><li>Repeat, but this time direct students to "think" the odd numbers and say the even numbers out loud.</li><li>Repeat. Have one student write corresponding numerals on board as we count.</li><li>Repeat. Students write numerals on individual whiteboards as we count.</li><li>Lay out 20 objects. Repeat above.</li></ul></li><li>Relate to number line.<ul><li>Demonstrate skip counting to 20 on number line.</li><li>Repeat. Have students join in.</li></ul></li></ul>
Guided Practice: Check for understanding	<ul><li>Individual white boards: "On your whiteboard, write the numbers to show how to skip count by 2s to 20. When you're done, hold them up."</li><li>Continue until students are fluent.</li><li>Choral count by 2s to 20.</li><li>Ask students:<ul><li>"What does it mean to skip count by 2s?"</li><li>"How do you know which numbers to skip?"</li></ul></li><li>Counting objects by 2s:<ul><li>Pair up.</li><li>Give each pair a baggie containing an even number of objects, and blank Post-It notes. In pairs, count the objects in their baggies and write the total.</li><li>"Square": Students trade with another pair and check each other's work. When both pairs agree on the answer, trade baggies (without answers) with another group and start over.</li><li>Monitor responses. Ask students to explain and justify their answers.</li><li>Continue until students are fluent.</li></ul></li></ul>

Independent Practice	Direct students to write the numbers to show how to skip count by 2s to 20 and draw a picture that illustrates their written numbers in their math journals.
Closure	Summary (elicit student responses): • "Today we learned to count by 2s. Whisper to your partner what that means." Call on individual students to share answers. • Students choral count by 2s. • Ask, "When could you use this? Share your idea with your partner." Call on individual students to share answers. Preview: "Tomorrow we will play a game to practice skip counting."

Explicit Instruction Lesson Plan Form
Lesson Objective:
Prerequisites & Background Knowledge:
Materials & Equipment:
Lesson Plan Outline

Introduction: Engage & activate background knowledge	
Lesson Presentation: Instructional input & modeling	
Guided Practice: Check for understanding	
Independent Practice	
Closure	

Appendix B: Games to Practice Basic Facts

Board Games to Practice +1 and +2 Facts

Give students a game board similar to the one shown below and one die labeled "1, 2, 3, 4, 5, 6" or "4, 5, 6, 7, 8, 9." To start the game, players take turns rolling the die, and the player who rolls the highest number will go first. That player rolls the die, adds one to the number rolled, and states the complete number fact. For example, if the player rolls a seven, he says, "Seven plus one is eight." He then advances his game piece eight spaces on the board. Players take turns rolling the die, adding one to the number rolled, stating the "plus one" math fact, and advancing their game piece that many spaces. Special directions can be written on some spaces, such as "Lose a turn" or "Move ahead 3 spaces," to make the game more exciting. The first player to move his game piece all around the board is the winner.

When the class is working on "plus two," the game is played as described except that players add two to the number rolled. To practice both strategies at once, students can be given two dice. The first die is labeled "1, 2, 3, 4, 5, 6" or "4, 5, 6, 7, 8, 9," just as described above. The six sides of the second die are labeled "+1, +1, +2, +2, one more, two more." Students roll both dice together, then follow the directions on the dice by adding one or two more to the number indicated on the first die, moving their game pieces accordingly. The game could be adapted to practice other facts by changing the numbers written on the second die.

Egg Carton Games to Practice +1 and +2 Facts

Using an empty egg carton and a magic marker, write a 1-digit number in each egg cup as shown below. A cardboard ramp may be taped to the front of the egg carton if desired. Give one egg carton and a small ball to each group of students. The students take turns rolling the ball up the ramp into one of the egg cups, then adding one to the number written in the cup where their ball landed and stating the complete number fact. For example, if a player rolls the ball into a cup labeled "8," she says, "Eight plus one is nine." The player who obtains the highest score for that round gets a point. If two players obtain the same high score, they each get one point for that round. The player with the highest point total after ten rounds (or when time is up) wins the game. To practice "plus two" facts, students add two to the number written in the cup where their ball landed.

Instead of rolling a ball up a ramp into the egg cups, students can also stand and drop a ball or paper clip into the egg carton. For a less noisy and exciting game, students can put a paper clip in the egg carton, close the lid, and shake. Their score is the number written in the cup where their paper clip lands, plus one or two, depending on the rules being used. The game can be adapted to practice other facts by changing the amount added to the number in the egg cup where the ball or paper clip lands.

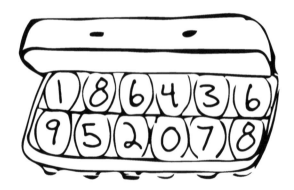

The Commutative Property: Fishy Facts

Young children enjoy "fishing" for math facts to practice the commutative property with addition facts. Create fishing poles from wooden or plastic dowels to which you attach a short length of string, with a small magnet tied to the end. Cut out paper fish shapes like the one shown below. Write an addition fact problem on each fish, attach a metal paper clip where the fish's mouth would be, and put all the fish in a container. Students take turns fishing. After catching a fish, the young fisherman reads the problem written on the fish, states the sum, and then uses the commutative property to state the related addition fact. For example, for the fish illustrated below the fisherman would say, "3 plus 4 is 7. So 4 plus 3 is also 7." Correctly identified fish may be kept, but if the facts are stated incorrectly, then the fish must be thrown back. This activity can be adapted to practice individual addition or subtraction facts, or, in addition to stating the related addition facts, students may also be asked to generate the related subtraction facts.

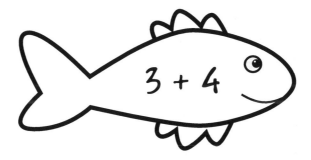

Games to Practice Adding Doubles

Double Trouble

Provide a pair of dice, a pencil, and a piece of paper per student. The object of the game is to see who can roll the most doubles in five minutes. When the teacher says, "Roll 'em," all students begin simultaneously rolling their dice. If a player rolls doubles, she writes the complete math fact on her paper. For example, if she rolls double fours, she writes 4 + 4 = 8 on her paper and then resumes rolling the dice. At the end of five minutes, the teacher calls, "Stop!" Players count the number of doubles each one rolled in the five minutes. The winner is the student who rolled the greatest number of doubles and accurately recorded each fact.

Egg Carton Doubles

This game is similar to the egg carton game, except it focuses on doubles instead of "plus one." Using an empty egg carton and a magic marker, write a 1-digit number in each egg cup. Tape a cardboard ramp on the front of the egg carton. Give one egg carton and a small ball to each group of students. Let the students take turns rolling the ball up the ramp into one of the egg cups, then doubling the number written in the cup where their ball landed and stating the complete number fact. For example, if the player rolls her ball into a cup labeled "8," she says, "8 plus 8 is 16." The player who obtains the highest score for that round gets a point. If two players obtain the same high score, they each get one point for that round. The player with the highest point total after ten rounds (or when time is up) wins the game.

Games to Practice Making Ten-Sums

Finding Ten-Sums

This game is played in pairs. Use four sets of ten-frame cards, or use a deck of playing cards with the face cards removed. The first player lays twelve cards on the table face up and then tries to find all the pairs of cards that total 10. He keeps each set of cards he finds. When the first player has exhausted all the possibilities he can find, play passes to the second player. That player deals more cards so there are again twelve cards on the table and then removes all the ten-sums she can find. Players take turns dealing cards and removing ten-sums until all the cards have been collected or no more combinations totaling ten can be found. The player who has collected the most cards is the winner.

Ten-Sums Fish

One deck of cards, with face cards removed, is needed for each group of two to four players. The goal is to be the first player to get rid of all the cards in your hand. The dealer shuffles the cards and gives seven cards to each player. The remaining cards are placed face down in the middle to form the draw pile. First, players look for all the pairs of cards in their own hand that total 10 and place those cards on the table. The player to the dealer's right selects a card in her hand and asks another player for a specific card that could be paired with the card in her own hand to make a ten pair. For example, if the first player has an 8 in her hand, she might ask the player to her left for a 2, which could be combined with her 8 to make 10. If the other player has the card requested, he must give it to the asker, and the recipient then places the newly formed pair on the table in front of her. She then gets another turn and may again ask any player for a card. If the person asked does not have the requested card, he says, "Go fish!" The asker must then draw the top card from the draw pile. If the card drawn is the card that she had requested, she gets another turn. If not, she keeps the card and the turn passes to the next player to the right. The game ends when one player is out of cards. If all the cards have been played before anyone goes out, then the winner is the person with the fewest cards in his or her hand at the end of the game.

Guess My Hand

This game is played in pairs using ten counters (snap cubes, chips, two-sided counters, etc.). Player #1 takes the ten counters, hides some in one hand, and shows his opponent the rest. Player #2 must figure out how many counters are hidden in Player #1's hand in order to make 10 in all. If she guesses correctly, she gets one point. Players take turns hiding counters and guessing. When time is up, the player with the most points wins the game.

Toss 'n' Cross

Students work together in pairs. Give each pair of students ten two-sided counters and a playing sheet listing all the possible combinations of two numbers that equal 10. Players take turns shaking the counters and tossing them onto the table, then writing one of the two ten-sum addition facts that can be created using the numbers tossed. For example, if a student's toss reveals 6 yellow counters and 4 red counters, he could record either 6 + 4 = 10 or 4 + 6 = 10. The team can then cross those facts off the list of possible combinations. The goal is to see how quickly they can roll all the possible combinations that equal 10.

Practicing Near-Tens: Make-Ten War

Play this game in groups of 2 to 4 players. Use ten-frame cards or a deck of playing cards with the face cards removed. To practice solving near-tens when one addend is 9, place one 9-card in the center of the table. To practice adding with eights, place one 8-card in the center. Place the remaining cards face down in the center of the table. To play, turn over the top card of the deck. The first player to correctly add the exposed card to the 8 or 9 card wins that card. When all of the cards have been played and counted, the student who collected the most cards is the winner.

Games to Practice Related Addition and Subtraction Facts

Triangle Fact Race

The purpose of this activity is for everyone in the group to practice generating related facts. Purchase or make triangle cards for each of the related fact families students need to master. One of the numbers in the fact family should be written on each point of the triangle, as shown below. Provide each student with a stack of triangle cards, or let students create their own stacks of cards. Each student should have the same number of triangle cards, but they do not need to be practicing the same fact families. Students will also need paper and pencil.

When the teacher says, "Go!" each student turns over the top card in his or her stack and writes the four related facts that can be created using the numbers on the triangle card. For example, for the card shown here, the student would list the four related facts: 6 + 7 = 13, 7 + 6 = 13, 13 − 6 = 7, 13 − 7 = 6. The object is to go through the stack and write as many facts as possible in the time allotted. When the teacher calls, "Time," all students put down their pencils. The winner is the student who has listed the greatest number of correct facts in the time allotted.

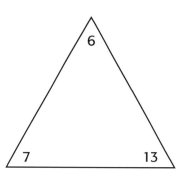

Subtraction Salute

This game is played in groups of three. It provides practice using missing addends to solve subtraction fact problems. Give students a deck of cards containing four sets of each of the numbers 0–9. One student is the general, and the other two are the soldiers. Deal half the deck to each soldier. The two soldiers each take one card off the top of their half of the deck and, without looking at their own cards, each salutes the general by holding the card up to their own forehead so that their opponent and the general can see it, but the soldier holding the card cannot see the number written on it. The general totals the two numbers and states the sum. Each of the two soldiers tries to be the first to identify the number on his or her own card. Whoever calls out the correct number first gets to keep both cards. When all the cards have been played, the soldier who has collected the most cards wins the round. Switch roles and play again, until everyone in the group has had a turn to be both a soldier and the general.

Games to Practice ×2 Facts

Egg Carton Roll

The egg carton game described to practice addition facts can be easily adapted to practice multiplication facts. Using an empty egg carton and a magic marker, write a 1-digit number in each egg cup. Tape a cardboard ramp on the front of the egg carton. Give one egg carton and a small ball to each group of students. Students take turns rolling the ball up the ramp into one of the egg cups, then multiplying the number written in the cup where their ball landed by whatever factor they need to practice. For example, if the player rolls her ball into a cup labeled "8," she says, "Two times eight is sixteen." The player who obtains the highest score for that round gets a point. If two players obtain the same high score, they each get one point for that round. The player with the highest point total after ten rounds (or when the teacher calls "time") wins the game. This game can be adapted to practice other times tables by simply changing the factor used to multiply the number in the cup where the ball lands.

Double Trouble

Provide a pair of dice, a pencil, and a piece of paper per student. The object of the game is to see who can roll the most doubles in five minutes. When the teacher says, "Roll 'em," all students begin simultaneously rolling their dice. If a player rolls doubles, she writes the complete math fact on her paper. For example, if a player rolls double fours, she writes $2 \times 4 = 8$ on her paper, then resumes rolling the dice. At the end of five minutes, the teacher calls, "Stop!" Players count the number of doubles each one rolled in the five minutes. The winner is the student who rolled the greatest number of doubles and accurately recorded each fact.

Games to Practice ×5 Facts

Tally Up!

This game is designed for two to four players to review the prerequisite skill of counting by fives. Provide one die for the group. Each player will need paper and pencil. Players take turns rolling the die and using tally marks to record the number rolled. When time is up, players skip-count by fives to see who has the most tallies.

Counting Nickels

This activity is designed for two to four players to practice counting by fives or multiplying ×5. Provide one die and a pile of pennies and nickels for the group. Each player will also need paper and pencil. Players take turns rolling the die and taking the number of pennies indicated on the die. Whenever a player accumulates five pennies, he exchanges them for a nickel. After eight rounds, players stop and calculate the value of their nickels, either by counting by fives to review skip-counting or multiplying ×5 to practice multiplication facts. The player with the highest total wins the round.

Star Points

This is a game for two to four players. Provide one pair of dice for the group, and paper and pencil for each student to record his or her own score. Players take turns rolling the dice to determine how many stars they earn on that turn. They record the number of points that are on that number of five-pointed stars. For example, if a player rolls a 6, she multiplies 5 points per star times 6 stars, for a total of 30 points for the round. The first player to earn 250 points wins the game. Use only one die to practice ×1 to ×6 facts. To practice a more limited set of facts, create a customized die using only those factors the students need to practice. For example, on the six sides of a blank die, write ×1 or ×2 on each side to practice just these two tables.

Practicing Division Facts: Connect Four

This game is designed for two players to each practice their own customized set of division facts while playing a game together. Each player needs a stack of ten or twenty flash cards containing multiple copies of two to four unfamiliar facts that the student needs to practice. Include several familiar facts for ongoing review and practice. Make sure that each student has at least one fact with an answer that uses each of the numbers 0–9. Give each player an erasable marker or a stack of counters or chips, using a different color for each player. Use a laminated 10 × 10 game board with one number from 0 to 9 written in each square in a random arrangement, as shown below (or give each student a blank 10 × 10 grid and let them write the numbers 0–9 in the squares in whatever arrangement they choose).

Players alternate turning over the top card in their stack and claiming a square on the game board that contains the answer to that fact. Players claim a square by using their colored marker to put an X on the square or by placing one of their colored chips on the square. If none of the unclaimed squares contains the needed quotient, then the player must skip that turn and the other player takes a turn.

The object of the game is to be the first player to claim four squares in a row, either horizontally, vertically, or diagonally. By strategically selecting boxes, players can block their opponent's efforts to connect four squares and increase their own chances of winning.

1	4	3	9	2	7	6	0	5	8
3	9	6	5	1	8	5	2	4	7
6	0	9	2	5	4	7	8	3	1
5	1	7	8	2	9	6	4	0	3
8	3	2	6	7	5	1	9	4	0
2	5	8	7	4	1	3	6	0	9
0	2	4	3	9	6	5	1	8	7
4	1	5	0	3	2	9	7	6	8
7	6	1	4	0	3	2	5	9	8
9	7	0	1	6	8	4	2	3	5

Games to Practice Related Multiplication and Division Facts

Two of the games described for practicing related addition and subtraction facts, Triangle Fact Race and Subtraction Salute, provide an excellent way to practice related multiplication and division facts. Play the games exactly as described previously, but substitute multiplication facts and their related division facts to develop proficiency with these fact families.

Card Games Easily Adapted to Differentiate Instruction

Games Involving Matching Pairs

(i.e., addition, subtraction, multiplication, or division fact on one card and the answer on the other card)

Make-a-Pair

Deck: 15–25 pairs of matching cards

Players: 2–3

Object: Be the first to run out of cards.

Deal: Shuffle the cards, and deal 8 cards to each player (6 cards if 3 people play). Turn the next card up to start the discard pile; then place the remaining cards face down to form the draw pile.

Play:

+ Players find any pairs in their hands, and place them face up on the table.
+ The player to the left of the dealer picks up the top card from the discard pile, or draws the top card from the draw pile. The player places any matched pairs face up on the table, then discards 1 card. Play then passes to the player to the left.
+ The game ends when someone runs out of cards.

Concentration (Memory)

Deck: 8, 10, or 12 pairs of matching cards

Players: 2–4

Object: Collect the most pairs of matching cards.

Deal: Shuffle the cards and place them face down in 4 rows of 4 cards, 4 rows of 5 cards, or 4 rows of 6 cards.

Play:

+ Players take turns. The player turns over 2 cards. If the cards match, the player takes them and his turn is finished. If the cards do not match, the player turns them back over in position, and the next player takes a turn.
+ Play continues until all the cards have been taken. The player with the most cards wins.

Old Maid/Old Dog

Deck: 24 pairs of cards and one card with a picture of a dog (or other picture of your choice), which is the Old Dog card.

Players: 2–4

Object: Avoid being left holding the Old Dog card when someone runs out of cards.

Deal: Shuffle the cards and deal them face down to the players. It is OK if the number of cards does not come out even.

Play:

- Players find any pairs in their hands and place them face up on the table.
- Beginning with the player to the left of the dealer, each player in turn offers his or her hand (face down) to the player on the left, who draws one card.
- Each time a player has a pair, it is placed face up on the table.
- The game ends when someone runs out of cards. The player left with the Old Dog card is the "Old Dog."

Snap

Deck: 12 sets of 4 matching/equivalent cards

Players: 2–4

Object: Collect all the cards. Players collect cards by being the first to identify pairs.

Deal: Shuffle the cards and deal them out among the players. Each player places her cards face down in a pile on the table.

Play:

- Each player in turn places a card face up in the center of the table on top of the last card played. If the card forms a pair with (is equivalent to) the last card played, the first player to shout SNAP! takes the entire center pile and places them face down under his pile.
- The player who collects all the cards wins.

Dominoes

Deck: Create 28 dominos. Each domino is a rectangular tile with a line down the center and a math fact or answer on each end. The items on a single domino should not match, but all the facts should have a matching answer written somewhere on one of the 28 dominoes. Math facts and answers may be used more than once, if desired.

Players: 2–4 students

Object: Be the first player to play all your dominoes.

Deal: Before the game begins, all dominoes are placed face down on the table and shuffled. Each player then takes 6 dominoes and arranges them so they cannot be seen by the other players.

Play:

- Play begins with the youngest player (or play can go in alphabetical order or reverse alphabetical order). The first player lays one domino right-side up on the table.
- Play progresses clockwise. The second player tries to place a domino on the table that matches one side of the domino already played. For example, if the first domino played contained $24 \div 8$ on one side and 5 on the other, the second player could use a domino containing the solution to $24 \div 8$ (i.e., 3) or a domino containing a problem whose answer is 5, such as $10 \div 2$ or $15 \div 3$. Dominoes are usually

joined lengthwise, end to end, so that a problem is matched with its corresponding answer. Dominoes that contain doubles (i.e., both halves of the tile are identical) are played crosswise, across the line of play. After a double is played, the next tile added is again played lengthwise. If a player does not have a domino that matches any of the open facts on the table, she picks a domino from the pile and skips that turn.

♦ Play continues clockwise around the table, with each player adding a tile or drawing a domino and skipping a turn.

♦ The winner is the first person to get rid of all his dominoes. If no one can go out, then the person with the fewest dominoes left is the winner.

Games Involving Creating Sets of Related Facts

Examples:

♦ Addition and subtraction related fact family: $1 + 2, 2 + 1, 3 - 1, 3 - 2$

♦ Multiplication and division related fact family: $2 \times 5, 5 \times 2, 10 \div 5, 10 \div 2$

♦ These games can also be played to practice other math concepts such as combinations that equal 10 (e.g., $6 + 4, 3 + 7, 8 + 2, 5 + 5$), or multiple representations of a given number (e.g., the numeral 4, 4 dots, 4 pictures, 4 tally marks), or sets of 4 equivalent fractions

Go Fish

Deck: 12 or 13 sets of 4 related facts

Players: 2–6

Object: Collect the most sets of 4 cards.

Deal: The dealer shuffles the cards and deals 5 cards to each player (7 for 2 players). The remaining cards are placed face down to form a draw pile.

Play:

♦ The player to the dealer's left starts. He selects a card in his hand and asks another player for any other card in that set. For example, if the object of the game is to collect sets of related multiplication and division facts, and the player holds a card labeled 2×5, he might say, "Michael, give me $10 \div 2$." If Michael has the card requested, he must hand it over. The recipient then gets another turn and may again ask any player for a card.

♦ If the person asked does not have the requested card, he says, "Go fish!" The asker must then draw the top card from the draw pile. If the card drawn is the card the player had requested, he gets another turn. If not, he keeps the card and the turn passes to the next player to the left.

♦ As soon as a player collects a set of 4 related facts, the four cards are placed in a pile on the table.

♦ The game continues until either someone has no cards left or the draw pile is empty. The winner is the player who has collected the most sets of related facts.

Rummy

Deck: 10–12 sets of 4 or 5 equivalent cards

Players: 2–4

Object: Players keep 6 cards in their hands at all times. The winner is the first player to form all 6 cards into *2 sets* of *3 related facts*.

Deal: Shuffle the cards, and deal 6 cards to each player. Turn the next card face up to start a discard pile, and then place the rest of the deck face down to form a draw pile.

Play:

♦ Play begins with the player to the dealer's right, and proceeds clockwise. On each turn, the player may either draw the top card from the draw pile or the top card from the discard pile, and then place one card on the discard pile.

♦ Play continues until someone has collected 2 sets of cards, with each set containing 3 related facts. That player then shouts "Rummy!" and reveals the cards.

Appendix C: Additional Resources for Teaching Basic Facts

Resources for Using Mnemonics to Master Basic Facts

Educational Memory Aids

www.memoryaids.com/math/html
Materials that use mnemonics to help students master basic facts.

Times Tales

www.TimesTales.com
Videos and other materials that use mnemonics to master the upper times tables.

City Creek Press

www.citycreek.com/
Offers several products for using mnemonics to master addition and multiplication facts.

Multiplication.Com

www.multiplication.com/resources/books
Books and flash cards that use mnemonics to master multiplication facts.

Songs and Raps for Math Facts

Addition and Subtraction Rap

www.rocknlearn.com/html/addition_subtraction_rap.htm
CDs, videos, and workbooks to practice addition and subtraction facts.

MathRap.com

www.mathrap.com/
Purchase CDs to practice addition and multiplication facts, with corresponding workbook.

Multiplication Hip Hop

http://edubasics.com/products/multiplication-hip-hop
This CD focuses on multiplication facts.

Multiplication Hip Hop for Kids

www.multiplicationhiphopforkids.com/samples-1.htm
Purchase CDs and video games to practice multiplication facts.

The Rappin' Mathematician

http://alexkajitani.com/rappin_mathematician.html
Purchase CDs and corresponding worksheets to practice multiplication
facts and other math skills.

Songs for Teaching

www.songsforteaching.com/math/additionsubtractionsongs.htm
This website provides numerous links to songs and raps that can be used
to practice a variety of math skills, including many that use the math
strategies we have described to help students master basic facts.

References

Akin-Little, K., Eckert, T., Lovett, B., & Little, S. (2004). Extrinsic reinforcement in the classroom: A best practice. *School Psychology Review, 23,* 344–362.

Alberto, P. A., & Troutman, A. C. (2012). *Applied behavior analysis for teachers* (9th ed.). Englewood Cliffs, NJ: Merrill.

Allsopp D. H., Kyger, M. M., Lovin, L., Gerretson, H., Carson, K. L., & Ray, S. (2008). Mathematics dynamic assessment: Informal assessment that responds to the needs of struggling learners in mathematics. *TEACHING Exceptional Children, 40*(3), 6–16.

Allsopp, D. H., McHatton, P. A., Ray, Sh. N. E., & Farmer, J. L. (2010). *Mathematics RTI: A problem-solving approach to creating an effective model.* Danvers, MA: LRP.

Archer, A. L. & Hughes, C. A. (2011). *Explicit instruction: Effective and efficient teaching.* New York: Guilford Press.

Aronson, J., Fried, C., & Good, C. (2002). Reducing the effects of stereotype threat on African American college students by shaping theories of intelligence. *Journal of Experimental Psychology, 38,* 113–125.

Ashlock, R. B. (2005). *Error patterns in computation: Using error patterns to improve instruction* (9th ed.). Upper Saddle River, NJ: Prentice Hall.

Axelrod, A. (1997). Pigs will be pigs. New York: Aladdin.

Baddeley, A. (1980). *Working memory.* New York: Oxford University Press.

Barrish, H. H., Saunders, M., & Wolf, M. M. (1969). Good behavior game: Effects of individual contingencies or group consequences on disruptive behavior in a classroom. *Journal of Applied Behavior Analysis, 2,* 119–124.

Batsche, G., Elliot, J., Graden, J. L., Grimes, J., Kovaleski, J. F., Prasse, D. et al. (2005). *Response to intervention: Policy considerations and implementation.* Alexandria, VA: Association of State Directors of Special Education.

Best Evidence Encyclopedia (BEE). (2009). *Effective programs for elementary mathematics: A best evidence synthesis educator's summary.* Author. Retrieved from http://www.bestevidence.org.

Blackwell, L., Trzesniewski, K., & Dweck, C. S. (2007). Implicit theories of intelligence predict achievement across an adolescent transition: A longitudinal study and an intervention. *Child Development, 78,* 246–263.

Bley, N. S., & Thornton, C. A. (2001). *Teaching mathematics to students with learning disabilities.* Austin, TX: Pro-Ed.

Bobis, J. (1996). Visualisation and the development of number sense with kindergarten children. In J. Mulligan & M. Muitchelmore, M. (Eds.),

Children's number learning: A research monograph of the mathematics education group of Australasia and the Australian Association of Mathematics Teachers. Adelaide: AAMT.

Brophy, J. (1981). Teacher praise: A functional analysis. *Review of Educational Research, 51*, 5–32.

Bruner, J. (1960). *The process of education.* Cambridge, MA: Harvard University Press.

Bryant, B. R., & Bryant, D. P. (2008). Introduction and special series: Mathematics and learning disabilities. *Learning Disability Quarterly, 31*(1), 3–10.

Bryant, B. R., Bryant, D. P., Kethley, C., Kim, S. A., Pool, C., & Seo, Y. (2008). Preventing mathematics difficulty in the primary grades: The critical features of instruction in textbooks as part of the equation. *Learning Disability Quarterly, 31*(1), 21–35.

Bryant, D. P., Kim, S. A., Hartman, P. H., & Bryant, B. R. (2006). Standards-based mathematics instruction and teaching middle school students with mathematical disabilities. In M. Montague & A. K. Jitendra (Eds.), *Teaching mathematics to middle school students with learning difficulties.* New York: Guilford Press.

Buschman, L. (2001). Using student interviews to guide classroom instruction. *Teaching Children Mathematics, 8*(4), 222–227.

Butler, F. M., Miller, S. P., Crehan, K., Babbitt, B., & Pierce, T. (2003). Fraction instruction for students with mathematics disabilities: Comparing two teaching sequences. *Learning Disabilities Research & Practice, 18*, 99–111.

Cameron, J., Bank, K., & Pierce, W. (2001). Pervasive negative effects of rewards on intrinsic motivation: The myth continues. *Behavior Analyst, 24*, 1–44.

Cameron, J., & Pierce, W. (1994). Reinforcement, rewards, and intrinsic motivation: A meta-analysis. *Review of Educational Research, 64*(3), 363–423.

Canter, L. & Canter, M. (2001). *Assertive discipline: Positive behavior management for today's classroom* (3rd ed.). Bloomington, IN: Solution Tree. Carnine, D. W., Silbert, J., Kame'enui, E. J., & Tarver, S. G. (2004). *Direct instruction reading* (3rd ed.). Upper Saddle River, NJ: Merrill/Prentice Hall.

Carpenter, S. L. & McKee-Higgins, E. (1996). Behavior management in inclusive classrooms. *Remedial & Special Education, (17)*4, 195–203.

Carpenter, T. P., Fennema, E., Franke, M. L., Levi, L., & Empson, S. B. (1999). *Children's mathematics: Cognitively guided instruction.* Portsmouth, NH: Heinemann.

Case, R. (1985). *Intellectual development.* Orlando, FL: Academic Press.

Case, R. (1998). A psychological model of number sense and its development. Paper presented at the annual meeting of the American Educational Research Association, San Diego.

Cathcart, W. G., Pothier, Y. M., Vance, J. H., & Bezuk, N. S. (2000). *Learning mathematics in elementary and middle schools.* Upper Saddle River, NJ: Merrill/Prentice-Hall.

Center on Instruction. (2008). *Mathematics instruction for students with learning disabilities or difficulty learning mathematics: A guide for teachers.* Retrieved from http://ww.centeroninstruction.org/.

Chance, P. (1992). The rewards of learning. *Phi Delta Kappan*, 200–207.

Cheng, L. (1998). Enhancing the communication skills of newly-arrived Asian American students. *ERIC/CUE Digest*, 136. New York: ERIC Clearinghouse on Urban Education. (ERIC Document Reproduction Service No. ED 420 726).

Cipani, E. (2008). *Classroom management for all teachers.* Upper Saddle River, NJ: Pearson.

Clements, D. H., & Sarama, J. (2007). Effects of a preschool mathematics curriculum: Summative research on the Building Blocks project. *Journal for Research in Mathematics Education, 38*, 136–163.

Cortiella, C. (2011). *A parent's guide to response-to-intervention.* National Center for Learning Disabilities. Retrieved 12/1/11 from www.ncld.org/images/stories/Publications/parentadvocacyguides/parents_guide_RTI_FINAL_101111-2.pdf.

Council for Exceptional Children. (2003). *What every special educator must know: Ethics, standards, and guidelines for special educators* (5th ed.). Upper Saddle River, NJ: Pearson.

Crespo, S., & Nicol, C. (2003). Learning to investigate students' mathematical thinking: The role of student interviews. *International Group for the Psychology of Mathematics Education, 2*, 261–268.

Curran, L. (1998). *Lessons for little ones: Mathematics cooperative learning lessons.* San Clemente, CA: Kagan Cooperative Learning.

Darch, C., Carnine, D., & Gersten, R. (1984). Explicit instruction in mathematics problem solving. *Journal of Educational Research, 77*(6), 351–359.

Deci, E. L. (1971). Effects of externally mediated rewards on intrinsic motivation. *Journal of Personality and Social Psychology, 22*, 113–120.

Deno, S. L., & Mirkin, P. K. (1977). *Data-based program modification: A manual.* Reston, VA: Council for Exceptional Children.

Downing, J. A. (1990). Contingency contracts: A step-by-step format. *Intervention in School and Clinic, 26*(2), 111–113.

Downing, J. A., Moran, M. R., Myles, B. S., & Ormsbee, C. K. (1991). Using reinforcement in the classroom. *Intervention in School and Clinic, 27*(2), 85–90.

Dweck, C. (2008). The perils and promises of praise. *Best of Educational Leadership 2007–2008, 65*(10), 34–39.

Epstein, M., Atkins, M., Cullinan, D., Kutash, K, & Weaver, R. (2008). *Reducing behavior problems in the elementary school classroom: A practice guide* (NCEE #2008-012). Washington, DC: National Center for Education Evaluation and Regional Assistance, Institute of Education Sciences,

U.S. Department of Education. Retrieved from http://ies.gov/ncee/wwc/practiceguides.

Fleischner, F. E., Garnett, K., & Shepherd, M. (1982). Proficiency in arithmetic basic fact computation by learning disabled and nondisabled children. *Focus on Learning Problems in Mathematics, 4*(2), 47–55.

Forbringer, L. (2007.) Using a mnemonic to develop effective incentive systems. *TEACHING Exceptional Children Plus, 4*(1), Article 6. Retrieved from http://journals.cec.sped.org/tecplus/vol4/iss1/art6.

Forbringer, L., & Fahsl, A. (2007). How one teacher used stations to differentiate instruction. *Illinois Mathematics Teacher, 58*(1), 31–38.

Forbringer, L., & Fahsl, A. (2009). Differentiating instruction to help students master basic facts. In *Mathematics for every student: Responding to diversity, grades pre-K–5.* Reston, VA: National Council of Teachers of Mathematics.

Fuchs, L. S., Compton, D. L., Fuchs, D., Paulsen, K., Bryant, J. D., & Hamlett, C. L. (2005). The prevention, identification, and cognitive determinants of math difficulty. *Journal of Educational Psychology, 97*(3), 493–513.

Fuchs, L. S., Fuchs, D., Craddock, C., Hollenbeck, K. N., & Hamlett, C. L. (2008). Effects of small-group tutoring with and without validated classroom instruction on at-risk students' math problem solving: Are two tiers of prevention better than one? *Journal of Educational Psychology, 100*(3), 491–509.

Fuchs, L. S., Fuchs, D., Finelli, R., Courey, S. J., & Hamlett, C. L. (2004). Expanding schema-based transfer instruction to help third graders solve real-life mathematical problems. *American Educational Research Journal, 4*(12), 419–445.

Fuchs, L. S., Fuchs, D., Hamlett, C. L., Walz, L., & Germann, G. (1993). Formative evaluation of academic progress: How much growth can we expect? *School Psychology Review, 22*(1), 27–48.

Fuchs, L. S., Fuchs, D., & Holleneck, K. N. (2007). Extending responsiveness to intervention to mathematics at first and third grades. *Learning Disabilities Research & Practice, 22*(10), 13–24.

Fuchs, L. S., Fuchs, D., & Karns, K. (2001). Enhancing kindergartners' mathematical development: Effects of peer-assisted learning strategies. *Elementary School Journal, 101*, 495–510.

Fuchs, L. S., Fuchs, D., Powell, S. R., Capizzi, A. M., & Seethaler, P. M. (2006). The effects of computer-assisted instruction on number combination skill in at-risk first graders. *Journal of Learning Disabilities, 39*(5), 467–475.

Fuchs, L. S., Fuchs, D., Prentice, K., Burch, M., Hamlett, C. L., Owen, R., et al. (2003a). Explicitly teaching for transfer: Effects on third-grade students' mathematical problem solving. *Journal of Educational Psychology, 95*(2), 293–305.

Fuchs, L. S., Fuchs, D., Prentice, K., Burch, M., Hamlett, C. L., Owen, R., et al. (2003b). Enhancing third-grade students' mathematical problem solving with self-regulated learning strategies. *Journal of Educational Psychology, 95*(2), 306–315.

Fuchs, L. S., Fuchs, D., Prentice, K., Hamlet, C. L., Finelli, R., & Courey, S. J. (2004). Enhancing mathematical problem solving among third-grade students with schema-based instruction. *Journal of Educational Psychology, 96*(4), 635–647.

Fuchs, L. S., Fuchs, D., Yazdian, L., & Powell, S. R. (2002). Enhancing first grade children's mathematical development with peer-assisted strategies. *School Psychology Review, 31*, 569–583.

Fuchs, L. S., Powell, S. R., Hamlett, C. L., & Fuchs, D. (2008). Remediating computational deficits at third grade: A randomized field trial. *Journal of Research on Educational Effectiveness, 1*(1), 2–32.

Fuchs, L. S., Seethaler, P. M., Powell, S. R., Fuchs, D., Hamlett, C. L., & Fletcher, J. M. (2008). Effects of preventative tutoring on the mathematical problem solving of third-grade students with math and reading difficulties. *Exceptional Children, 74*(2), 155–173.

Geary, D. C. (1993). Mathematical disabilities: Cognitive, neuropsychological, and genetic components. *Psychological Bulletin, 114*, 345–362.

Geary, D. C. (2003). *Learning disabilities in arithmetic: Problem-solving differences and cognitive deficits.* In H. L. Swanson, K. R. Harris, & S. Graham (Eds.), *Handbook of learning disabilities* (pp. 199–212). New York: Guilford.

Geary, D. C. (2004). Mathematics and learning disabilities. *Journal of Learning Disabilities, 37*, 4–15.

Gersten, R., Beckmann, S., Clarke, B., Foegen, A., Marsh, L., Star, J. R., & Witzel, B. (2009). *Assisting students struggling with mathematics: Response to Intervention (RtI) for elementary and middle schools* (NCEE 2009-4060). Washington, DC: National Center for Education Evaluation and Regional Assistance, Institute of Education Sciences, U.S. Department of Education. Retrieved from http://ies.ed.gov/ncee/wwc/publications/practiceguides/.

Gersten, R., & Clarke, B. S. (2010). Effective strategies brief: Effective strategies for teaching students with difficulty in mathematics. Retrieved from www.nctm.org/news/content.aspx?id=8452.

Gersten, R., Fuchs, L. S., Compton, D., Coyne, M., Greenwood, C., & Innocenti, M. S. (2005). Quality indicators for group experimental and quasi-experimental research in special education. *Exceptional Children, 71*, 149–164.

Ginsburg, H. P., Jacobs, S. F., & Lopez, L. S. (1998). *The teacher's guide to flexible interviewing in the classroom: Learning what children know about math.* Boston: Allyn & Bacon.

Goldman, S. R., Pellegrino, J. W., & Mertz, D. L. (1988). Extended practice of addition facts: Strategy changes in learning disabled students. *Cognition & Instruction, 5*(3), 223–265.

Good, C., Aronson, J., & Inzlicht, M. (2003). Improving adolescents' standardized test performance: An intervention to reduce the effects of stereotype threat. *Journal of Applied Developmental Psychology, 24,* 645–662.

Greene, G. (1999). Mnemonic multiplication fact instruction for students with learning disabilities. *Learning Disabilities Research & Practice, 14*(3), 141–148.

Griffin, S., & Case, R. (1997). Re-thinking the primary school math curriculum: An approach based on cognitive science. *Issues in Education, 3,* 1–49.

Hallahan, D. P., Lloyd, J. W., Kauffman, J. M., Weiss, M. P., & Martinez, E. A. (2005). *Learning disabilities: Foundations, characteristics, and effective teaching* (3rd ed.). Boston: Pearson.

Halpern, D., Aronson, J., Reimer, N., Simpkins, S., Start, J., & Wentzel, K. (2007). *Encouraging girls in math and science* (NCER 2007-2003). Washington, DC: National Center for Education Research, Institute of Education Sciences, U.S. Department of Education. Retrieved from http://ies.ed.gov/ncee/wwc/publications/practiceguides.

Hanich, L. B., Jordan, N. C., Kaplan, D., & Dick, J. (2001). Performance across different areas of mathematical cognition in children with learning difficulties. *Journal of Educational Psychology, 93*(3), 615–626.

Harris, C. A., Miller, S. P., & Mercer, C. D. (1995). Teaching initial multiplication skills to students with disabilities in general education classrooms. *Learning Disabilities Research & Practice, 10,* 180–195.

Harris, V. W. & Sherman, J. A. (1973). Use and analysis of the "Good Behavior Game" to reduce disruptive classroom behavior. *Journal of Applied Behavior Analysis, 6,* 405–417.

Harrison, M., & Harrison, B. (1986). Developing numeration concepts and skills. *Arithmetic Teacher, 33,* 1–21.

Hasselbring, T. S., Goin, L. I. & Bransford, J. D. (1988). Developing math automaticity in learning handicapped children: The role of computerized drill and practice. *Focus on Exceptional Children, 20,* 1–7.

Hazekamp, J. (2011). *Why before how: Singapore math computation strategies.* Peterborough, NH: Crystal Springs Books.

Hecht, S. A., Vogi, K. J., & Torgesen, J. K. (2007). Fraction skills and proportional reasoning. In D. B. Berch & M. M. Mazzocco (Eds.), *Why is math so hard for some children? The nature and origin of mathematical learning difficulties and disabilities* (pp. 121–132). Baltimore, MD: Paul H. Brooks.

Heller, L. R., & Fantuzzo, J. W. (1993). Reciprocal peer tutoring and parent partnership: Does parent involvement make a difference? *School Psychology Review, 22*(3), 517–534.

Heward, W. L. (1996). Everyone participates in this class. *Teaching Exceptional Children,* winter, 4–10.

Heyman, G. D., Dweck, C. S., & Cain, K. M. (1992). Young children's vulnerability to self-blame and helplessness: Relationship to beliefs about goodness. *Child Development, 63,* 401–415.

Hiebert, J., Carpenter, P. P., Fennema, E., Fuson, K. C., Wearned, D., Murray, H., & Oliver, A. (1997). *Making sense: Teaching and learning mathematics with understanding.* Portsmouth, NH: Heinemann.

Hodges, T. E., Cady, J., & Collins, L. (2008). Fraction representation: The not-so-common denominator among textbooks. *Mathematics Teaching in the Middle School, 14*(2), 78–84.

Hong, Y. Y., Chiu, C., Dweck, C. S, Lin, D., & Wan, W. (1999). Implicit theories, attributions, and coping: A meaning system approach. *Journal of Personality and Social Psychology, 77*, 588–599.

Hosp, M. K., Hosp, J. L., & Howell, K. W. (2007). *The ABCs of CBM: A practical guide to curriculum-based measurement.* New York: Guilford Press.

Hudson, P. J., & Miller, S. P. (2006). *Designing and implementing mathematics instruction for students with diverse learning needs.* Boston: Pearson.

Hudson, P. J., Peterson, S. K., Mercer, C. D., & McLeod, P. (1988). Place value instruction. *TEACHING Exceptional Children, 20*(3), 72–73.

Hulme, C., & Mackenzie, S. (1992). *Working memory and severe learning difficulties.* Hillsdale, NJ: Erlbaum.

Hunter, R. (2004). *Madeline Hunter's mastery teaching: Increasing instructional effectiveness in elementary and secondary schools.* Thousand Oaks, CA: Corwin Press.

Huntington, D. J. (1995). Instruction in concrete, semi-concrete, and abstract representation as an aid to the solution of relational problems by adolescents with learning disabilities. *Dissertation Abstracts International, 56*, 512.

Individuals with Disabilities Education Improvement Act P.L. 108–446 (2004). Retrieved from http://idea.ed.gov/explore/home.

Izsak, A., Tillema, E., & Tunc-Pekkan, Z. (2008). Teaching and learning fraction addition on numberlines. *Journal for Research in Mathematics Education, 39*(1), 33–62.

Jayanthi, M., Gersten, R., & Baker, S. (2008). *Mathematics instruction for students with learning disabilities or difficulty learning mathematics: A guide for teachers.* Portsmouth, NH: RMC Research Corporation, Center on Instruction.

Jitendra, A. K., Friffin, C. C, McGoey, K., Gardill, M. C., Bhat, P., & Riley, T. (1998). Effects of mathematical word problem solving by students at risk or with mild disabilities. *Journal of Educational Research, 91*(6), 345–355.

Jordan, N. C., Hanich, O. B., & Kaplan, D. (2003). A longitudinal study of children with specific mathematics difficulties versus children with comorbid mathematics and reading difficulties. *Child Development, 74*(3), 834–850.

Kagan, S. (1994). *Cooperative learning.* San Clemente, CA: Resources for Teachers.

Kahnemann, P. (1973). *Attention and effort.* Englewood Cliffs, NJ: Prentice Hall.

Kame'enui, E. J., & Simmons, D. C. (1990). *Designing instructional strategies: The prevention of academic learning problems.* Columbus, OH: Merrill.

Kamins, M. L., & Dweck, C. (1999). Person versus process praise and criticism: Implications for contingent self-worth and coping. *Developmental Psychology, 35*(3), 835–847.

Kemp, K. A. (2009). *RTI & math: The classroom connection.* Port Chester, NY: Dude.

Kampwirth, T. J. (1988). Behavior management in the classroom: A self-assessment guide for teachers. *Education & Treatment of Teachers, 19*(1), 1–10.

Kouba, V. L., Brown, C. A., Carpenter, T. P., Lindquist, M. M., Silver, E. A., & Swafford, I. L. (1988). Results of the fourth NAEP assessment of mathematics: Number, operations, and word problems. *Arithemtic Teacher, 35*(8): 14–19.

Kroesbergen, E. H., & Van Luit, J. E. H. (2003). Mathematical interventions for children with special educational needs. *Remedial and Special Education, 24,* 97–114.

Kumar, K. (September 5, 2004). Money for grades: How much should it pay to be smart? *St. Louis Post Dispatch.*

Lepper, M. R., Greene, D., & Nisbett, R. E. (1973). Undermining children's intrinsic interest with extrinsic reward: A test of the overjustification hypothesis. *Journal of Personality and Social Psychology, 28,* 129–137.

Lesh, R., Post, T., & Behr, M. (1987). Representations and translations among representations in mathematics learning and problem solving. In C. Janvier (Ed.), *Problems of representation in the teaching and learning of mathematics* (pp. 33–40). Hillsdale, NJ: Erlbaum.

Lockwood, A. T., & Secada, N. G. (1999). *Transforming education for Hispanic youth: Exemplary practices, programs, and schools.* NCBE Resource Collection Series, No 12. Washington, DC: National Clearinghouse for Bilingual Education. (ERIC Document Reproduction Service No. ED 434 788).

Logan, G. D. (1985). Executive control of thought and action. *Acta Psychologica, 60*(2–3), 193–210.

Long, M. J. & Ben-Hur, M. (1991). Informing learning through the clinical interview. *Arithmetic Teacher, 38*(6), 44–46.

Ma, L. (1999). *Knowing and teaching elementary mathematics: Teachers' understanding of fundamental mathematics in China and the United States.* Mahwah, NJ: Erlbaum.

Mabbott, D. J., & Bisanz, J. (2008). Computational skills, working memory, and conceptual knowledge in older children with mathematics learning disabilities. *Journal of Learning Disabilities, 41*(1), 15–28.

Maccini, P., & Gagnon, J. A. (2000). Best practices for teaching mathematics to secondary students with special needs. *Focus on Exceptional Children, 32*(5).

Maccini, P., & Hughes, C. A. (2000). Effects of a problem-solving strategy on the introductory algebra performance of secondary students with learning disabilities. *Learning Disabilities Research and Practice, 15*(1), 10–12.

Marshall, S. P. (1990). The assessment of schema knowledge for arithmetic story problems: A cognitive science perspective. In G. Kulm (Ed.),

Assessing higher order thinking in mathematics. Washington, DC: American Association for the Advancement of Science. (ERIC Document Reproduction Service No. ED 324 201).

Marshall, S. P., Pribe, C. A., & Smith, J. D. (1987). *Schema knowledge structures for representing and understanding arithmetic story problems* (Tech. Rep. Contract No. N00014-85-K-0061). Arlington, VA: Office of Naval Research.

Martella, R. C., Nelson, J. R., & Marchand-Martella, N. E. (2003). *Managing disruptive behaviors in the schools: A schoolwide, classroom, and individualized social learning approach.* Boston: Allyn & Bacon.

Marzano, R. J., Pickering, D. J., & Pollock, J. E. (2001). *Classroom instruction that works: Research-based strategies for increasing student achievement.* Alexandria, VA: ASCD.

Mastropieri, M. A., & Scruggs, T. E. (1991). *Teaching students ways to remember: Strategies for learning mnemonically.* Cambridge, MA: Brookline Press.

Mastropieri, M. A., & Scruggs, T. E. (2005). Feasibility and consequences of response to intervention: Examination of the issues and scientific evidence as a model for the identification of individuals with learning disabilities. *Journal of Learning Disabilities 38,* 525–531.

Mazzocco, M. M. (2007). Defining and differentiating mathematical learning disabilities and difficulties. In D. B. Berch & M. M. Mazzocco (Eds.), *Why is math so hard for some children? The nature and origins of mathematical learning difficulties and disabilities.* Baltimore, MD: Paul H. Brookes.

McDougall, D., & Brady, M. P. (1998). Initiating and fading self-management interventions to increase math fluency in general education classes. *Exceptional Children, 64,* 151–166.

Medland, M. B. & Stachnik, T. J. (1972). Good-behavior Game: A replication and systematic analysis. *Journal of Applied Behavior Analysis, 5,* 45–51.

Mercer, C. D., Jordan, L., & Miller, S. P. (1996). Constructivistic math instruction for diverse learners. *Learning Disabilities Research & Practice, 11,* 147–156.

Mercer, C. D., & Miller, S. P. (1992). Teaching students with learning problems in math to acquire, understand, and apply basic math facts. *Remedial and Special Education, 13*(3), 19–35.

Miller, G. A. (1956). The magical number seven, plus or minus two: Some limits on our capacity for processing information. *Psychological Review, 63,* 81–97.

Miller, S. P. (1996). Perspectives in mathematics instruction. In D. D. Deshler, E. S. Ellis, & B K. Lenz, *Teaching adolescents with learning disabilities: Strategies and methods* (2nd ed.). Denver, CO: Love.

Miller, S. P., Harris, C. A., Strawser, S., Jones, W. P., & Mercer, C. D. (1998). Teaching multiplication to second graders in inclusive settings. *Focus on Learning Problems in Mathematics, 21*(4), 49–69.

Miller, S. P., Mercer, C. D., & Dillon, A. S. (1992). CSA: Acquiring and retaining math skills. *Intervention in School and Clinic, 28*, 105–110.

Montague, M. (2006). Self-regulation strategies for better math performance in middle school. In M. Montague & A. K. Jitendra (Eds.), *Teaching mathematics to middle school students with learning difficulties.* New York: Guilford Press.

Montague, M., & Applegate, B. (1991). Middle school students' mathematical problem solving: An analysis of think-aloud protocols. *Learning Disability Quarterly, 16*(1), 19–32.

Montague, M., & Applegate, B. (1993a). Mathematical problem-solving characteristics of middle school students with learning disabilities. *The Journal of Special Education, 227*, 175–201.

Montague, M., & Applegate, B. (1993b). Middle school students' mathematical problem solving: An analysis of think-aloud protocols. *Learning Disability Quarterly, 16*, 19–32.

Montague, M., Applegate, B., & Marquard, K. (1993). Cognitive strategy instruction and mathematical problem-solving performance of students with learning disabilities. *Learning Disabilities Research & Practice, 8*(4), 223–232.

Montague, M., & Dietz, S. (2010). Evaluating the evidence base for cognitive strategy instruction and mathematical problem solving. *Exceptional Children, 75*(3), 285–302.

Montague, M., & Jitendra, A. K. (Eds.). (2006). *Teaching mathematics to middle school students with learning difficulties.* New York: Guilford Press.

Morgan, M. (1984). Reward-induced decrements and increments in intrinsic motivation. *Review of Educational Research, 54*, 5–30.

Morin, V. A., & Miller, S. P. (1998). Teaching multiplication to middle school students with mental retardation. *Education and Treatment of Children, 21*(1), 22–36.

Moser, J. M. (1992). Arithmetic operations on whole numbers: Addition and subtraction. In T. R. Post (Ed.), *Teaching mathematics in grades K–8: Research-based methods.* Boston: Allyn & Bacon.

Moxley, R. A. (1998). Treatment-only designs and student self-recording as strategies for public school teachers. *Education and Treatment of Children, 21*(1), 37–61.

Moyer, P. S., Bolyard, J. J., & Spikell, M. (2002). What are virtual manipulatives? *Teaching Children Mathematics, 8*(6), 372–377.

Moyer, P. S., Niezgoda, D., & Stanley, J. (2005). Young children's use of virtual manipulatives and other forms of mathematical representations. In W. J. Masalski & P. C. Elliott (Eds.), *Technology-supported mathematics learning environments: Sixty-seventh yearbook (17–34).* Reston, VA: NCTM.

Moyer-Packenham, P. S., Salkind, G., & Bolyard, J. J. (2008). Virtual manipulatives used by K–8 teachers for mathematics instruction: Considering mathematical, cognitive, and pedagogical fidelity. *Contemporary Issues in Technology and Teacher Education, 8*(3), 1–17.

Mueller, C. M., & Dweck, C. S. (1998). Intelligence praise can undermine motivation and performance. *Journal of Personality and Social Psychology, 75*, 33–52.

National Center for Learning Disabilities. (2010). Parent advocacy brief: A parent's guide to response to intervention. New York, NY: Author.

National Center on Response to Intervention (RtI). (2010). *Essential components of RtI: A closer look at Response to Intervention*. Washington, DC: U.S. Office of Special Education Programs.

National Council of Teachers of Mathematics (NCTM). (1989; 2000). *Principles and standards for school mathematics*. Reston, VA: Author.

National Council of Teachers of Mathematics (NCTM). (2006). *Curriculum focal points for mathematics in prekindergarten through grade 8 mathematics*. Reston, VA: Author.

National Governors Association Center for Best Practices, Council of Chief State School Officers. (2010). *The common core state standards for mathematics*. Washington, DC: Author.

National Institute for Literacy. (2006). *What is scientifically based research? A guide for teachers*. Washington, DC: Author.

National Mathematics Advisory Panel (NMAP). (2008). *Foundations for Success: The Final Report of the National Mathematics Advisory Panel*. Washington, DC: U.S. Department of Education. Retrieved from http://www.ed.gov/MathPanel.

Nussbaum, A. D., & Dweck, C. S. (2008). Defensiveness vs. remediation: Self-theories and modes of self-esteem maintenance. *Personality and Social Psychology Bulletin, 34*, 599–612.

Pascual-Leone, J. (1970). A maturational model for the transition rule in Piaget's developmental stages. *Acta Psychologica, 32*, 301–345.

Pashler, H., Bain, P., Bottge, B., Graesser, A., Koedinger, K., McDaniel, M., & Metcalfe, J. (2007). *Organizing instruction and study to improve student learning* (NCER 2007-2004). Washington, DC: National Center for Education Research, Institute of Education Sciences, U.S. Department of Education. Retrieved from http://ncer.ed.gov.

Pierangelo, R., & Guiliani, G. A. (2008). *Classroom management for students with emotional and behavioral disorders: A step-by-step guide for educators*. Thousand Oaks, CA: Corwin Press.

Pellegrino, J. W., & Goldman, S. R. (1987). Information processing and elementary mathematics. *Journal of Learning Disabilities, 20*, 23–32.

Peterson, S. K., Mercer, C. D., & O'Shea, L. (1988). Teaching learning disabled students place value using the concrete to abstract sequence. *Learning Disabilities Research, 4*(1), 52–56.

Polya, G. (1957). *How to solve it*. Garden City, NY: Doubleday.

Polya, G. (1965). *Mathematical discovery: On understanding, learning, and teaching problem solving* (vol. 2). New York: Wiley.

Polya, G. (2004). *How to solve it: A new aspect of mathematical method*. Princeton, NJ: Princeton University Press.

Porter, A. (1989). A curriculum out of balance: The case of elementary school mathematics. *Educational Researcher, 18*(5), 9–15.

Pressley, M., & Afflerbach, P. (1995). *Verbal protocols of reading: The nature of constructively responsive reading.* Hillsdale, NJ: Erlbaum.

Pressley, M., Borkowski, J. G., & O'Sullivan, J. (1984). Memory strategy instruction is made of this: Meta-memory and durable strategy use. *Educational Psychologist, 19,* 94–107.

Pressley, M., Borkowski, J. G., & O'Sullivan, J. (1984). Children's metamemory and the teaching of memory strategies. In D. L. Forrest-Presley, G. E. MacKinnon, & T. G. Walker (Eds.), *Metacognition, cognition and human performance.* (pp. 111–153). Orlando, FL: Academic Press.

Pressley, M., Harris, K. R., & Marks, M. B. (1982). The mnemonic key word method. *Review of Educational Research, 52*(1), 61–91.

Pressley, M., Levin, J. R., & Ghatala, E. S. (1988). Strategy comparison opportunities promote long-term strategy use. *Contemporary Educational Psychology, 13,* 137–168.

Pressley, M., & McCormick, C. B. (1995). *Cognition, teaching, and assessment.* New York: Harper Collins.

Pressley, M., Ross, K. A., Levin, J. R., & Ghatala, E. S. (1984). The role of strategy utility knowledge in children's strategy decision making. *Journal of Experimental Child Psychology, 38,* 491–504.

Pressley, M., & Woloshyn, V. (1995). *Cognitive strategy instruction that really improves children's academic performance.* Cambridge, MA: Brookline Books.

Reimer, K., & Moyer, P. S. (2005). Third graders learn about fractions using virtual manipulatives: A classroom study. *Journal of Computers in Mathematics and Science Teaching, 34*(1), 5–25.

Reiss, S. (2005). Extrinsic and intrinsic motivation at 30: Unresolved scientific issues. *Behavior Analyst, 28,* 1–14.

Rhode Island Department of Elementary and Secondary Education. (2010). *Rhode Island Criteria and Guidance for the Identification of Specific Learning Disabilities.* Providence: Author.

Riccomini, P. J. (2005). Identification and remediation of systematic error patterns in subtraction. *Learning Disability Quarterly, 28*(3), 1–10.

Riccomini, P. J., & Witzel, B. S. (2010). *Response to intervention in math.* Thousand Oaks, CA: Corwin.

Ripley, A. (April 19, 2010). Is cash the answer? *Time, 175*(15), 41–47.

Rock, M. L. (2005). Use of strategic self-monitoring to enhance academic engagement, productivity, and accuracy of students with and without exceptionalities. *Journal of Positive Behavior Interventions, 7*(1), 3–17.

Scheuermann, A. M., Deshler, D. D., & Schumaker, J. B. (2009). The effects of the explicit inquiry routine on the performance of students with learning disabilities on one-variable equations. *Learning Disability Quarterly, 32*(2), 103–120.

Schmidt, W. H., McKnight, C. C., & Raizen, S. A. (1997). *A splintered vision: An investigation of U.S. science and mathematics education.* Dordrecht, Netherlands: Kluwer.

Schmidt, W. H., Wang, H. C., & McKnight, C. C. (2005). Curriculum coherence: An examination of U.S. mathematics and science content standards from an international perspective. *Journal of Curriculum Studies, 37*(5), 525–559.

Schneider, W., Dumais, S. T., & Shiffrin, R. M. (1984). Automatic and control processing and attention. In R. Parasuraman & D. R. Davies (Eds.), *Varieties of attention.* Orlando, FL: Academic Press.

Schunk, D. H. (1983). Reward contingencies and the development of children's skills and self-efficacy. *Journal of Educational Psychology, 75,* 511–518.

Schunk, D. H., & Cox, P. D. (1986). Strategy training and attributional feedback with learning disabled students. *Journal of Educational Psychology,* 201–209.

Shea, T. M., & Bauer, A. M. (1987). *Teaching children and youth with behavior disorders* (2nd ed.). Upper Saddle River, NJ: Prentice Hall.

Siegler, R. S. (1988). Strategy choice procedures and the development of multiplication skills. *Journal of Experimental Psychology: General, 111,* 258–275.

Siegler, R., & Jenkins, E. (1989). *How children discover new strategies.* Hillsdale, NJ: Lawrence Erlbaum Associates.

Smith, D. D., & Rivera, D. M. (1993). *Effective discipline.* Austin, TX: Pro-Ed.

Sophian, C. (2004). Mathematics for the future: Developing a Head Start curriculum to support mathematics learning. *Early Childhood Research Quarterly, 19,* 59–81.

Sousa, D. A. (2002). *How the special needs brain learns.* Thousand Oaks, CA: Corwin.

Sousa, D. A. (2007). *How the brain learns mathematics.* Thousand Oaks, CA: Corwin.

Sprick, R., Garrison, M., & Howard, L. M. (1998). *CHAMPs: A proactive and positive approach to classroom management.* Longmont, CO: Sopris West.

Steen, K., Brooks, D., & Lyon, T. (2006). The impact of virtual manipulatives on first grade geometry instruction and learning. *Journal of Computers in Mathematics and Science Teaching, 25*(4), 373–391.

Sternberg, R. (2005). Intelligence, competence, and expertise. In A. Elliot & C. Dweck (Eds.), *Handbook of competence and motivation.* New York: Guilford Press.

Suh, J., & Moyer, P. S. (2007). Developing students' representational fluency using virtual and physical algebra balances. *Journal of Computers in Mathematics and Science Teaching, 26*(2), 155–173.

Suh, J., Moyer, P. S., & Heo, H. J. (2005). Examining technology uses in the classroom: Developing fraction sense using virtual manipulative concept tutorials. *Journal of Interactive Online Learning, 3*(4), 1–22.

Suydam, M. N., & Higgins, J. L. (1977). *Activity-based learning in elementary school mathematics: Recommendations from research.* Columbus, OH: ERIC Center for Science, Mathematics, and Environmental Education.

Swanson, H. L. (1987). Information-processing theory and learning disabilities: An overview. *Journal of Learning Disabilities, 20,* 3–7.

Swanson, H. L. (1990). Instruction derived from the strategy deficient model: Overview of principles and procedures. In T. E. Scruggs & B. Y. L. Wong (Eds.), *Intervention research in learning disabilities* (pp. 34–65). New York: Springer-Verlag.

Swanson, H. L. (1993). Principles and procedures in strategy use. In L. Meltzer (Ed.), *Strategy assessment and instruction for students with learning disabilities* (pp. 61–92). Austin, TX: Pro-Ed.

Swanson, H. L., & Cooney, J. B. (1991). Learning disabilities and memory. In B. Y. L. Wong (Ed.), *Learning about learning disabilities* (pp. 104–127). San Diego, CA: Academic Press.

Swanson, H. L., Cooney, J. B., & O'Shaughnessy, T. E. (1998). Learning disabilities and memory. In B.Y.L. Wong (ed.), *Understanding learning and learning disabilities.* San Diego, CA: Academic Press.

Swanson, H. L., Jerman, O., & Zheng, Z. (2009). Math disabilities and reading disabilities: Can they be separated? *Journal of Psycho-educational Assessment, 27*(3), 175–196.

Tarver, S. G., & Jung, J. S. (1995). A comparison of mathematics achievement and mathematics attitudes of first and second graders instructed with either a discovery-learning mathematics curriculum or a direct instruction curriculum. *Effective School Practices, 14*(1), 49–56.

Tournaki, N. (2003). The differential effects of teaching addition through strategy instruction versus drill and practice to students with and without learning disabilities. *Journal of Learning Disabilities, 36*(5), 449–458.

Tucker, B. F., Singleton, A. H., & Weaver, T. L. (2002). *Teaching mathematics to all children.* Upper Saddle River, NJ: Pearson.

U.S. Department of Education. (2001). *No Child Left Behind Act of 2001.* Retrieved from www.ed.gov/policy/elsec/leg/esea02/index.html.

U.S. Department of Education. (2003). *Mathematics and science initiative concept paper.* Retrieved from www.ed.gov/rschstat/research/progrs/mathscience/concept_paper.pdf.

U.S. Department of Education. (2009). *National Assessment of Educational Progress (NAEP).* Author.

U.S. Department of Education. (2011). *National Assessment of Educational Progress (NAEP).* Author.

U.S. Department of Health and Human Services, Administration on Children, Youth and Families/Head Start Bureau. (2001). *The Head Start path to positive child outcomes.* Washington, DC: Author.

VanDerHeyden, A. M., & Burns, M. K. (2005). Using curriculum-based assessment and curriculum-based measurement to guide elementary accountability scores. *Assessment for Effective Intervention, 30*(30), 15–31.

VanDerHeyden, A. M., Witt, J. C., & Gilbertson, D. (2007). A multiyear evaluation of the effects of a Response to Intervention (RtI) model on identification of children for special education. *Journal of School Psychology, 45*(2), 225–256.

Van de Walle, J. A. (1988). The early development of number relations. *Arithmetic Teacher, (35)*6, 15–21.

Van de Walle, J. A. (2004). *Elementary and middle school mathematics: Teaching developmentally* (5th ed.). Boston: Pearson.

van Garderen, D., & Montague, M. (2003). Visual-spatial representation, mathematical problem solving and students of varying abilities. *Learning Disabilities Research and Practice, 18*(4), 246–254.

Vaughn, S., Gersten, R., & Chard, D. J. (2000). The underlying message in L.D. intervention research: Findings from a research synthesis. *Exceptional Children, 67*, 99–114.

Viorst, J., & Cruz, R. (1978). *Alexander, who used to be rich last Sunday.* New York: Atheneum.

Vygotsky, L. S. (1978). *Mind in society: The development of higher psychological processes.* Cambridge, MA: Harvard University Press.

Walker, D. W., & Poteet, J. A. (1989). A comparison of two methods of teaching mathematics story problem-solving with learning disabled students. *National Forum of Special Education Journal, 1*, 44–51.

Walker, J. E., & Shea, T. M. (1999). *Behavior management: A practical approach for educators.* Upper Saddle River, NJ: Merrill.

Walqui, A. (2000). Access and engagement: Program design and instructional approaches for immigrant students in secondary school. Topics in immigrant education 4, Language in education: Theory and practice, 94. Washington, DC: Center for Applied Linguistics.

Wearne, D., & Kouba, V. L. (2000). Rational numbers. In E. A. Silver & P. A. Kenny (Eds.), *Results from the seventh mathematics assessment of the National Assessment of Educational Progress*, pp. 163–191. Reston, VA: National Council of Teachers of Mathematics.

Wehmeyer, M. L., Yeager, D., Bolding, N., Agran, M., & Hughes, C. (2003). The effects of self-regulation strategies on goal attainment for students with developmental disabilities in general education classrooms. *Journal of Developmental and Physical Disabilities, 15*(1), 79–91.

Wei, S., & Zhang, J. (2001). Teaching addition and subtraction facts: A Chinese perspective. *Teaching Children Mathematics*, September, 28–31.

Wilson, C. L., & Sindelar, P. T. (1991). Direct instruction in math word problems: Students with learning disabilities. *Exceptional Children, 57*(6), 512–519.

Wirtz, R. (1974). *Mathematics for everyone.* Washington, DC: Curriculum Development Associates.

Witzel, B. S. (2005). Using CRA to teach algebra to students with math difficulties in inclusive settings. *Learning Disabilities: A Contemporary Journal, 3*(2), 49–60.

Witzel, B. S., Mercer, C. D., & Miller, M. D. (2003). Teaching algebra to students with learning difficulties: An investigation of an explicit instruction model. *Learning Disabilities Research and Practice, 18*, 121–131.

Witzel, B. S., & Riccomini, P. J. (2009). *Computation of fractions: Math interventions for elementary and middle grades students.* Upper Saddle River, NJ: Pearson.

Wolfe, P. (2001). *Brain matters: Translating research into classroom practice.* Alexandria, VA: ASCD.

Wolgemuth, J. R., Cobb, R. B., & Alwell, M. (2008). The effects of mnemonic interventions on academic outcomes for youth with disabilities: A systematic review. *Learning Disabilities Research & Practice, 23*(1), 1–10.

Wong, B. Y. L., Harris, K. R., Graham, S., & Butler, D. L. (2003).Cognitive strategies instruction research in learning disabilities. In H. L. Swanson, K. R. Harris, & S. Graham (Eds.), *Handbook of learning disabilities* (pp. 383–402). New York: Guilford Press.

Woodward, J. (2006). Developing automaticity in multiplication facts: Integrating strategy instruction with timed practice drills. *Learning Disability Quarterly, 29*(4), 269–289.

Woodward, J., & Baxter, J. (1997). The effects of an innovative approach to mathematics on academically low achieving students in mainstreamed settings. *Exceptional Children, 63*(3), 373–388.

Xin, Y. P., & Jitendra, A. K. (2006). Teaching problem solving skills to middle school students with learning difficulties: Schema-based strategy instruction. In M. Montague & A. K. Jitendra (Eds.), *Middle School Students with Mathematics Difficulties* (pp. 51–71). New York: Guilford Press.

Xin, Y. P., Jitendra, A. K., & Deatline-Buchman, A. (2005). Effects of mathematical word-problem-solving instruction on middle school students with learning problems. *Journal of Special Education, 39*(3), 181–192.

Made in the USA
Columbia, SC
31 August 2022

66412618R00167